ITALIAN FAMILY COOKING

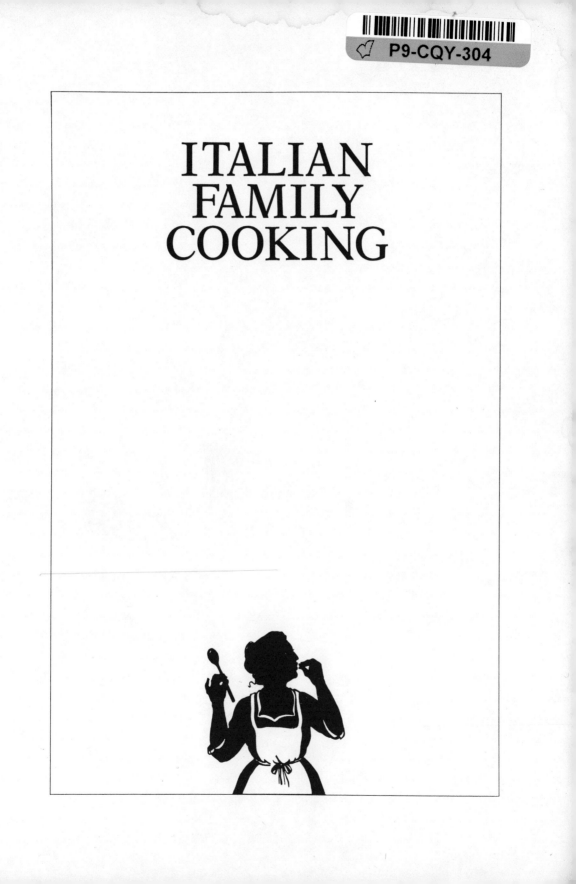

ITALIAN FAMILY COOKING

Like Mama Used to Make

Anne Casale

FAWCETT COLUMBINE
NEW YORK

A Fawcett Columbine Book
Published by Ballantine Books
Copyright © 1984 by Anne L. Casale
Illustration copyright © 1984 by Lauren Jarrett
Silhouettes copyright © 1984 by Heather Taylor
Design by Beth Tondreau

Cover design by James R. Harris
Silhouette by Heather Taylor

All rights reserved under International and
Pan-American Copyright Conventions.
Published in the United States by Ballantine Books,
a division of Random House, Inc., New York,
and simultaneously in Canada by
Random House of Canada Limited, Toronto.

Library of Congress Catalog Card Number: 84–90841
ISBN 0–449–90133–5

Manufactured in the United States of America
First Edition: November 1984
10 9 8 7

Many years ago, my husband was asked by an inquisitive three-year-old to explain the meaning of the word "pal." Patiently and lovingly he knelt down and explained, "A pal is your closest friend, someone you admire and love." The child thought for a moment, looked up and beamed, saying, "Then that's what you are to me—you're my pal!" To this day my husband, John, is known as Pal to everyone in the family. It is to him, my husband and Pal, that this book is dedicated.

Anne L. Casale

Contents

SALADS   □   257

DESSERTS ☐ 271

Acknowledgments

I gratefully acknowledge and thank: My daughter, Amy; my wonderful agent, Amy Berkower, at Writers House; my dear friend, David Wald, who helped put so many of my thoughts into words; and my family and friends for their support, encouragement and patience during the many months of writing.

Preface

I grew up in an Italian household where hospitality and food were a natural part of my heritage, a heritage rich in tradition and gastronomic delight. Being introduced to good food at an early age gave me an inquisitive, demanding palate that has flourished for a lifetime.

Both my parents, Rose and Amadeo Lovi, were excellent cooks. My mother's side of the family came from the region of Campania and my father's from Liguria and Tuscany, so we always had a diversity of magnificent dishes at our table.

When I was a child, it was always an exciting experience to go shopping with my father on Saturdays. We would start out early in the morning and visit a string of specialty shops where he would select the finest, freshest ingredients—whether produce, fowl, fish or meats. As he made his selections, he would lean over and tell me, "Learn to use your eyes, Anna, as well as your nose. The best needs no embellishment." He never sacrificed quality in whatever was to be served. I watched him prepare many of his Tuscan specialties, from a simple risotto to an intricate veal roast which was alive with flavor. "Cooking," he would say, "is a form of self-expression. Don't be afraid to explore new gastronomic territories. A good cook must always keep an open mind for new ideas, new tastes and new combinations."

From Mamma, the first culinary rule I learned was cleanliness and organization before getting started. If Mamma were baking, everything would be pre-measured into little bowls and set out on the counter waiting to be systematically assembled. In this manner, nothing was ever left out of a recipe. The same attention was given to all her food preparation. Each vegetable was meticulously cleaned, then chopped, minced or diced to perfection before being added to any dish. She stressed the idea that cooking and baking were acts of love and passed that love on to me.

Her food was beautifully arranged on handsome serving platters.

"Always remember, Anna," she would advise me, "when food looks good, it tastes even better."

My father-in-law, Vincenzo Casale, owned and operated La Bella Palermo, an Italian pastry shop in lower Manhattan, for over forty years. He was respected by his fellow *pasticceri* (pastry men) as one of the finest bakers of his time. He was also an excellent Sicilian cook. We lived with him for fourteen years after his retirement. I can remember spending hours in the kitchen to please this man of impeccable taste. Most of the time I was rewarded with unstinting compliments, but once in a while his "compliment" after a meal was, "Anna, this is good, but don't make it any more." Needless to say, I wanted to die right on the spot. I learned much in the years he lived with us and am grateful for the many techniques and methods he taught me. He always used an Italian expression, *Quello che ci mette, ci trova,* meaning, "What one puts into a dish one will find." Papa Casale was right—and in complete accord with my parents' philosophies. Love is a basic and the best ingredient in every recipe I offer. I have shared this love with my family, friends and students for many years and now I am happy to share this heritage with others. What one puts into a dish one will find!

Introduction

Prized family recipes are creations that not only satisfy the palate, but warm the heart with the memories they generate. Every family-inspired recipe created for this book has been developed to capture the original magic I recall. *Italian Family Cooking* has been designed to share my culinary heritage with today's cook in today's kitchen.

The recipes in this collection are presented in a clear, precise manner. The procedures are written in simple steps as they are needed. Incorporated in the procedures are specific cooking techniques that will instruct the beginning cook or reinforce, refine and expand the skills of the more experienced one. Ingredients are listed in the order in which they are used. Each measurement is standard and allows the reader to reproduce the selections without guesswork and with confidence. I recommend that you read the chapter on ingredients before starting any of the recipes. An understanding of the ingredients being used can only add to a cook's security and confidence.

Planning is the key to carefree cooking. It is extremely important to have all your ingredients and utensils readily at hand before you start to cook. Consult your recipes in advance and jot down all the ingredients you'll need, even the most obvious. Without your list you may find yourself up a creek minus the salt and pepper, or waiting for an oven to preheat. Note when the same ingredients—such as chopped onion or minced parsley—must be readied for several recipes: do all the preparation, then divide the ingredients and place required amounts in separate bowls. Clean up as you go along. Read through each recipe again before starting. If you are properly prepared, cooking can be easy and fun.

One of the most versatile kitchen appliances available to today's cook is the food processor. This time-saving device opens up a world of culinary possibilities, for it is capable of performing a large percentage of the tedious work in the kitchen. Many recipes found in this book incorporate the food processor. However, specific directions are always included for those who may not yet have a processor. My strong suggestion to you is—buy one; you won't be sorry.

If you find yourself torn between enthusiasm for entertaining and dread of spending long hours in the kitchen, stop. Remember that an elegant menu needn't mean a lot of last-minute fussing. Once again, planning is essential. Read through the recipes carefully to select ones that don't require last-minute preparation. Many desserts can be made a day or two in advance. You can also find any number of pasta sauces that can be done ahead of time and reheated. While suggestions for menus and pointers for successful menu planning appear in a later chapter, hints for variations on recipes as well as additional menu suggestions are listed before many recipes.

If you are a novice at cooking, I would not advise your starting off with Rotolo di Pasta. Buy some good imported or fresh pasta and begin with one of the simple sauces. You can have dinner in no time flat. Remember, confidence is gained through experience.

I hope this cookbook will send you directly into the kitchen, charged with excitement over new methods, ingredients and taste combinations.

Glossary: Ingredients

When it comes to selecting the ingredients for the recipes you have chosen, I implore you to follow the words of Papa Casale: "What one puts into a dish, one will find." Since you want your guests to be served food that's nothing short of wonderful, insist on starting with nothing less.

Many of my students have little cooking experience. While they learn recipes, techniques and procedures in class, they also come to appreciate the range of top-quality ingredients that are essential for all dishes.

ARROWROOT

This is obtained by drying and grinding the rootstalks of a tropical plant of the same name. It is used as a thickening agent which leaves no floury aftertaste. Arrowroot gives a clearer sauce than other thickening agents such as cornstarch or flour. Always dissolve arrowroot in a little broth, wine or water before adding to any sauce or gravy. Remove pan from heat before adding dissolved mixture.

BREADCRUMBS, DRY AND FRESH

Dry—Arrange slices of bread in a single layer on cookie sheet. Preheat oven to 250° and toast bread until crisp and golden, about 30 minutes. Break into 1-inch chunks and whirl in food processor fitted with metal blade until finely ground. Place crumbs in fine mesh strainer and sift into large bowl. Discard any large crumbs or whirl again in food processor. Pack into jars and keep in cool dry place until needed. Should be stored in refrigerator during summer months.

Fresh—Cut up fresh or day-old bread, including crust, or tear it gently with fingers. Place in food processor fitted with metal blade. Run machine until bread is reduced to coarse crumb consistency.

BUTTER

For the finest flavor use unsalted (sweet) butter for cooking and baking. Purchase only U.S. Grade AA butter, which is made from the highest quality fresh sweet cream.

CAPERS

These are the flower buds from a low, trailing shrub called a caper bush. The unopened buds are packed in vinegar or salt and must be thoroughly rinsed and drained before being added to any dish. Buy either the Spanish or Italian varieties.

CREAM

Heavy or whipping cream should be whipped in a well chilled bowl for best results. Cream can be whipped, covered and refrigerated up to two hours before serving. Always check before serving, as whipped cream may separate slightly. This can be corrected by mixing again very briefly with a wire whisk.

EGGS

Sizes will be specified with each recipe. If they are to be separated, use eggs taken directly from refrigerator. A cold egg breaks cleanly and the yolk is less likely to rupture than in one at room temperature. It is critical that no egg yolk find its way into the whites, for even a trace of yolk will prevent them from reaching full volume. If part of the yolk should fall into the white, use the shell to scoop it out. If egg whites are used in dessert, cream of tartar is added to stabilize them.

FLOUR

Recipes in this book call for different varieties of flour. Read labels and recipes carefully.

Unbleached flour is a blend of hard and soft wheat. It is recommended for bread, pasta (if semolina flour is unavailable) and some pastry doughs.

All purpose enriched flour is a bleached variety and will produce a more delicate pastry dough (especially if the dough is to be rolled). It is also suitable for all cakes in this book. For recipes calling for this type of flour, the term *all purpose* will be used.

Cake flour has a silky consistency and is particularly good for sponge cake. If unavailable, all purpose flour can be substituted but the texture will be a little heavier.

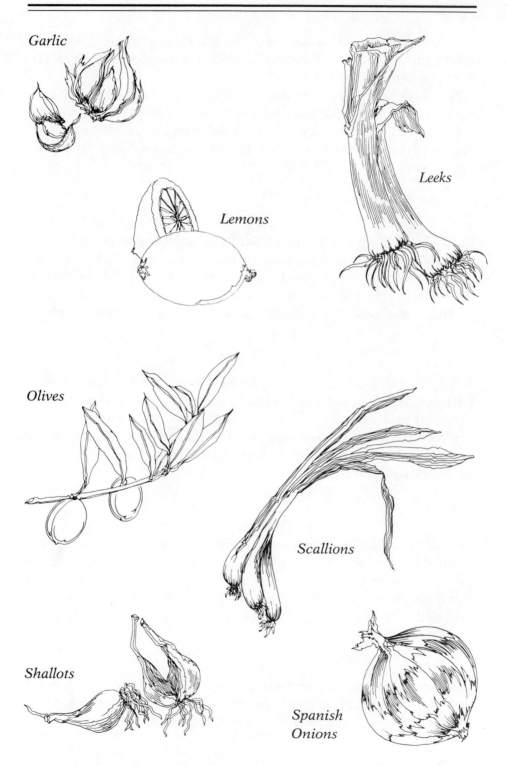

Garlic

Lemons

Leeks

Olives

Scallions

Shallots

Spanish
Onions

To measure, use cups designed for dry measurement. Spoon the flour lightly into cup; do not shake the cup or pack or press the flour. Level lightly with the back of a knife.

Semolina flour is used in making pasta. It is weighed rather than measured into cups. See introduction to pasta (page 33) for details.

For coating, I recommend Gold Medal Wondra, an instantized all purpose flour that pours like salt. It will give a much lighter coating for sautéing.

GARLIC

Buy bulbs that are tightly closed, with unwrinkled skins of white, pink to purple, or white with purple streaks. Store in cool, dark place. For easy peeling, place a clove under the side of a large knife blade. Thump the blade to split the garlic's clinging skin; it will slip off easily. It is better to chop garlic finely with a knife than to mash through a press.

LEEKS

Buy leeks with crisp, green, unwithered tops and clean white bottoms. Leeks should be straight and cylindrical. If the ends are very bulbous, they will probably be tough and woody inside. To clean, trim roots and a portion of the fibrous leaf tops. Cut the stalks in half lengthwise and wash thoroughly under running water, while holding the layers apart, until no sand appears.

LEMONS

An indispensable flavoring in many of my dishes. Try to pick smooth-skinned lemons, which have more juice. The juice can be substituted for vinegar in salad dressing. Use only fresh, never the reconstituted juice, which leaves a bitter aftertaste. Make sure you scrub the outer skin well to remove any coating before using the rind in any dish.

MUSHROOMS, DRIED

Look for the large, light brown type imported from Italy and labeled Porcini. They are rather expensive, but a little goes a long way. Store in jar with tight-fitting lid and they will keep indefinitely.

OLIVE OIL

Only purchase the imported oil. For cooking, I prefer a lighter olive oil from Tuscany, such as Bertolli or Berio. Olive oil does not have to be kept in the refrigerator, but it should be kept sealed in a cool, dark place. Refrigerate on lower shelf only in extraordinarily hot weather. (Refrigerated oil turns cloudy but will not lose flavor.) A sealed oil can may be kept for several years, but do not leave oil in an open can; decant into a capped bottle. For a special treat on salads and plain boiled vegetables try one of the extra virgin olive oils. The best extra virgin oils are made entirely by hand and use only the finest olives, which are picked by hand and pressed in a manually operated cold-stone press; the resulting oil is then filtered through cheesecloth. This is the primary reason for the oils' high cost. My personal favorites are Raineri from Liguria and Badia a Coltibuono from Tuscany. Once sampled, you will never forget their fruity taste.

SCALLIONS

Select those with crisp, green, unwithered tops and clean white bottoms. Try to pick scallions with large, bulbous ends. Trim roots and any brown or limp tops. Wash thoroughly and blot dry with paper towel. Wrap in paper towel and store in plastic bag in refrigerator. Use within four to five days.

SHALLOTS

Halfway between onion and garlic. Store in cool, dark place. To use, divide the cloves. Cut off tops and tails of the shallots. Peel with a small paring knife, pulling away the first layer of flesh with the skin that is usually firmly attached to it.

SPANISH ONION

I prefer using this large yellow onion because of its sweet taste. Store in a cool, dark place. If only using a portion for a recipe, the unused part can be wrapped in plastic and stored in the refrigerator for a couple of days.

VINEGAR

Recipes call for either red or white wine vinegar. Use a good imported brand of vinegar for best results, especially in salads. The three brands I use are Badia a Coltibuono and Bertolli for red and Sasso for white.

Herbs

I have always enjoyed cooking with herbs. They are so important to my cuisine that I grow them in my garden in the summer, but during the winter months we have to use the dried variety. In this book, both fresh and dry measurements are provided. A general rule of thumb: one tablespoon of minced or chopped fresh herbs is equivalent to one teaspoon dried. When buying dried herbs, always look for those that are green rather than pale or powdered, which usually have less flavor. Buy herbs in see-through packages or glass jars so that you can see the color and judge the freshness. Store in jars with tight screw-top lids away from sunlight and heat. When using the dried variety, rub the herb between your palms to bring out its full aroma and flavor.

BASIL

Best when fresh leaf is available in summer. Pluck off the leaves just before you use them, so they won't go limp. Wash in cold water, drain well and blot dry with paper towel. The fresh leaves can be stored for winter in a jar with sea salt or kosher salt. Place about five layers of leaves in a jar and sprinkle with one teaspoon salt. Continue to layer, pressing down leaves and salting until jar is filled. Seal with lid and store in refrigerator. When ready to use, wipe off salt with damp cloth. The leaves will definitely darken in refrigerator, but will still have full, aromatic flavor. This herb marries perfectly with tomato, whether in salads or sauces.

BAY LEAF

Always buy whole leaf, never crumbled or powdered. Look for those that are still tinged with green; if they are more than a year old, they will have lost their flavor as well as their color. Wonderful flavoring for roast pork, beef soup and stews.

FENNEL

Fresh fennel, better known among Italians as *finocchio*, is usually available from late October to January. It looks somewhat like a large head of celery with a large bulb at the bottom. Trim off the green fronds (the tender leaflike part of the top of the bulb), rinse and dry with paper towel. Freeze in plastic bags. Finely chop and add to sautéed peas, artichokes or broiled fish for a faint licorice flavor. Most produce people throw the tops away, so just ask for them. The lower portion or bulb is usually served thinly sliced after dinner to cleanse the palate, or in recipes such as Fennel and Mushrooms (page 244). If fresh fennel is unavailable, dried fennel seed can be substituted. Fennel seed is usually found in Italian sausage. If it is unavailable in your area, just add about ½ teaspoon of the dried seeds to the water when steaming sausage for added seasoning.

MINT

Sometimes the dried variety is sold under the name of peppermint. Very easy to grow and dry. Collect the leaves on a hot, sunny day, preferably just before flowering time. Wipe the leaves with a damp cloth and dry on paper towel for a couple of days. A wonderful flavoring with roast lamb, broiled fish or cold seafood salads, and of course used fresh in cold summer drinks.

OREGANO

Always use sparingly because of the herb's strong, spicy flavor. Try to buy whole bunches of the dried plant, which hold their flavor longer in storage. The best quality comes from Italy, Greece and Mexico. Oregano has a great affinity for marinara sauce, and is a must on roasted peppers and on tomato salad simply dressed with olive oil, salt and pepper.

PARSLEY

The Sicilians often refer to a busybody as *putrusino* because, like parsley, he is found in everything. It can be used in almost any meat, fowl, fish or vegetable, and finely minced it will dress up any dreary-looking dish. The flat leafed variety known as Italian parsley is more pungent in taste than the curly leaf; use curly leaf for garnishing. Use leaves for flavoring. Stems can be wrapped in bundles, frozen and saved for soups. To store parsley leaves, wash and air dry on paper towel or spin dry in a salad spinner. Pack in jar and place a folded piece of paper towel on top to absorb additional moisture. Cover tightly and refrigerate. Parsley stored in this manner will stay green and fresh up to one week in refrigerator.

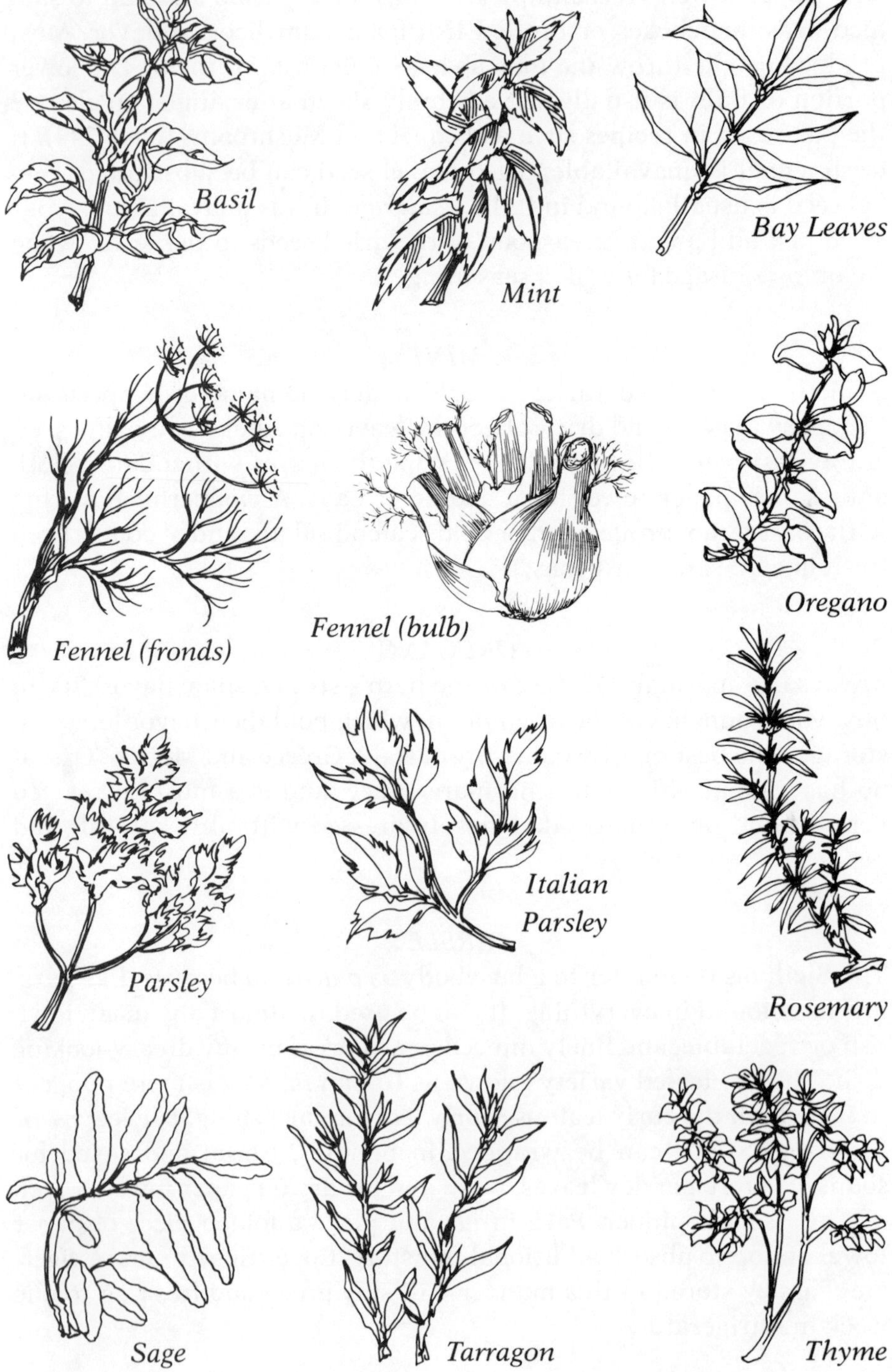

Basil

Mint

Bay Leaves

Fennel (fronds)

Fennel (bulb)

Oregano

Parsley

Italian Parsley

Rosemary

Sage

Tarragon

Thyme

ROSEMARY

Here again, fresh is best. When this herb is dried it has needle-like leaves and must be crumbled with a mortar and pestle. This is one herb that I do use powdered; ½ teaspoon powdered is equivalent to one teaspoon dried. Excellent flavoring on baked or broiled chicken, roast loin of pork or leg of lamb.

SAGE

Slightly musky taste; must be used sparingly. Fresh sage can be packed and stored with salt like basil in refrigerator for winter. Adds zesty flavoring to stuffings for roast chicken or pork.

TARRAGON

A slight anise taste. Fresh tarragon, available through the summer months, harmonizes beautifully with all egg dishes and broiled chicken. You might also want to try some snipped into your tossed green salad.

THYME

A hardy plant and easy to grow. Leaf thyme or common thyme is used for the recipes in this book. To dry, just hang in bunches in a warm, dry place, then rub the leaves off and store in a jar. A pungent flavoring for stews and beef soup; a must for bouquet garni. If available, use lemon thyme, which has a faint citrus flavor and is excellent on broiled chicken and sautéed eggplant or zucchini.

Spices

Store in jars with tight-fitting screw-top lids, away from sunlight and heat.

CINNAMON

Whole stick and good imported ground should be kept on hand. Whole stick can be ground with a mortar and pestle.

NUTMEG

Select whole nutmeg and grate with a small grater whenever needed. Much better flavor than the powdered variety.

PEPPER

Only use the finest quality whole black pepper. I buy the type known as Tellicherry Black, which comes from India. Freshly grind the pepper each time you use it. White pepper is black pepper with the outer black skin removed. I recommend it for white sauces and mayonnaise.

SAFFRON

Buy in thread form, not powdered. The threads are the dried stigmas from the flower of a crocus plant that grows around the Mediterranean. The stigmas are all removed by hand, which explains why the spice is so costly. It provides a brilliant orange-red tint and unique flavor to risotto.

Cheeses

To store all of these cheeses, wrap in foil, place in a plastic bag and refrigerate until needed (see note for storing Parmigiano Reggiano).

ASIAGO
Very similar to Provolone, but not as sharp. A good table cheese that can also be freshly grated for many pasta dishes. Made from cow's milk. Both domestic and imported varieties are excellent.

FONTINA
The real Fontina comes from only one place, the Valley of Aosta in the province of Piedmont. Before buying, ask to see the wheel and make sure the name Fontina is imprinted on top of the cheese. It is still prepared as it was many centuries ago, with unskimmed and unpasteurized milk. A very sweet and delicate semi-soft cheese and one of the greatest Italian culinary treasures. Can you tell it's one of my favorites?

FONTINELLA
Do not confuse this with Fontina. This cheese has a sharper flavor and is more like a very young Provolone in texture. A light-tasting table cheese from goat and cow's milk. Try it for a grilled cheese sandwich.

GORGONZOLA
Mold-ripened blue cheese—gray-green in color rather than blue—which tastes like blue but has a light, spicy flavor and buttery texture. For a truly special treat try Torta di Gorgonzola, which is made of layers of Mascarpone (solidified cream) and Gorgonzola. It is excellent served with crusty Italian bread and pears.

MOZZARELLA
If you must buy the packaged kind, make sure you purchase the one labeled "whole milk." I prefer the fresh variety, which is usually found soaking in water in Italian specialty shops. To store, rinse several times in cold water. Place in jar filled with water and a little salt. Cover securely with lid. Mozzarella is very perishable, and must be kept refrigerated and used within one week of purchase.

PARMIGIANO REGGIANO

This rich, nutty flavor is essential to many dishes. Parmigiano should be grated just before using so that flavor is at its best. The production of Parmigiano is very strictly controlled. Ask to see the wheel before purchasing and make sure it is stamped Reggiano. To store, wrap in a thin layer of dampened cheesecloth, then plastic wrap and an outer layer of foil before refrigerating. It must be stored in this manner because it dries out much more quickly than other cheeses. When freshly cut and moist it is also an excellent table cheese.

PECORINO ROMANO

Pecorino is the family name given to a group of cheeses made from ewe's milk. There are several different grades of Pecorino. This sharp cheese is used for robust flavoring in pastas and other dishes. It should be freshly grated just before using. For recipes in this book, I have dropped the Pecorino and just call it Romano.

PROVOLONE

You will usually find this cheese, in many different shapes, hung from the ceiling in Italian specialty stores. Made from cow's milk, Provolone comes in many varieties from very mild to very piquant. The mild type is usually packed in a thin, smooth, waxed rind and has only been aged for about two to three months. The more piquant type is matured from six months to two years, and has a dark honey color with a spicy, sharp taste.

RICOTTA SALATA

There are two different types; one is semi-soft, and the other is matured to a dry, hard consistency. Both are pressed and salted ricotta cheeses. For recipes in this book, I use the semi-soft variety. For a quick snack with a truly different flavor, try a thin slice of the semi-soft variety on a piece of banana. The hard type is excellent grated on pasta that has been tossed just with butter.

SARDO

Made from ewe's milk, this is another member of the Pecorino family. Dark yellow in color, it is often mistaken for Parmigiano but has a much sharper taste. Excellent in all pesto sauces and must be grated right from the refrigerator or it will crumble. Also a wonderful table cheese, thinly sliced. It is usually imported from Sardinia or South America; both are excellent.

Pork Products

CAPOCOLLA

Italian cured ham, hot or sweet. Either can be used for recipes in this book. Wonderful with a thin slice of melon as an appetizer.

PROSCIUTTO

The finest you can buy is from Parma, but there are many domestic prosciuttos that are of very good quality. It is air cured and when properly matured is a pale red. Prosciutto is added to many of my dishes for a wonderfully different flavor.

MORTADELLA

Italian style bologna, this is a very large, tasty sausage which has been boiled. Mouthwatering for an appetizer or in a sandwich. For full flavor, do not have it sliced too thin.

PANCETTA

Italian cured bacon, not smoked. Looks like a jelly roll and should be purchased very lean. I usually have it sliced and freeze it in 4-ounce packages. Can be frozen up to 2 months. When ready to use, take right from freezer and chop (it will also be easier to chop or dice when frozen). Pancetta is available in many gourmet shops and Italian specialty shops.

SOPRASSATA

Sometimes spelled sopressata—an Italian salami or dried sausage made with spices. It will be much easier to chop for the several recipes in this book if the casing is removed. To do this, run about 4 inches of the dried sausage under hot water until the casing feels soft, about 5 minutes. Pull casing off part of the sausage, then slice and chop. This is a good tip to remember when slicing pepperoni as well.

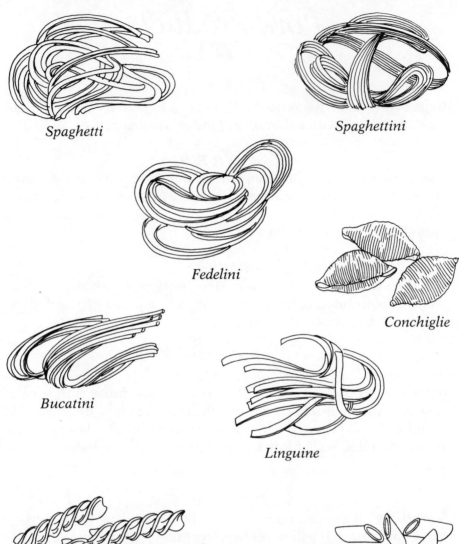

Spaghetti

Spaghettini

Fedelini

Conchiglie

Bucatini

Linguine

Fusilli

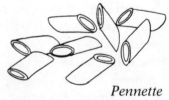

Pennette

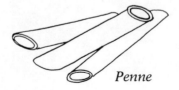

Penne

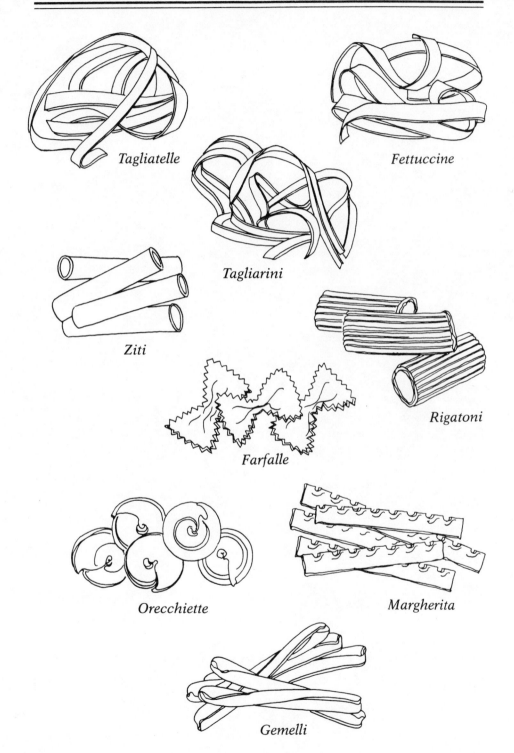

Tagliatelle

Fettuccine

Tagliarini

Ziti

Rigatoni

Farfalle

Orecchiette

Margherita

Gemelli

APPETIZERS

(Antipasti)

MARINATED ARTICHOKE HEARTS

SICILIAN EGGPLANT RELISH

BELGIAN ENDIVE WITH PROSCIUTTO

MARINATED MUSHROOMS

ROASTED PEPPER SALAD

CLAM-STUFFED MUSHROOMS

FRIED MOZZARELLA

SHRIMP WITH CAPER DRESSING

GARLIC BREAD

SAUSAGE BREAD

Whenever I mentioned the word "antipasto," Papa Casale would tease me and tell me that I was going to ruin everyone's appetite. "Anna," he would say, "everyone must come to the table so that they can enjoy the entire meal. Forget the cocktails and the appetizers—no one will have room for the pasta!"

If I am entertaining a small group, I prefer serving something such as marinated artichoke hearts, mushrooms or eggplant caponata. Anything with a vinegar base is said to open the appetite. I may select a small wedge of Asiago or Provolone cheese to accompany the vegetables.

For a large party, I serve more involved appetizers such as sausage bread, marinated shrimp or stuffed mushrooms, or a platter made up of one or two Italian cold pork products such as prosciutto, soprassata salami, capocolla or mortadella which I arrange in an outer border with marinated mushrooms or roasted peppers in the center.

The appetizers that I suggest in the following chapter can also be served as a luncheon or as a salad to accompany your entrée.

ARRANGING ANTIPASTI PLATTER (Opposite)
Roll or fold cold cuts into triangles and arrange as outer border of the antipasti platter.

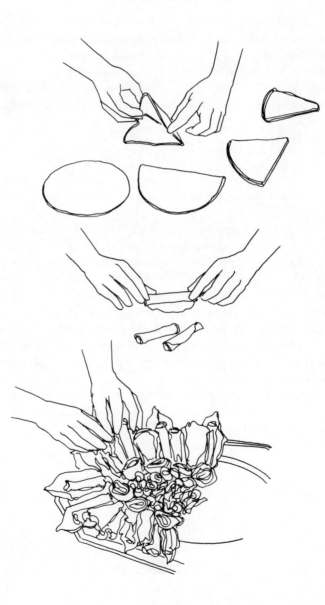

MARINATED ARTICHOKE HEARTS
Carciofi Marinati

Artichoke hearts can be prepared up to 4 days before serving. Make sure you turn jar at least once a day to keep artichoke hearts completely coated with marinade.

SERVES 8 TO 10—APPETIZER

2 packages (9 ounces each) frozen artichoke hearts
1 teaspoon salt
2 Tablespoons finely minced shallots
¼ cup imported white wine vinegar
½ cup olive oil
1 teaspoon salt
½ teaspoon freshly milled black pepper
½ teaspoon sugar
2 Tablespoons minced Italian parsley leaves (garnish)

1. Rinse frozen artichoke hearts in a strainer under warm running water to defrost.
2. In a 12-inch skillet, bring 2 cups of water to a boil and add 1 teaspoon salt. Arrange artichokes in a single layer in pan and cook, covered, over medium heat until barely tender when tested with a fork, about 4 minutes. Transfer to a strainer and refresh under cold water. Place strainer over a bowl. With your hands, gently squeeze artichokes to get rid of excess liquid.
3. In a large bowl, mix remaining ingredients except parsley. Beat dressing thoroughly with a fork. Add artichoke hearts to bowl and toss well in marinade. Transfer mixture to a 1½-quart jar with a tight-fitting lid and marinate overnight, turning jar once or twice so that artichokes are completely covered with marinade.
4. Remove artichoke hearts from refrigerator at least 2 hours before serving. Drain off some of the marinade. Transfer artichoke hearts to small bowls and garnish with chopped parsley. Serve with fancy frill picks and unsalted crackers.

SICILIAN EGGPLANT RELISH
Caponata

The zesty flavors of capers, olives and vinegar make this wonderful dish come alive. Caponata can be served with unsalted crackers as an appetizer. It can also be served as a vegetable or as an excellent topping for omelets. It is equally delicious with cold meats or poached chicken. Caponata can be made 3 days before serving, stored in jars and refrigerated until needed. It can also be packed into small plastic containers and frozen up to 3 months. Allow 4 hours to defrost before serving.

SERVES 12—APPETIZER
SERVES 8—VEGETABLE

½ cup olive oil

2 cups diced celery (strings removed), cut into ¼-inch cubes

2 cups finely chopped yellow onion

2 medium-size red or green bell peppers (10 ounces), washed, halved, cored and diced into ¼-inch cubes

2 medium-size firm eggplants (2½ pounds), washed, ends trimmed, diced into ½ inch cubes

1 cup medium-size black pitted olives (about 24), well drained and thinly sliced

½ cup medium-size pimiento-stuffed green olives (about 12), well drained and thinly sliced

3 Tablespoons capers, rinsed and well drained

1 can (6 ounces) tomato paste

¼ cup imported red wine vinegar

2 Tablespoons water

2 Tablespoons sugar

2 Tablespoons minced fresh basil or 2 teaspoons crumbled dried basil

1 teaspoon salt

1 teaspoon freshly milled black pepper

½ cup toasted almonds, coarsely chopped (optional garnish)

1. In a 5-quart Dutch oven, heat olive oil over medium heat until haze forms. Add celery and cook, stirring frequently with a wooden spoon, until barely tender, about 3 minutes. Add onion and cook, stirring frequently, until soft but not brown, about 3 minutes. Stir in peppers and cook, stirring frequently, until tender when tested with fork, about 4 minutes. Stir in eggplant and continue to cook, stirring frequently, until barely tender when tested with fork, about 5 minutes.

2. Remove pan from heat and stir in olives and capers; mix well with wooden spoon to incorporate.
3. In a small bowl, combine tomato paste, vinegar, water and sugar. Add to vegetable mixture and blend thoroughly with a wooden spoon. Add basil and season with salt and pepper.
4. Turn heat to low and cook caponata partially covered, stirring frequently with wooden spoon, for an additional 15 minutes. Remove from heat and let cool to room temperature before serving.
5. To serve as an appetizer, transfer to small bowls and garnish with chopped almonds. Serve with crackers on the side.
6. To serve as a vegetable, transfer to a large platter and garnish with chopped almonds.

BELGIAN ENDIVE WITH PROSCIUTTO
Endivia con Prosciutto

This makes a very light appetizer before a pasta course. You may want to accent the platter with a few marinated artichoke hearts.

SERVES 6—APPETIZER

2 medium heads Belgian
  endive (5 ounces)
8 ounces thinly sliced
  prosciutto

1. Very carefully remove outer leaves of Belgian endive and wipe with a damp cloth. (Save center section for salad.)
2. Tightly roll each slice of prosciutto jelly roll fashion; slice each roll in half.
3. Open each leaf of Belgian endive and place ½ roll of prosciutto in center.
4. To serve, arrange in a slightly overlapping pattern on a small platter.

MARINATED MUSHROOMS
Funghi Marinati

Make this appetizer when you can find small white button mushrooms no larger than 1 inch in diameter with tight-fitting stems. The mushroom caps can be prepared up to 3 days before serving; just remember to turn jar at least once a day to keep caps completely coated with marinade.

SERVES 8—APPETIZER
SERVES 6—SALAD

2 pounds small white mushrooms
3 cups water
1 cup distilled white vinegar
1 Tablespoon salt
¾ cup olive oil
¼ cup imported white wine vinegar

2 cloves garlic, split in half
1 teaspoon salt
½ teaspoon freshly milled white pepper
2 Tablespoons minced Italian parsley leaves (garnish)

1. Wipe mushrooms with a damp cloth. Cut off stems and save for another purpose. Divide mushrooms into three batches.
2. In a 3-quart saucepan, bring water and distilled vinegar to a boil and then add 1 Tablespoon salt.
3. Drop one batch of mushrooms into boiling vinegar-water mixture. When water returns to a boil, cook mushrooms for about 45 seconds. With a slotted spoon, transfer mushrooms to a strainer. Repeat with remaining two batches of mushrooms. Place strainer over a bowl. Put a flat plate on top of strainer with a weight on top to expel all the liquid. Let mushrooms drain for at least 30 minutes.
4. In a large bowl, combine olive oil, white wine vinegar, garlic, salt and pepper; thoroughly blend with a fork. Toss mushrooms with marinade and mix to incorporate. Transfer mixture to a 1½-quart jar with a tight-fitting lid and marinate overnight, turning jar once or twice so that mushroom caps are completely covered with marinade.
5. Remove mushroom caps from refrigerator at least 1 hour before serving. Transfer to a bowl, remove garlic, garnish with parsley and serve with fancy frill picks. Note: To serve as a salad, add 1 cup finely chopped celery to mushroom caps upon removing from refrigerator. Arrange on individual salad plates and garnish with chopped parsley.

ROASTED PEPPER SALAD
Insalata di Peperoni

Every Italian cook has his or her own technique for roasting peppers. Several years ago my Aunt Lucy taught me her method, which insures crispness and makes the peppers a lot easier to clean. When red bell peppers are in season, buy several pounds of them. Roast the peppers, peel, place in plastic containers and freeze until needed. Defrost peppers 1 day before serving, blot dry with paper towel and marinate overnight in dressing.

SERVES 8—APPETIZER

SERVES 6—SALAD

6 large firm red bell peppers (3 pounds)
2 large cloves garlic, split in half
½ cup olive oil

1 Tablespoon minced fresh oregano or 1 teaspoon crumbled dried oregano
1 teaspoon salt
½ teaspoon freshly milled black pepper

1. Adjust oven rack to 6 inches from broiler and preheat to broil setting.
2. Wash peppers in cold water, blot dry with paper towel and slice in half lengthwise. Remove core and seeds.
3. Place peppers cut side down on a baking sheet. Broil peppers until partially charred, about 5 minutes. Remove from oven, wrap in paper towels and place in a plastic bag. Secure the end with a twist tie or twine and let stand for at least one hour to cool. Remove from bag and peel peppers with a small paring knife. Pat dry with paper towel and cut lengthwise into ½-inch strips.
4. In a medium bowl, mix remaining ingredients. Add peppers and toss well. Transfer mixture to a 1-quart jar with a tight-fitting lid and refrigerate overnight, turning jar once or twice so that peppers are completely covered with dressing.
5. Remove from refrigerator 1 hour before serving. Transfer to a platter, remove garlic and serve with a basket of crusty garlic bread.

CLAM-STUFFED MUSHROOMS
Funghi Imbottiti Vongole

For the loveliest presentation, hand pick pure white mushrooms all the same size.

SERVES 8 TO 10

24 medium to large mushrooms (about 1 pound)
3 Tablespoons unsalted butter
1 teaspoon finely minced garlic
1 can (6½ ounces) minced clams, well drained
1 cup fresh breadcrumbs
2 Tablespoons minced Italian parsley leaves
1 Tablespoon minced fresh oregano or 1 teaspoon crumbled dried oregano
1 teaspoon salt
½ teaspoon freshly milled black pepper
2 Tablespoons olive oil
1 bunch curly parsley (garnish)

1. Adjust oven rack to upper portion of oven and preheat to 450°F.
2. Wipe mushrooms with a damp cloth. Snap out stems, trim ends and chop finely. (Can be chopped in food processor fitted with metal blade.)
3. Melt butter in a small skillet over low heat. Add garlic and cook until soft but not brown, about 2 minutes. Add chopped mushroom stems and cook, stirring constantly, for another 30 seconds. Transfer mixture to bowl and add remaining ingredients, except olive oil; mix well.
4. Fill mushroom caps with mixture, mounding slightly in center.
5. Arrange on a cookie sheet and drizzle ¼ teaspoon olive oil over each. Bake until lightly golden, about 5 to 7 minutes.
6. Arrange parsley on a flat platter and place stuffed mushrooms on top; serve immediately.

FRIED MOZZARELLA
Mozzarella Fritta

Nothing more is needed with this filling appetizer than a glass of chilled white wine.

SERVES 6 TO 8

8 ounces whole milk
  Mozzarella cheese
¼ cup Wondra flour
2 extra large eggs
1 teaspoon salt

½ teaspoon freshly milled
  black pepper
1½ cups fine dry breadcrumbs
1½ cups vegetable oil,
  preferably corn

1. Cut Mozzarella into ½-inch slices and then into ½-inch strips.
2. Place flour in a shallow bowl. In another shallow bowl, beat eggs, salt and pepper thoroughly with a fork. Place bread crumbs in third bowl.
3. Dip Mozzarella strips in flour, then in beaten eggs. Dredge thoroughly in breadcrumbs, making sure cheese is thoroughly coated with crumbs so that it does not ooze in frying. Arrange strips in a single layer on a large platter lined with waxed paper. Chill for at least 1 hour (chilling will prevent breadcrumb coating from falling off when frying).
4. In a 12-inch skillet, heat vegetable oil over medium-high heat until haze forms. Fry Mozzarella in two batches, turning once, until lightly golden on both sides. Drain on paper towels.
5. To serve, arrange on platter and serve immediately.

SHRIMP WITH CAPER DRESSING
Insalata di Gamberetti

A great do-ahead appetizer that will tantalize your guests! Soaking the shrimp in ice water and lemon will keep it tender and moist.

SERVES 10 TO 12

1 teaspoon salt
2 pounds medium shrimp,
  shelled and deveined

½ lemon, seeded and sliced
  into 4 wedges

1. In a 5-quart pot, bring 3 quarts of water to a boil and add 1 teaspoon salt. Place shrimp in pot and cover. As soon as water returns to a boil, uncover and cook shrimp just until they turn pink, about 2 minutes; do not overcook or shrimp will be tough. Drain in a colander and rinse under cold water.

2. Place shrimp in a 3½-quart jar, layering lemon wedges in between. Fill jar with cold water, cover and refrigerate for at least 6 hours or overnight.

DRESSING

¼ cup fresh lemon juice
½ cup olive oil
1 Tablespoon Dijon mustard
½ cup Italian parsley leaves, well packed
¾ cup celery, cut into ½-inch pieces, strings removed
¾ cup scallions, cut into 1-inch pieces

1 teaspoon salt
1 teaspoon freshly milled black pepper
¼ cup capers, rinsed and well drained
1 medium head romaine lettuce (about 1 pound), garnish

1. Place all ingredients except capers in food processor fitted with metal blade. Run machine nonstop until the dressing is creamy and vegetables and parsley are finely minced. Transfer to a bowl and mix in capers. (Dressing can be made one day ahead, covered and refrigerated.)

2. Discard any bruised outer leaves from romaine. Trim tough bottom ends and wash several times in cold water to remove grit. Spin dry in a salad spinner or blot with paper towel.

3. Two hours before serving, drain shrimp, discard lemon and blot shrimp thoroughly dry with paper towel.

4. In a large bowl, combine shrimp with dressing, cover with plastic wrap, and refrigerate for 2 hours (do not marinate any longer or shrimp will become soggy).

5. To serve, arrange a border of romaine on a platter. Toss shrimp in marinade again and pile in center of platter. Serve with toothpicks.

GARLIC BREAD
Pane Untata

This garlic bread can be made with regular olive oil, but if extra virgin oil is available, by all means use it. The fragrance and taste are truly unforgettable.

SERVES 8

1 large loaf French or Italian bread, split in half lengthwise
1 large clove garlic, split in half

¼ cup (approximately) extra virgin olive oil
Salt and freshly milled black pepper

1. Adjust oven rack to 6 inches from boiler and preheat oven to broil setting.
2. Place bread cut side down on a baking sheet and toast on both sides until lightly golden. Remove from oven and transfer to a cutting board with split side up.
3. Immediately rub garlic over cut side of bread. (It does not take much rubbing to give the bread a strong flavor of garlic; the more you rub, the stronger the flavor.) Generously brush olive oil on top; sprinkle with salt and freshly milled black pepper. Slice into 1½-inch wedges, transfer to platter or basket and serve immediately.

SAUSAGE BREAD
Pane di Salsicce

If you are looking for a finger food with a savory filling that is just a little different, this appetizer is always a crowd pleaser.

YIELDS 3 LOAVES
SERVES 12

DOUGH

¼ cup warm water (105 to 115°F)
1 teaspoon sugar
1 package active dry yeast
3½ cups unbleached flour
1½ teaspoons salt
2 Tablespoons sugar

1 Tablespoon nonfat dry milk powder
2 extra large eggs, lightly beaten
6 Tablespoons warm water
1 Tablespoon unsalted butter, softened

FOOD PROCESSOR METHOD

1. In a small mixing bowl, combine ¼ cup warm water and 1 teaspoon sugar. Add yeast and stir until completely dissolved. Set aside until foamy, about 5 minutes.
2. Fit processor with metal blade. Measure flour, salt, 2 Tablespoons sugar and dry milk into work bowl. Process until mixed, about 10 seconds.
3. Add yeast mixture to work bowl and process until blended, about 20 seconds.
4. Remove cover and pour lightly beaten egg over flour mixture. Process again until blended, about 20 seconds. Remove cover and scrape down sides of work bowl with rubber spatula. Spoon half of the water onto dough. Cover and process for 20 seconds. Remove cover and scrape down sides of work bowl with spatula. Drizzle remaining water onto dough and process until dough forms a ball that cleans sides of the bowl. Process until dough turns around bowl about 25 times. Turn off processor and let dough rest 1 to 2 minutes. Turn machine on and process until dough turns around bowl about 15 times. At this point, the dough should be soft, smooth and satiny, but not sticky; if it is sticky, add 2 more Tablespoons flour and process until satiny.
5. Turn dough onto lightly floured surface. Knead until extremely smooth, about 3 minutes. Shape dough into a ball.

6. Grease sides and bottom of a 3-quart bowl with softened butter. Place ball of dough in greased bowl, turning once to bring greased side up. Cover with plastic wrap and then a dishtowel. Let rise in a warm place (80 to 85°F) until doubled in bulk, about 1 hour.

HAND METHOD

1. In a small mixing bowl, combine ¼ cup warm water and 1 teaspoon sugar. Add yeast and stir until completely dissolved. Set aside until foamy, about 5 minutes.

2. In a large mixing bowl, sift 1 cup flour, salt, 2 Tablespoons sugar and dry milk.

3. Add yeast mixture and beat thoroughly with a wooden spoon. Add lightly beaten eggs and remaining water; beat with wooden spoon to incorporate. Add another cup of flour and beat again with wooden spoon until completely incorporated. At this point the dough should be soft and sticky. Transfer dough to a lightly floured surface. Gradually add remaining flour ½ cup at a time, kneading with your hands until the dough is smooth and satiny, but not sticky. If dough is sticky, add about 2 more Tablespoons flour and knead until smooth and satiny. Total kneading time will be approximately 20 minutes. Shape dough into a ball.

4. Grease sides and bottom of 3-quart bowl with softened butter. Place ball of dough in greased bowl, turning once to bring greased side up. Cover with plastic wrap and then a dishtowel. Let rise in a warm place (80 to 85°F) until doubled in bulk, about 1 hour.

FILLING

1¼ pounds Italian sweet sausage with fennel

8 ounces Mozzarella cheese, grated (2 cups)

8 ounces thinly sliced Genoa salami, cut into ½-inch strips

6 ounces Asiago or Provolone cheese, grated (1½ cups)

1 cup finely minced Italian parsley leaves, well packed

1. In a 1½-quart saucepan, combine sausage and 1½ cups water. Cover and bring to a boil. Reduce heat to low and simmer, covered, for 15 minutes. Let sausage cool in cooking liquid. Remove casing and chop coarsely (can be chopped in food processor fitted with metal blade). Set aside with remaining ingredients.

TO ASSEMBLE AND BAKE

1 large egg
1 Tablespoon water

1. Divide dough into 3 pieces. Remove 1 piece and keep remaining dough covered with plastic wrap so that it will not dry out.
2. Line bottom of a 10 × 15-inch jelly roll pan with parchment paper.
3. Adjust oven rack to center of oven and preheat to 375°F.
4. On a lightly floured work surface, stretch dough into a rectangular shape with fingers. Roll out dough evenly into a 14 × 10-inch rectangle. Transfer dough to a cutting board with long end facing you.
5. Leaving a ½-inch border on all four sides, sprinkle dough with ⅓ of each of the filling ingredients in this order: sausage, Mozzarella cheese, salami, Asiago or Provolone and parsley. Tightly roll up dough jelly roll fashion. Pinch seam down center and ends to seal. Place in pan with seam side down. Cover with dishtowel while assembling the other 2 loaves. Make remaining loaves and arrange in pan 2½ inches apart.
6. In a small bowl, combine egg with water and beat with a fork. Brush top and sides of each loaf with egg wash.
7. Bake breads until tops are lightly golden, about 25 minutes. Transfer to a wire rack and let cool for 10 minutes.
8. To serve, slice loaves at a 20° angle. Arrange in an overlapping pattern on large platter.

Note: To freeze, let sausage bread cool completely on wire rack. Wrap in plastic and then in aluminum foil. Loaves can be kept frozen up to 2 months. Defrost, unwrapped, for 3 hours. Place on cookie sheet and warm in preheated 325°F oven for 20 minutes.

SOUPS

(Zuppe)

BEEF BROTH

CHICKEN BROTH

CARROT—PANCETTA SOUP

ESCAROLE, RICE AND TINY MEATBALL SOUP

LENTIL SOUP WITH PENNETTE

POTATO—PARSLEY SOUP

TUSCAN BEAN SOUP

VEGETABLE SOUP

As a child I can remember the weekly ritual that started each Monday morning. As I would come into the kitchen for breakfast before leaving for school, there would always be a large pot of chicken or beef broth simmering on the stove. While Monday was traditionally Mamma's wash day, it was also her day to make broth. Kissing Mamma goodbye, I'd catch a final glimpse of the broth pot. The sight signified more than merely letting me know I'd be having soup that night; it assured me that Mamma would be replenishing her supply of the magically clear liquid she seemed to add to so many of her wonderful creations.

As I grew older and more inquisitive, Mamma shared with me many of her secrets for making a variety of soups. In recalling these pointers, I realize her soup suggestions are all broth-based.

- Broth should always be clear. To insure clear broth, always bring it to a slow boil; rapid boiling makes for cloudy broth. It can take almost an hour to bring a large pot of broth to a slow boil.
- Froth must be skimmed from the broth several times, depending on the type and amount being made.
- Garlic should be unpeeled when it is added to broth. Peeled garlic will fall apart as it cooks and tends to make broth cloudy.
- The ribcages left over from boning chicken breasts have enough meat on the bones to produce an excellent broth.
- Simmer broth slowly to bring out its full flavor. To extract the most flavor from the meat and vegetables, be sure to allow broth to rest for at least an hour before straining.
- Once broth is chilled or frozen, the fat will rise to the surface. This fat acts as a seal for preserving freshness. Do not remove

it until ready to use for soups or sauces. Beef broth should not be used until it has had time to be sufficiently chilled and its surface fat removed.

Perhaps her best secret, and the lesson I wish to share with you, is the knowledge that a good broth is more than just a simple soup. It is an essential ingredient in any number of wonderful culinary creations.

The reaction of many of the students at one of my hearty soup courses is, "This isn't soup—it's a meal!" I think you'll agree with them as you sample some of the robust soups that follow.

Remember: *the heartiest, most robust soup has as its base the same clear, golden chicken or richly amber beef broth I trust will soon be simmering on your kitchen stove.*

BEEF BROTH
Brodo di Manzo

This rich, amber broth forms the base not only for soups, but for many of the sauces used throughout this book. When shin sold for less than a dollar a pound, one wouldn't hesitate discarding it. At today's prices, however, I recommend reserving it, removing any fat or sinew and thinly slicing it for sandwiches. If beef soup is desired, cut shin into ½-inch cubes and return with chopped vegetables to the strained broth.

YIELDS ABOUT 3½ QUARTS

3 pounds beef bones (including marrow)
1 beef shin, 2½ to 3 pounds
4½ quarts cold water
2 Tablespoons salt
1 large yellow onion (8 ounces), peeled and halved
3 medium carrots (8 ounces), trimmed and peeled
3 large celery ribs (9 ounces), trimmed and halved, including leaves
1 large parsnip (3 ounces), trimmed and peeled

5 canned Italian plum tomatoes, well drained
1 large bay leaf
6 parsley stems or sprigs, tied together with kitchen twine
2 large cloves garlic, unpeeled
10 peppercorns

1. Place bones and beef shin in an 8-quart pot. Add water and salt, cover and very slowly bring to a boil over low heat. Skim off all the foam that rises to the surface with a skimmer or small strainer (you may have to skim 4 to 5 times). Simmer partially covered for 2 hours. Add remaining ingredients and continue cooking, partially covered, over low heat for 1 hour. Turn heat off and let broth rest for 1 hour.
2. Remove shin and set aside to cool. Discard bones from broth with tongs.
3. Strain broth through a fine mesh strainer lined with a double thickness of dampened cheesecloth into a large bowl. Remove carrots, celery, parsnip and pieces of tomato. Finely dice vegetables and save for soup, or discard. Discard remaining solids.
4. Cool broth to room temperature and pour into jars with tight-fitting lids; do not use broth the same day you make it, because it will be too greasy. Broth can be kept in refrigerator for 1 week. It can also be frozen in plastic containers up to 5 months. When ready to use, discard fat from surface.

CHICKEN BROTH
Brodo di Pollo

Many of the sauces and hearty soups found in this book begin with this richly golden broth. If a chicken soup is desired, return boned, skinned chicken pieces and chopped vegetables to the strained broth.

YIELDS 4 QUARTS

1 5-pound roasting chicken or 5 pounds chicken parts, such as necks, backs, wings and ribcages from boned breasts

5 quarts cold water

2 Tablespoons salt

1 large yellow onion (8 ounces), peeled and halved

3 medium carrots (8 ounces), trimmed and peeled

3 large celery ribs (8 ounces), trimmed and halved, including leaves

1 large or 2 small parsnips (3 ounces), trimmed and peeled

10 parsley stems, tied together with kitchen twine

2 large cloves garlic, unpeeled

6 peppercorns

1. Rinse chicken or parts well in cold water and place in a 10-quart pot. If using whole chicken, place in pot breast down. Add water and salt, cover and slowly bring to a boil over low heat. Skim all the foam that rises to the surface with a skimmer or small strainer (you may have to skim 2 or 3 times). Simmer partially covered for 2 hours. Add remaining ingredients and continue cooking, partially covered, over low heat for another 45 minutes. Turn heat off and let broth rest for 1 hour.
2. With a slotted spoon, remove chicken carcass or parts. Reserve chicken for soup. If using parts, discard.
3. Strain broth through a fine mesh strainer lined with a double thickness of dampened cheesecloth into another pot. Remove carrots, celery and parsnip. Finely dice vegetables and save for soup, or discard. Discard remaining solids.
4. Cool broth to room temperature and pour into jars with tight-fitting lids. Broth can be kept in refrigerator for 1 week. Broth can also be frozen in plastic containers up to 3 months. When ready to use, discard fat from surface.

CARROT–PANCETTA SOUP
Zuppa di Carote e Pancetta

A colorful, fresh-tasting soup that can be the mainstay of a luncheon or supper and can double as a first course. If you have a food processor, use it! All the vegetables can be finely chopped in processor fitted with metal blade, which makes this soup a breeze to prepare. Cut vegetables into 1-inch chunks before placing in processor.

YIELDS 3 QUARTS
SERVES 12

4 sprigs Italian parsley
1 large bay leaf
2 sprigs fresh thyme or 1 teaspoon dried thyme
½ cup (1 stick) unsalted butter, cut into 8 pieces
4 ounces pancetta or very lean bacon, finely diced
½ large yellow onion (4 ounces), finely chopped
2 pounds carrots, peeled and finely chopped
4 large celery ribs (8 ounces), strings removed, finely chopped

2 large Russet potatoes (1 pound), peeled and finely chopped
½ cup flour
2½ quarts chicken broth
1 teaspoon salt
1 teaspoon freshly milled black pepper
½ cup sour cream (garnish)
1 Tablespoon minced Italian parsley leaves (garnish)

1. To make bouquet garni, place parsley sprigs, bay leaf and thyme in the center of a 6-inch square of cheesecloth. Tie securely into a bundle with kitchen twine and set aside.
2. In a heavy 6-quart pot, melt butter over medium heat. Add pancetta or bacon and cook, stirring constantly, until soft but not brown, about 3 minutes. Add onion, carrots, celery and potatoes. Sauté, stirring frequently, until vegetables are slightly softened, about 5 minutes. Stir in flour and cook, stirring constantly, until well incorporated into vegetable mixture, about 2 minutes. Add chicken broth, turn heat to high and bring to a boil. Add bouquet garni, salt and pepper. Turn heat to low, cover pot and simmer, stirring occasionally, for another 45 minutes. Remove from heat and let soup cool to almost room temperature. Remove bouquet garni.
3. Ladle 3 cups of soup at a time into food processor fitted with metal blade. Run machine nonstop until you have a creamy puree. Transfer soup to a clean pot and repeat until all the soup is pureed. If you do not have a food

processor, puree soup in batches through the fine disc of a food mill set over a bowl.

4. When ready to serve, reheat over low heat. Ladle into individual bowls and garnish each with a dollop of sour cream and a sprinkling of minced parsley.

Note: Soup freezes very well and can be kept frozen up to 2 months.

ESCAROLE, RICE AND TINY MEATBALL SOUP
Zuppa di Scarola e Riso con Polpettine

Mamma always made this soup when anyone in the family had a cold. This makes an excellent first course or, again, it can be a whole meal!

SERVES 6

8 ounces very lean chopped sirloin or top round steak

2 Tablespoons freshly grated Parmigiano cheese

2 Tablespoons finely minced Italian parsley leaves

¼ teaspoon salt

¼ teaspoon freshly milled black pepper

1 extra large egg, lightly beaten

1 medium head escarole (¾ to 1 pound)

½ cup Arborio or converted long-grain rice, picked over and any dark grains removed

½ teaspoon salt

1½ quarts chicken broth

Freshly grated Parmigiano cheese (for serving)

1. In a shallow bowl, combine chopped meat, Parmigiano cheese, parsley, ¼ teaspoon salt and pepper; blend together with a fork. Add lightly beaten egg and mix with your hands until all the ingredients are well incorporated. Shape into meatballs the size of marbles (about ½ inch in diameter). Arrange in a single layer on a platter lined with waxed paper and refrigerate for at least 1 hour (chilling will prevent meatballs from falling apart when added to soup).

2. Discard any bruised or wilted leaves from escarole. Cut off tough bottom ends of greens. Wash leaves several times in cold water. Place escarole in a 3-quart saucepan (do not add water; the final rinse water clinging to leaves

will be sufficient to steam them). Cook, covered, over medium heat until tender when tested with a fork, about 6 minutes. Transfer to a colander and refresh under cold water. Squeeze out excess moisture with your hands. Transfer to a cutting board and chop coarsely. Set aside.

3. Cook rice in 1 quart boiling water with ½ teaspoon salt until al dente, about 8 minutes. Drain in a strainer and rinse under cold running water. Set aside.

4. In a 4-quart saucepan, bring chicken broth to a boil. Turn heat to medium and add meatballs a few at a time. Cover pan and cook for 6 minutes. Add escarole and rice to soup. Continue to cook, covered, until heated through, about 3 minutes.

5. Ladle soup into individual bowls and serve with freshly grated Parmigiano cheese.

LENTIL SOUP WITH PENNETTE
Zuppa di Lenticchie

This soup can be the main event of a hearty one-dish meal. A large bowl with good bread and a salad is a good reminder that simple is best! You may want to double this recipe and use the whole bag of lentils (1 pound); eat half and freeze half (do not add pasta if you are going to freeze). Soup can be kept frozen up to 3 months.

SERVES 6 TO 8

8 ounces dried lentils
3 Tablespoons olive oil
3 Tablespoons unsalted butter
4 ounces pancetta or very lean bacon, finely diced
1 large leek (4 ounces), trimmed, split in half, thoroughly washed and thinly sliced
3 large celery ribs (6 ounces), strings removed, cut into ¼-inch cubes
2 large carrots (6 ounces), peeled and cut into ¼-inch cubes

1 small parsnip (2 ounces), peeled and cut into ¼-inch cubes
1 cup canned Italian plum tomatoes, coarsely chopped, juice included
4½ cups beef broth, heated
2 teaspoons salt
1 teaspoon freshly milled black pepper
1 cup pennette or any short tubular pasta
1 teaspoon salt
Freshly grated Romano cheese (for serving)

1. Spread lentils in a single layer on a large plate and discard any bits of foreign matter. Rinse lentils in a strainer with cold water and soak in 3 quarts of cold water for at least 3 hours.
2. In a 6-quart pot, heat olive oil over medium heat until haze forms, then add butter. Add pancetta or bacon and cook, stirring constantly, until soft but not brown, about 3 minutes. Add leek, celery, carrots and parsnips. Sauté, stirring frequently, until vegetables are slightly softened, about 5 minutes. Add tomatoes and cook, stirring frequently, for an additional 5 minutes.
3. Drain lentils. Add to pot with heated broth, and season with 2 teaspoons salt and pepper. Cover pot, turn heat to low, and cook, stirring frequently, until lentils are tender, about 1 hour. Remove from heat and let soup rest for at least 1 hour.
4. Cook pasta in 2 quarts boiling water with 1 teaspoon salt until al dente. Drain well in a colander and add to soup.
5. When ready to serve, reheat soup over low heat. Ladle into individual bowls and serve with freshly grated Romano cheese.

Note: If you do not have beef broth on hand, you can substitute water. After cooking, the soup must rest for at least 4 hours or overnight before serving so that all the flavors meld together.

POTATO–PARSLEY SOUP
Zuppa di Patate e Prezzemolo

A very creamy, smooth soup—unlike anything you'll find in a can! Excellent served hot or cold.

SERVES 8

3 Tablespoons unsalted butter

2 large leeks (8 ounces), trimmed, split in half, thoroughly washed and thinly sliced

4 large celery ribs (8 ounces), strings removed, finely chopped

2 large baking potatoes (1½ pounds), peeled and coarsely shredded

4½ cups chicken broth

1 bay leaf

1 teaspoon salt

½ teaspoon freshly milled white pepper

2 cups light cream or half and half

½ cup finely minced Italian parsley leaves

1. In a 5-quart heavy pot, melt butter over medium heat. Add leeks and celery and sauté until soft but not brown, stirring frequently, about 10 minutes.
2. Add potatoes, chicken broth, bay leaf, salt and pepper. Cook partially covered over medium heat, stirring frequently, for 30 minutes. (Frequently stirring will prevent potatoes from sticking to bottom of pot). Remove from heat and let soup rest for 1 hour. Discard bay leaf.
3. Ladle 3 cups of soup at a time into food processor fitted with metal blade. Run machine nonstop until you have a smooth puree. Transfer soup to a clean pot and repeat until all the soup is pureed. If you do not have a food processor, puree the soup in batches through the fine disc of a food mill set over a bowl.
4. Stir minced parsley into soup and add light cream. Reheat over low heat, stirring constantly.

Note: This soup is also excellent served cold. After you have pureed all the soup, dilute with light cream. Add parsley and mix well. Cover and chill until ready to serve.

TUSCAN BEAN SOUP
Zuppa di Cannellini

My grandfather, Donato, often made this Tuscan soup but did not add pasta. You may want to try his version: After the soup had finished cooking, he would remove about 4 cups, puree it in a food mill and return it to the pot (it can also be pureed in a food processor fitted with the metal blade). He would then toast day-old Italian bread, line the bottoms of the soup plates with it, ladle the hot soup over and top it off with plenty of freshly grated Romano or Parmigiano cheese. This soup freezes very well; do not add pasta if you are going to freeze it. Can be kept frozen up to 3 months.

YIELDS 4 QUARTS

1 pound dried white kidney beans (cannellini) or 4 cans (20 ounces each) cannellini beans, well drained

¼ cup olive oil

6 ounces pancetta or very lean bacon, finely diced

1 cup finely chopped yellow onion

1 cup finely chopped celery

1 Tablespoon minced fresh basil or 1 teaspoon crumbled dried basil

1 teaspoon salt

1 teaspoon freshly milled black pepper

1½ quarts (6 cups) chicken broth

8 ounces (2 cups) ditalini or any short tubular pasta

1 teaspoon salt

3 Tablespoons minced Italian parsley leaves

Freshly grated Romano or Parmigiano cheese (for serving)

1. If using dried beans, spread in a single layer on a large plate and discard any bits of foreign matter. Place beans in a large bowl, cover with 5 cups cold water and soak overnight.
2. Drain beans and place in a 6-quart pot. Add 10 cups cold water, cover pot and bring to a boil over medium heat. Reduce heat to low and cook until beans are tender, about 1 hour. (Beans can be cooked up to 2 days in advance, transferred to a bowl or jars along with cooking liquid and refrigerated until needed.)
3. In an 8-quart pot, heat olive oil over medium heat until haze forms. Add pancetta or bacon and cook, stirring constantly, until soft but not brown, about 3 minutes. Add onion and celery and continue cooking, stirring frequently, until soft but not brown, about 5 minutes. Add basil, 1 teaspoon salt and pepper.

4. Add chicken broth, cover pot and bring to a boil over medium heat.
5. Drain beans in strainer, add to soup, cover pot and simmer over low heat for 30 minutes.
6. Meanwhile, cook pasta in 4 quarts boiling water with 1 teaspoon salt until al dente. Drain well in colander and add to soup.
7. Stir in minced parsley just before serving. Ladle into individual bowls and serve with freshly grated cheese.

VEGETABLE SOUP
Minestrone

Every Italian family has its own recipe for minestrone. Our version is very substantial, richly satisfying and an ideal one-dish meal. Make this whole recipe—eat some and freeze some. Can be placed in containers and kept frozen up to 3 months.

YIELDS 5 QUARTS

1 large head cabbage (2 pounds), preferably Savoy
3 Tablespoons olive oil
1 pound very lean Italian sweet sausage, casing removed, crumbled
1 large yellow onion (8 ounces), finely chopped
1 can (35 ounces) Italian plum tomatoes, coarsely chopped, juice included (can be chopped in food processor fitted with metal blade)
1 Tablespoon salt
1 teaspoon freshly milled black pepper
2 teaspoons sugar
2 Tablespoons minced fresh basil or 2 teaspoons crumbled dried basil

6 large carrots (1 pound), peeled and diced into ¼-inch cubes
8 large celery ribs (1 pound), strings removed, diced into ¼-inch cubes
2½ quarts chicken broth
½ cup Arborio or converted long-grain rice, picked over and any dark grains removed
1 can (20 ounces) white cannellini beans, well drained
1 can (20 ounces) kidney beans, well drained
Freshly grated Parmigiano or Romano cheese (for serving)

1. Discard any bruised outer leaves from cabbage. Wash cabbage and blot dry with paper towel. Quarter cabbage and remove center core. Shred each quarter on the large holes of a grater or in food processor fitted with shredding disc. Set aside.

2. In an 8-quart stockpot, heat olive oil over medium heat until haze forms. Add crumbled sausage, turn heat to low and sauté just until it loses its pinkness, about 3 minutes. Add onion and sauté until soft but not brown, about 5 minutes. Add tomatoes, salt, pepper, sugar and basil. Cook sauce uncovered, stirring frequently, for 15 minutes. Add cabbage and cook, stirring frequently, until limp, about 5 minutes. Add carrots and celery. Continue to cook, stirring frequently, for an additional 5 minutes. Pour in chicken broth and bring to boil over high heat. As soon as soup reaches a boil, turn heat to low, cover pot and simmer, stirring frequently, until vegetables are cooked, about 45 minutes.

3. Stir in rice, cover pot and cook undisturbed over low heat for 10 minutes. Stir in both beans; cook, covered, for an additional 5 minutes. Remove pot from heat and let soup rest for 2 hours before serving so that all the flavors meld together.

4. If sausage is not lean, you will have to skim off any surface grease with a large spoon.

5. When ready to serve, reheat over low heat. Ladle into individual bowls and serve with freshly grated Parmigiano or Romano cheese.

PASTA AND SAUCES

PASTA
TOMATO-BASED SAUCES
VEGETABLE AND CREAM SAUCES
SEAFOOD SAUCES
PASTA SPECIALTIES

Pasta

COOKING PASTA

EGG PASTA
Food Processor Method and Hand Method
Pasta Machine and Hand Method

SPINACH PASTA
Food Processor Method and Hand Method

Today everyone's eyes seem to light up whenever the words "fresh pasta" are mentioned. There is nothing better tasting than a dish of homemade pasta. Once sampled, it is hard to be satisfied with anything else.

Some traditionalists believe that the very best pasta is hand rolled and hand cut. I can still remember sitting in my Nonna Louisa's kitchen and watching her skillfully make pasta with what seemed to me, at the time, no effort at all. She would begin by placing a mound of flour on her kitchen table. Using three fingers, she would make a well in the center, add lightly beaten eggs, a little salt, a few drops of olive oil and a sprinkling of water. Gradually, using the same three fingers, she would incorporate the flour into the egg mixture. Everything seemed to blend neatly into a mass in a matter of seconds. She would scrape away any caked dough with a large knife, sprinkle a little more flour on the table and start to knead with the heels of her palms until it was smooth. Nothing was ever measured; everything was done by eye, touch and feel. I can remember her telling me, "Anna, you must always rub the dough with a little olive oil to make it relax so that it rolls out easier." The dough would then be placed in a bowl and covered with a damp cloth for about forty minutes. At this point, I would be sent out to play until she called me back to help. Watching her roll out the dough was always an exciting experience for me. She used a dowel about three inches thick and three feet long that Nonno Chico had made for her.

Nonna Louisa was a rather large woman who could work the dough into a paper-thin sheet in a matter of seconds. She would lightly flour the sheet of dough, wrap it loosely around the rolling pin, slip it off and cut it into thin strips. My job was to separate *the strands and place them on a lightly floured, large white linen tablecloth to dry out for a few minutes before cooking.*

Several years after she died, I tried making the dough by myself—only to find that it was not as easy as it had seemed while watching Nonna Louisa. After many attempts, I finally arrived at a formula that successfully carries me back to the warmth of my grandmother's kitchen.

When I purchased my first food processor, I started adapting my version of Nonna's recipe and was amazed with the results. It is almost miraculous how quickly and easily—in less than a minute—the food processor mixes and kneads fresh pasta dough.

The task is reduced when the dough is rolled out with the aid of a pasta machine. If someone were to blindfold me, I would not be able to tell the difference in texture between the hand-cut and the machine-cut variety.

A word of warning before you start making pasta: Do not try to make it on a hot, humid day, because the dough will take on moisture and will not roll out properly.

Nonna Louisa always used unbleached flour for making pasta, but I prefer semolina. It is available in most Italian specialty or gourmet shops. Semolina is made from durum wheat and produces a firmer type of pasta that holds up better in cooking. There are different textures of semolina. I prefer one that is finely ground and resembles a cake flour to the coarsely ground variety that resembles cornmeal. If semolina is unavailable, use unbleached all purpose flour. The texture will be a little different but it will still produce an exceptionally tender pasta.

After teaching many pasta courses, I find the easiest method of measurement is to weigh the flour. A half pound of semolina flour is about 1¾ cups, while a half pound of unbleached flour is about 1½ cups. A kitchen scale is a worthwhile investment for all cooks.

Eggs vary in size and will absorb flour a little differently, so be sure you weigh the eggs (in the shell) before starting. Be sure the eggs are at room temperature so that the dough will stay soft and easy to handle.

Letting the dough rest for at least 30 minutes will relax it so that the dough will not shrink back to its original shape when you try to roll it out.

Once you have learned the technique of making fresh pasta, don't stop at one batch. Make at least three, using one and drying or freezing the other two. With practice, you too can be as proficient a pasta maker as Nonna Louisa was.

Cooking Pasta

There are just a few simple rules to remember in cooking perfect pasta, whether homemade or commercial. The first of these is that the pasta must be cooked in a large pot (at least 8 quarts) so that it can swim freely; otherwise it will stick together.

For 1 pound of pasta, bring 6 quarts of water to a rolling boil and add 1 Tablespoon of salt. If cooking homemade pasta, also add 2 teaspoons vegetable or olive oil. Add the pasta slowly, so that the water never stops boiling. If the boiling should subside a little, cover the pot briefly to bring the water back to a rolling boil.

Stir the pasta frequently with a wooden fork to separate the pieces. A metal fork will break long strands, especially if the pasta is homemade. Don't leave the pot once the pasta has been added to the boiling water. The cooking time will vary with the size and shape. Fresh homemade pasta will be ready in about 2 minutes; dried homemade, in about 5 minutes. Frozen pasta, cooked directly from the freezer, will take 4 to 6 minutes. Commercial pasta will take anywhere from 5 to 20 minutes of boiling. The only way to tell whether it is done is to lift a piece from the water with the wooden fork and bite into it. The pasta should be cooked *al dente*, which means it should be slightly resistant to the bite—literally, "to the tooth."

Begin testing fresh pasta 1 minute after it is in the pot, dried homemade pasta after 2 minutes of cooking time, and frozen pasta after 3 minutes. Commercial pastas should be tested after 4 minutes. Keep tasting every few minutes until al dente. The moment the pasta is done, drain quickly in a large colander, shaking vigorously to remove excess liquid.

Transfer to a bowl containing 1 Tablespoon olive oil or dotted with 1 Tablespoon softened unsalted butter, depending on the sauce that will be used. Briefly toss the pasta and oil or butter together to separate the strands.

The next step is to immediately toss the sauce with the pasta. Since pasta cools very rapidly, make sure your sauce is ready before you drain the pasta. As my father always says, "The guests wait for the pasta—the pasta never waits for the guests."

EGG PASTA
Pasta all'uovo

YIELDS ABOUT 12 OUNCES

8 ounces superfine semolina
  flour or unbleached flour
½ teaspoon salt
4 ounces eggs, room
  temperature (2 jumbo)

1 Tablespoon olive oil
1 to 2 Tablespoons warm
  water
½ teaspoon olive oil (for
  coating)

FOOD PROCESSOR METHOD

1. Place flour and salt in work bowl of food processor fitted with metal blade. Turn machine on/off once.

2. Beat eggs lightly with fork in a glass measuring cup or small pitcher (this makes pouring easier). Turn machine on, pour eggs through the feed tube and let machine run until mixture resembles coarse meal, about 30 seconds. With machine running, pour 1 Tablespoon olive oil through feed tube in a thin steady stream. Pour 1 Tablespoon water through feed tube a few drops at a time and let machine run nonstop for 30 seconds. Remove cover and scrape down sides of work bowl with a plastic spatula. Cover work bowl and let machine run again nonstop for another minute or until dough forms a ball; if dough is not forming a ball, stop machine, remove cover and scrape bottom of work bowl with plastic spatula to loosen any dough that might be stuck. Run machine again, adding remaining Tablespoon of water through feed tube a few drops at a time. Let machine run again for an additional 1 to 2 minutes or until dough forms a ball. Remove metal blade first, then remove dough from machine. Pick up any little pieces of dough left in bottom of work bowl and knead into large pieces of dough. (Usually a ball is formed in a matter of seconds. There may be times, depending on weather and temperature of

ingredients, when dough will not form a ball after machine is run nonstop for 2 minutes. If this happens, stop machine, remove metal blade, gather all the dough and knead with your hands to form a ball.)

3. Shape dough into a flat 6-inch disc and rub with ½ teaspoon olive oil. Place dough in bowl and cover with a damp cloth. Let rest for 30 minutes before rolling through pasta machine or hand rolling.

HAND METHOD

1. Sift flour and salt onto a board or smooth work surface. Pile flour into a mound and make a well in center.

2. In a glass measuring cup or small pitcher, combine eggs with olive oil and beat lightly with a fork.

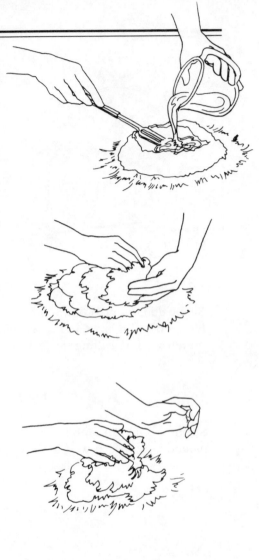

3. Support the outside of well with the palm of one hand. Pour half of the egg mixture into center of well. Working in a circular motion, incorporate some of the flour from the inside of well with a fork. This must be done very fast so that you do not break the wall of flour with the egg mixture. Add remaining egg mixture to center of well and again mix very quickly in a circular motion, taking more of the flour from inside of well. Work the rest of the flour into the dough with both hands. At this point the dough should feel sticky and crumbly. Add 1 Tablespoon of water and keep working the dough with your fingertips until it starts to adhere into a ball. If the dough feels too dry and crumbly, add a few more drops of water and keep working with your fingertips until it forms a ball. Scrape any dough left on fingers and work into ball. Set dough aside.

4. Scrape off any excess caked flour from work surface. Sprinkle a thin film of flour on work surface.

5. Wash and dry hands. Rub your hands with a little flour and knead the dough with the heels of your palms, pushing it away from you, folding it over and turning it as you knead. You will have to knead the dough for at least 10 to 15

minutes. The consistency will
change from sticky to smooth and
satiny as you knead.

6. Shape dough into a flat 6-inch disc
and rub with ½ teaspoon olive oil.
Place dough in bowl, cover with a
damp cloth, and let rest for at
least 30 minutes before rolling
through pasta machine or hand
rolling.

TO SHAPE NOODLES USING PASTA MACHINE

1. Divide dough into 4 pieces.
Remove 1 piece and keep the
remaining dough covered to
prevent drying.

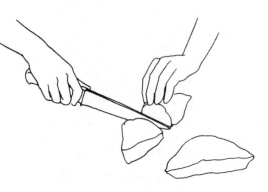

2. Adjust rollers on pasta machine to
widest setting.

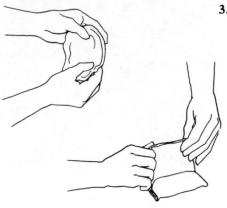

3. Flatten dough into a rectangular shape and flour lightly. Run the dough through the rollers once. Fold in thirds and run through rollers again. Repeat folding and rolling, lightly flouring dough only as necessary, until dough is smooth and satiny (may take 4 or 5 times).

4. Reset rollers for next thinner setting. *Do not fold dough.* Run dough through machine. Repeat on each thinner setting until dough is a long, thin, translucent sheet about 1/16 inch thick. Place dough on towels to dry out a little for about 15 minutes. Repeat with remaining pieces of dough. Do not allow dough to over-dry or it will become too brittle to cut.

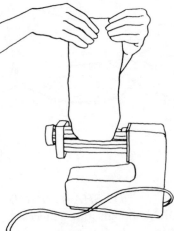

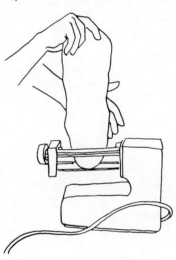

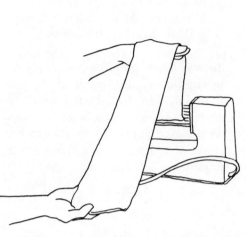

5. Cut each strip of dough into 15-
   inch lengths with a sharp knife.

6. Feed the dough into the cutters,
   keeping the dough even with the
   rollers; if it goes in crooked it will
   not cut properly. Remove strands
   of pasta from machine by looping
   them over your hand and lifting
   up. To make tagliarini, feed the
   dough through the narrow cutting
   blades of pasta machine. To make
   tagliatelle, feed dough through the
   wide blades.

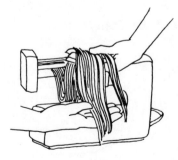

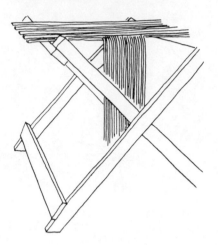

7. Separate strands and arrange on pasta rack or lightly floured dishtowels. At this point, the pasta is ready to cook, dry or freeze.

To dry: Leave pasta on pasta rack or lightly floured dishtowels to thoroughly air-dry, about 3 hours. To store, place pasta in a large box lined with waxed paper. The pasta can be stored in a dry place up to one month.

To freeze: Take about 14 strands of fresh pasta, fold in half and give one twist in center. Lay bundles between lightly floured sheets of waxed paper, place in plastic bag, tie end with twist tie and freeze. When ready to cook, take directly from freezer and drop into boiling water.

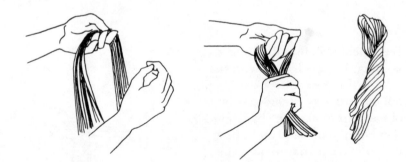

TO SHAPE NOODLES BY HAND

1. Divide dough in half and keep the other half covered to prevent drying.

2. Sprinkle a little flour on a board or smooth surface. Shape each piece of dough into a rectangle.

Roll dough with a floured rolling pin into a 1/16-inch-thick sheet. Cut each piece into 2 even lengths. Brush off any excess flour with a soft pastry brush. Place on a lightly floured towel and allow to dry for about 10 minutes. Do not allow dough to over-dry or it will become too brittle to cut.

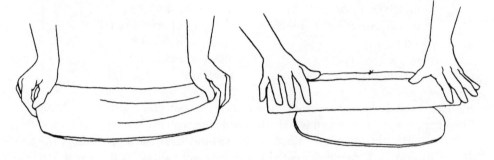

3. Starting at short end, roll the sheet of dough jelly roll fashion. Using a sharp knife, cut into the following desired widths:
Fettuccine–1/4 inch wide
Tagliatelle–3/8 inch wide
Tagliarini–1/8 inch wide

4. Separate strands and arrange on pasta rack or clean towels. At this point, pasta is ready to cook, dry or freeze. See directions for drying and freezing, page 42.

SPINACH PASTA
Pasta Verde

YIELDS ABOUT 1 POUND

8 ounces fresh young tender spinach or 1 package (10 ounces) frozen leaf spinach, defrosted
4 ounces eggs, room temperature (2 jumbo)

1 Tablespoon olive oil
½ teaspoon salt
12 ounces superfine semolina flour or unbleached flour
½ teaspoon olive oil (for coating)

Stem spinach and wash several times in warm water. Place spinach in 2-quart saucepan; cover. Do not add water; the final rinse water clinging to leaves will be sufficient to steam them. Cook over medium heat until spinach is limp, about 3 minutes. If using defrosted frozen spinach, add 2 Tablespoons water to pan and reduce cooking time to 2 minutes. Transfer to colander, rinse under cold water and drain well. Squeeze out excess moisture with your hands. Place spinach in a double layer of cheesecloth or a tea towel and squeeze again until there is not a drop of moisture left.

FOOD PROCESSOR METHOD

1. Place spinach in work bowl of food processor fitted with metal blade. Run machine nonstop until spinach is finely chopped, about 1 minute.
2. In a small bowl, combine eggs, 1 Tablespoon olive oil and salt. Add egg mixture to food processor and run machine nonstop until thoroughly incorporated. Add flour to work bowl and let machine run nonstop for 30 seconds. Remove cover and scrape down sides of work bowl with a rubber spatula. Run machine again nonstop for another minute. If dough feels too sticky, add 2 more Tablespoons flour and process for another minute or until dough forms a ball. The dough should be smooth and satiny. Remove metal blade first, then remove dough from machine. Pick up any little pieces of dough left in bottom of work bowl and knead into large piece of dough.
3. Shape dough into a flat 6-inch disc and rub with ½ teaspoon olive oil. Place dough in bowl, cover with a damp cloth, and let rest for at least 45 minutes.
4. If you are using a pasta machine, divide dough into 6 pieces. If hand rolling, divide dough into 3 pieces. Follow directions for pasta machine rolling on page 39, or directions for hand rolling on page 42.

HAND METHOD

1. Chop spinach very fine.
2. In a medium bowl, combine eggs, olive oil and salt. Beat mixture thoroughly with fork. Add chopped spinach and mix again until thoroughly incorporated.
3. Sift flour onto a board or smooth surface. Pile it into a mound and make a deep well in center. Place egg-spinach mixture in center of well. Support the outside of well with the palm of your hand. Working in a circular motion, incorporate some of the flour from the inside of the well with a fork. Try to keep the well intact until most of the egg-spinach mixture has been absorbed into the flour. Work the rest of the flour into the dough with fingertips. Keep working the dough in a circular motion until the dough starts to adhere into a ball. If at this point the dough feels too moist or sticky, add about 2 to 3 Tablespoons of flour to mixture and work in again with fingertips until it forms a ball. Scrape off any dough left on fingers and work into ball. Set dough aside.
4. Scrape off any excess caked flour from work surface. Sprinkle a thin film of flour on work surface.
5. Wash and dry hands. Knead the dough with the heels of your palms, pushing it away from you, folding it over and turning it as you knead. You will have to knead the dough for 10 to 15 minutes. The consistency of the dough will change as you knead from sticky to smooth and satiny.
6. Shape the dough into a flat 6-inch disc and rub with ½ teaspoon olive oil. Place dough in bowl, cover with a damp cloth, and let rest for at least 45 minutes.
7. If you are using a pasta machine, divide dough into 6 pieces. If hand rolling, divide dough into 3 pieces. Follow directions for pasta machine rolling on page 39, or directions for hand rolling on page 42.

Tomato-Based Sauces

PREPARING SAUCES

BUCATINI WITH PLAIN TOMATO SAUCE

CONCHIGLIE WITH TOMATO, MOZZARELLA AND FRESH HERBS

FEDELINI WITH TOMATO AND DRIED MUSHROOM SAUCE

FUSILLI WITH TOMATOES AND OLIVES

LINGUINE WITH TOMATO–GARLIC SAUCE

SPAGHETTI WITH TOMATO SAUCE, EGGPLANT AND RICOTTA

SPAGHETTI WITH TOMATO AND CHICKEN SAUCE

SPAGHETTINI WITH OLIVE AND CAPER SAUCE

RAVIOLI WITH TOMATO–PANCETTA SAUCE

Preparing Sauces

Whenever I tell someone I teach Italian cooking, nine times out of ten the question asked is, "How do you prepare your sauce?" My reply is, "Which sauce are you talking about?" Most people think the only way to envelop a noodle is with a thick tomato sauce. They probably visualize an Italian kitchen with a pot of red sauce on the back burner simmering for hours and hours. The mystique of the long-cooking tomato is more prevalent in this country than in Italy.

Pasta cooking should be looked upon as an opportunity for creative improvisation. Whichever sauce you choose should reflect the whim of the moment: sometimes a subtly elegant light one, at other times a more earthy and robust selection. Whatever sauce you choose to make, here are a few pointers for guaranteed success.

As you read through the next chapter, you will notice that most of the sauces are cooked in a sauté pan. I prefer using this type of pan because the sides are a little higher than a skillet. If you do not have a sauté pan, use a large skillet. Either of these pans should be at least 12 inches in diameter. By using this size pan, the vegetables can be tossed and cooked quickly so that they remain crisp and do not become watery. Any tomato-based sauce cooked in this type of pan will remain fairly sweet and cook down faster. Remember, the longer you cook tomatoes, the more acidic and bitter the sauce will become.

A sauce will only be as good as its ingredients. Using the finest olive oil, freshest produce and best imported cheese you can find are essential. If at all possible, use fresh herbs; the flavor is much more pungent than that of dried. If you do have to use dried herbs, rub them between the palms of your hands to bring out their full aromatic flavor.

Olive oil, an unsaturated fat, has a higher burning point than butter, which is a saturated fat. When using an olive oil-butter combination in any cooking, heat the olive oil first until a haze or slight ripple forms, then add the butter, which has been cut into small pieces, to the oil. Using this technique, the butter will melt down instantly into the oil and will not burn.

Since many sauces are based on sautéed onions, there are a few tricks here, too. If you sauté onions slowly they become mild and sweet, and will complement the tomato or vegetable sauce. A quick sauté over medium-high heat will give your sauce a more robust flavor.

The addition of garlic to any sauce must be kept under control. Never use a heavy hand. Whenever an onion-garlic combination is used, sauté the onion first, then add the garlic and cook for only a few minutes. Never sauté onion and garlic together, because by the time the onion is cooked, the garlic will be burned. If you only want a slight hint of garlic in any sauce, heat the skillet with olive oil or an oil-butter combination over medium-high heat. Remove pan from heat, add the chopped or sliced garlic, and tilt pan to a 45° angle. With a wooden spoon, push all the garlic down to one spot, sauté until lightly golden and then discard with a slotted spoon. By tilting the pan, you will be better able to keep the garlic from burning. This is a good little tip to remember whenever sautéing garlic, even if you are going to leave it in the sauce.

There are almost as many shapes of pasta as there are sauce possibilities; the range is just unbelievable. Everyone always asks which shape to use with what sauce. There is no rigid rule governing this, but in general, fresh homemade pasta or thin commercial pastas are good with lighter sauces, whereas heavier-textured sauces are generally reserved for the thicker pastas.

A common English expression indicating company's coming has always been "put up the pot," meaning put on the coffee or tea. In an Italian household, when they say "put up the pot," they mean "PASTA!" So when faced with only a few minutes to whip up a meal, or when planning a dinner party, you too can "put up the pot" and choose one of the many sauces in the next chapter.

BUCATINI WITH PLAIN TOMATO SAUCE
Bucatini con Salsa di Pomodore

This is the fastest of all the tomato sauces to make. I happen to like bucatini with it, but it is equally delectable with spaghetti, linguine or home-made pasta. The slow sautéing of the onion creates a mild, sweet taste to complement the tomatoes.

SERVES 4—MAIN COURSE
SERVES 6—FIRST COURSE

2 Tablespoons olive oil
2 Tablespoons unsalted butter
½ cup finely chopped yellow onion
2 large cloves garlic, split in half
1 can (28 ounces) concentrated crushed tomatoes (see note)
1½ Tablespoons minced fresh basil or 1½ teaspoons crumbled dried basil

½ teaspoon sugar
1 teaspoon salt
½ teaspoon freshly milled black pepper
1 pound bucatini (tubular pasta)
1 Tablespoon salt
1 Tablespoon unsalted butter, softened
Freshly grated Romano cheese (for serving)

1. In a 3-quart heavy saucepan, heat olive oil over medium heat until haze forms, then add 2 Tablespoons butter. Add onions and turn heat to low; cook, stirring frequently, until soft but not brown, about 5 minutes. Add garlic and continue cooking until soft but not brown, about 4 minutes. Stir in tomatoes, basil, sugar, 1 teaspoon salt and pepper. Increase heat to high. Bring sauce to a boil, stirring constantly, then turn heat down to low. Cook partially covered, stirring frequently, until slightly thickened, about 25 minutes. Remove from heat, cover pan, and let sauce rest for at least 1 hour before cooking pasta. Reheat sauce over low heat while cooking pasta; remove garlic.
2. Cook pasta in 6 quarts boiling water with 1 Tablespoon salt until al dente. Drain pasta in a colander, transfer to a bowl containing 1 Tablespoon softened butter and toss quickly. Mix ¾ of the sauce with pasta and spoon remaining sauce on top. Serve with grated Romano cheese.

Note: If concentrated crushed tomatoes are unavailable, use one 35-ounce can of Italian plum tomatoes, coarsely chopped, juice included (can be chopped in food processor fitted with metal blade). Increase cooking time by 10 minutes.

CONCHIGLIE WITH TOMATO, MOZZARELLA AND FRESH HERBS
Conchiglie Estivi

*Make this sauce only when you have good summer-ripened plum toma-
toes and fresh herbs. The hot, drained pasta tossed with cubed Mozzarella
and marinated tomatoes will intrigue the palate with its contrasting
tastes and textures. This is on my menu quite often in the summer
months.*

SERVES 4—MAIN COURSE
SERVES 6—FIRST COURSE

10 large ripe plum tomatoes (2
   pounds)
½ cup olive oil
½ cup minced fresh basil
½ cup minced Italian parsley
   leaves
3 Tablespoons minced fresh
   oregano
3 Tablespoons bottled capers,
   rinsed and well drained
½ cup freshly grated
   Parmigiano cheese
½ teaspoon sugar

1 teaspoon salt
½ teaspoon freshly milled
   black pepper
1 pound conchiglie (medium-
   size shells)
1 Tablespoon salt
1 Tablespoon olive oil
4 ounces whole milk
   Mozzarella cheese, cut into
   ½-inch cubes
   Freshly grated Parmigiano
   cheese (for serving)

1. Blanch fresh tomatoes in boiling water for 1 minute. Transfer to a colander
   and rinse under cold water. Peel skins with a small paring knife. Cut each
   tomato in half lengthwise. Gently squeeze out the seeds, keeping as much
   moisture in the tomatoes as possible. Cut the tomatoes into ½-inch cubes.
2. Place the tomatoes in a large glass or porcelain bowl. Add ½ cup olive oil,
   basil, parsley, oregano, capers, Parmigiano cheese, sugar, 1 teaspoon salt
   and pepper. Toss sauce well, cover with plastic wrap and refrigerate for at
   least 4 hours or overnight.
3. Thirty minutes before cooking pasta, remove sauce from refrigerator.
4. Cook pasta in 6 quarts boiling water with 1 Tablespoon salt until al dente.
   Drain pasta in a colander, transfer to a bowl containing 1 Tablespoon olive
   oil and toss quickly. Add ¾ of the sauce and half of the cubed Mozzarella
   cheese to the pasta; toss well. Spoon remaining sauce on top of pasta and
   garnish with remaining cubed Mozzarella. Serve with additional freshly
   grated Parmigiano cheese.

FEDELINI WITH TOMATO AND DRIED MUSHROOM SAUCE
Fedelini con Pomodoro e Funghi Secchi

The pungent flavor of dried mushrooms combined with tomatoes goes particularly well with fedelini or any type of spaghetti or homemade pasta. An excellent sauce with polenta as well. Perfect for anyone who dislikes or cannot digest garlic.

SERVES 4—MAIN COURSE
SERVES 6—FIRST COURSE

½ ounce dried Italian
 mushrooms (porcini)
2 Tablespoons olive oil
2 Tablespoons unsalted
 butter
3 ounces pancetta or
 prosciutto, finely diced
¼ cup finely chopped shallots
1 can (35 ounces) Italian
 plum tomatoes, coarsely
 chopped, juice included
 (can be chopped in food
 processor fitted with metal
 blade)
1 Tablespoon minced fresh
 basil or 1 teaspoon
 crumbled dried basil

½ teaspoon sugar
1 teaspoon salt
½ teaspoon freshly milled
 black pepper
1 pound fedelini (thin
 spaghetti)
1 Tablespoon salt
1 Tablespoon unsalted butter,
 softened
½ cup freshly grated
 Parmigiano cheese
 Freshly grated Parmigiano
 cheese (for serving)

1. Soak dried mushrooms in 1 cup warm water for 30 minutes. Drain mushrooms in a strainer, reserving liquid. Pour liquid through strainer lined with paper towel to remove sand; set aside. Rinse mushrooms in cold water, blot dry with paper towel and chop finely. Set aside.
2. In a large sauté pan, heat olive oil over medium heat until haze forms, then add 2 Tablespoons butter. Add pancetta or prosciutto and cook, stirring constantly, until soft but not brown, about 2 minutes. Turn heat to low and add shallots. Cook, stirring constantly, until lightly golden, about 2 minutes. Stir in tomatoes, mushrooms, strained liquid from mushrooms, basil, sugar, 1 teaspoon salt and pepper. Cook sauce uncovered over low heat, stirring frequently, until slightly thickened, about 35 minutes.
3. Cook pasta in 6 quarts boiling water with 1 Tablespoon salt until al dente. Drain pasta in a colander, transfer to a bowl containing 1 Tablespoon soft-

ened butter and toss quickly. Mix ¾ of the sauce with pasta and Parmigiano cheese. Spoon remaining sauce on top and serve with additional Parmigiano.

Note: If dried porcini mushrooms are unavailable, substitute 4 ounces fresh mushrooms, wiped and thinly sliced. Sauté in 1 Tablespoon unsalted butter over medium-high heat just until liquid starts to exude from mushrooms. Stir mushrooms and liquid into sauce during the last 5 minutes of cooking.

FUSILLI WITH TOMATOES AND OLIVES
Fusilli con Pomodoro e Olive

The sparkling flavor of tomatoes marinated with Gaeta olives (available in Italian specialty stores) or oil-cured olives makes this uncooked sauce quite zesty. A great do-ahead summer pasta, and wonderful for a buffet.

SERVES 4—MAIN COURSE
SERVES 6—FIRST COURSE

12 large ripe plum tomatoes (2½ pounds)
½ cup olive oil
3 large cloves garlic, peeled and pierced with toothpicks (see note)
½ cup Gaeta or oil-cured black olives, pitted and sliced into thin strips
3 Tablespoons minced fresh basil or 1 Tablespoon crumbled dried basil

¼ cup minced Italian parsley leaves
1 teaspoon salt
½ teaspoon freshly milled black pepper
1 pound fusilli (twists)
1 Tablespoon salt
1 Tablespoon olive oil
Freshly grated Romano cheese (for serving)

1. Blanch fresh tomatoes in boiling water for 1 minute. Transfer to a colander and rinse under cold water. Peel skins with a small paring knife. Cut each tomato in half lengthwise. Squeeze each half and discard all of the seeds. Slice into ¼-inch strips, place in strainer set over a bowl and reserve juice.
2. In a medium bowl, combine tomatoes, ½ cup olive oil, garlic, olives, basil, parsley, 1 teaspoon salt and pepper; mix well with wooden spoon. Transfer

to a 1½-quart jar with a tight-fitting lid. Refrigerate sauce for at least 6 hours or overnight, turning jar 3 to 4 times so that tomatoes will be well coated with marinade. Pour reserved juice into a small jar, cover and refrigerate.

3. Remove sauce and reserved juice from refrigerator and let stand at room temperature for 2 hours before serving. Discard garlic from sauce just before tossing with pasta.

4. Cook pasta in 6 quarts boiling water with 1 Tablespoon salt until al dente. Drain pasta in a colander, transfer to a bowl containing 1 Tablespoon olive oil and toss quickly. Toss pasta with ¾ of the sauce. If pasta is a little dry when tossing, add about ½ cup of the reserved juice to moisten. Spoon remaining sauce on top and serve with freshly grated Romano cheese.

Note: Piercing each garlic clove with a toothpick before adding to sauce will simplify its removal.

LINGUINE WITH TOMATO–GARLIC SAUCE
Linguine con Salsa Marinara

Adding the oregano after this robust sauce has finished cooking will give perfect flavor and prevent a bitter aftertaste. Anyone who adores garlic will just love this! The sauce is not served with cheese, so you can truly taste the flavor of garlic, tomato and oregano.

SERVES 4—MAIN COURSE
SERVES 6—FIRST COURSE

¼ cup olive oil
2 Tablespoons finely minced garlic
1 can (35 ounces) Italian plum tomatoes, coarsely chopped, juice included (can be chopped in food processor fitted with metal blade)
1 teaspoon salt
½ teaspoon freshly milled black pepper
½ teaspoon sugar
2 Tablespoons minced fresh oregano or 2 teaspoons crumbled dried oregano
1 pound linguine
1 Tablespoon salt
1 Tablespoon olive oil
2 Tablespoons minced Italian parsley leaves (garnish)

1. In a large sauté pan, heat ¼ cup olive oil over medium-high heat until haze forms. Remove pan from heat, add garlic and tilt pan to a 45° angle. With a wooden spoon, push all the garlic to one spot and sauté until lightly golden (sautéing garlic in this manner will prevent it from burning).
2. Return pan to burner and turn heat to high. Stir in the tomatoes and immediately cover with lid to prevent olive oil from splattering. Remove lid, add 1 teaspoon salt, pepper and sugar and mix well with wooden spoon. Bring sauce to a boil, turn heat to low and cook uncovered, stirring frequently, until sauce is slightly thickened, about 25 minutes. Remove from heat and stir in oregano.
3. Cook pasta in 6 quarts boiling water with 1 Tablespoon salt until al dente. Drain pasta in a colander, transfer to a bowl containing 1 Tablespoon olive oil and toss quickly. Mix half of the sauce with the pasta, spoon remaining sauce on top and garnish with minced parsley. Serve immediately.

SPAGHETTI WITH TOMATO SAUCE, EGGPLANT AND RICOTTA
Spaghetti con Salsa di Pomodoro, Melanzana e Ricotta

This dish looks better than an ice cream sundae when finished. Best served in summer or early fall when fresh basil is available. You need nothing more than a salad, crisp Italian bread and a good bottle of dry red wine, such as Bardolino, to complete this Sicilian gastronomic delight.

SERVES 4—MAIN COURSE

Single recipe of Plain Tomato Sauce, page 49.
1 medium-size firm eggplant (1½ pounds)
Salt (approximately 3 Tablespoons)
1 cup Wondra flour
¾ cup (approximately) olive oil
1 pound spaghetti

1 Tablespoon salt
1 Tablespoon unsalted butter, softened
8 ounces whole milk ricotta cheese
3 Tablespoons snipped fresh basil
Freshly grated Romano cheese (for serving)

1. Prepare tomato sauce; set aside.
2. Wash eggplant; dry and trim both ends. Slice into ¼-inch-thick rounds. Place in a colander and sprinkle about ½ teaspoon salt over each layer. Place a flat plate over top layer. Weight down with a heavy object (I use an antique iron, but Webster's Dictionary works as well). Place colander in bowl or sink and let eggplant drain for at least 1 hour. Wipe slices with a damp cloth and blot dry with paper towel.
3. Place flour in a shallow bowl and dredge slices on both sides; shake off excess. (Dredge just before frying or flour coating will become gummy.)
4. In a large skillet, heat olive oil over medium-high heat until haze forms. Fry eggplant in two batches until golden on both sides. Drain on paper towels.
5. Cook pasta in 6 quarts boiling water with 1 Tablespoon salt until al dente. Reheat tomato sauce. Drain pasta in a colander, transfer to a bowl containing 1 Tablespoon softened butter and toss quickly. Toss pasta with half of the sauce. Place individual servings of pasta in bowls and spoon remaining sauce on top of each. Place 2 or 3 slices of fried eggplant atop each serving. Spoon 2 heaping Tablespoons of ricotta onto eggplant and garnish each serving with snipped basil. Serve with the remaining ricotta and freshly grated Romano cheese.

SPAGHETTI WITH TOMATO AND CHICKEN SAUCE
Spaghetti alla Nonna

A memorable sauce Nonna Louisa always made, featuring the delicate flavor of chicken breasts combined with mushrooms and tomato.

SERVES 4—MAIN COURSE
SERVES 6—FIRST COURSE

2 Tablespoons olive oil
1 large whole chicken breast (1½ pounds), rinsed, dried and split in half
½ cup finely chopped onion
½ cup finely chopped carrot
1 can (35 ounces) Italian plum tomatoes, coarsely chopped, juice included (can be chopped in food processor fitted with metal blade)
1 teaspoon salt
¼ teaspoon crushed red pepper flakes or ½ teaspoon freshly milled black pepper
½ teaspoon sugar
2 Tablespoons minced fresh basil or 2 teaspoons crumbled dried basil
8 ounces medium mushrooms, wiped and thinly sliced
1 pound spaghetti
1 Tablespoon salt
1 Tablespoon olive oil
Freshly grated Parmigiano cheese (for serving)

1. In a large sauté pan, heat 2 Tablespoons olive oil over medium heat until haze forms. Add chicken skin side down and sauté on both sides until lightly golden. Transfer to a platter. Turn heat to low and sauté onion and carrot, stirring constantly, until soft but not brown, about 4 minutes. Add tomatoes, 1 teaspoon salt, pepper, sugar and basil. Return chicken to pan, skin side down; cook sauce partially covered, stirring frequently, until slightly thickened, about 35 minutes. Add sliced mushrooms, turn heat to medium-high and cook, stirring constantly, for an additional 5 minutes. Remove from heat, cover pan and let sauce cool to room temperature. Remove chicken from sauce; skin and bone. Slice breast in half horizontally and slice into ¼-inch strips. Return chicken to sauce and mix well. When ready to serve, reheat sauce, covered, over low heat.
2. Cook pasta in 6 quarts boiling water with 1 Tablespoon salt until al dente. Drain pasta in a colander, transfer to a bowl containing 1 Tablespoon olive oil and toss quickly. Mix half of the sauce with pasta and spoon remaining sauce on top. Serve with freshly grated Parmigiano cheese.

SPAGHETTINI WITH OLIVE AND CAPER SAUCE
Pasta alla Puttanesca

There are many tales as to how this "harlot's" sauce got its name. Some stories say that it was a fast dish to make between clients; others claim that when the ladies were cheating on their husbands in the afternoons, it was a quick dish to prepare before their spouses returned home. If I were cheating on my husband, I think I would pick another sauce, because it does take a little time to pit the olives!

SERVES 4—MAIN COURSE
SERVES 6—FIRST COURSE

¼ cup olive oil
3 large cloves garlic, split in half
1 cup oil-cured black olives (about 24), pitted and quartered
1 can (35 ounces) Italian plum tomatoes, coarsely chopped, juice included (can be chopped in food processor fitted with metal blade)

½ teaspoon salt
½ teaspoon freshly milled black pepper
3 Tablespoons bottled capers, rinsed and well drained
2 Tablespoons minced Italian parsley leaves
1 pound spaghettini
1 Tablespoon salt
1 Tablespoon olive oil
Freshly grated Romano cheese (for serving)

1. In a large sauté pan, heat ¼ cup olive oil over medium heat until haze forms. Add garlic and sauté until lightly golden; discard garlic. Stir in olives and cook, stirring constantly, until slightly puffed, about 2 minutes. Stir in tomatoes, ½ teaspoon salt and pepper. Cook sauce uncovered, stirring frequently, until slightly thickened, about 15 minutes. Stir in capers and cook for an additional 5 minutes. Remove from heat and add minced parsley.
2. Cook pasta in 6 quarts boiling water with 1 Tablespoon salt until al dente. Drain pasta in a colander, transfer to a bowl containing 1 Tablespoon olive oil and toss quickly. Mix ¾ of the sauce with pasta and spoon remaining sauce on top. Serve with grated Romano cheese.

RAVIOLI WITH TOMATO–PANCETTA SAUCE
Ravioli con Salsa di Pomodoro e Pancetta

Cooking the ravioli in batches will prevent them from sticking together. They are just as tasty when served with Plain Tomato Sauce, page 49, or Tomato and Dried Mushroom sauce, page 51. If you are going to cook the whole batch of homemade ravioli, you will have to double the sauce recipes; see directions for making ravioli, page 99. The following sauce is also excellent on one pound of spaghetti, linguine or homemade pasta.

SERVES 6—MAIN COURSE
SERVES 8—FIRST COURSE

2 Tablespoons olive oil
1 Tablespoon unsalted butter
3 ounces pancetta or prosciutto, finely diced
½ cup finely chopped yellow onion
½ cup finely chopped carrot
2 large cloves garlic, split in half
1 can (35 ounces) Italian plum tomatoes, coarsely chopped, juice included (can be chopped in food processor fitted with metal blade)
1 teaspoon salt
½ teaspoon freshly milled black pepper

½ teaspoon sugar
1 Tablespoon minced fresh basil or 1 teaspoon crumbled dried basil
2 Tablespoons minced Italian parsley leaves
1 Tablespoon salt
2 teaspoons vegetable or olive oil
48 ravioli (2-inch-square size), preferably homemade
½ cup freshly grated Parmigiano cheese
Freshly grated Parmigiano cheese (for serving)

1. In a large sauté pan, heat olive oil over medium heat until haze forms, then add butter. Add pancetta or prosciutto and cook, stirring constantly, until soft but not brown, about 2 minutes. Turn heat to low and add onion and carrot. Cook, stirring constantly, until soft but not brown, about 4 minutes. Add garlic and continue to cook, stirring constantly, until soft but not brown, about 1 minute. Stir in tomatoes, 1 teaspoon salt, pepper, sugar and basil. Turn heat to high and bring to a boil, stirring constantly. Reduce heat to medium, partially cover pan and cook, stirring frequently, until slightly thickened, about 30 minutes. Remove from heat, cover pan, and let sauce rest for at least 1 hour before cooking ravioli. Reheat sauce, covered,

over low heat while cooking ravioli. Remove from heat and discard garlic. Add parsley and mix well.

2. In a 10-quart pot, bring 7 quarts of water to a boil. Add 1 Tablespoon salt and 2 teaspoons oil.

3. Adjust rack to center of oven and preheat to 200°F.

4. Drop half of the ravioli into rapidly boiling water and stir gently with a wooden fork. When water returns to a boil, cook ravioli uncovered until tender, about 8 minutes. (Remove one ravioli and cut off tip. Bite into it and taste; it should be tender, yet firm. If it isn't tender, boil for another minute and test again.) As soon as they are done, transfer a few at a time with a skimmer or slotted spoon to a colander and drain well. Repeat with second batch of ravioli.

5. Spoon a thin layer of sauce into the bottom of an ovenproof platter. Arrange ravioli on platter in a single layer. Cover with a thin layer of sauce and half of the Parmigiano cheese. Transfer to oven to keep warm while cooking second batch. After second batch has been drained well, arrange in another single layer over first batch, spoon another thin layer of sauce on top and sprinkle with remaining cheese.

6. Serve with remaining sauce and additional Parmigiano cheese.

Vegetable and Cream Sauces

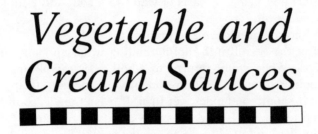

FETTUCCINE WITH ARTICHOKE HEARTS

LINGUINE WITH BROCCOLI

MARGHERITA WITH FRIED CAULIFLOWER

CONCHIGLIE WITH BROCCOLI, CAULIFLOWER AND ANCHOVIES

GREEN NOODLES WITH CARROTS AND MUSHROOMS

ZITI WITH EGGPLANT AND ROASTED PEPPERS

SPAGHETTI WITH LIMA BEANS, ARTICHOKE HEARTS AND PEAS

PENNE WITH MUSHROOMS AND PROSCIUTTO

TAGLIATELLE WITH ZUCCHINI AND MUSHROOMS

LINGUINE WITH FRIED ZUCCHINI AND RICOTTA

PASTA PRIMAVERA

TAGLIARINI WITH BASIL PESTO SAUCE

FARFALLE WITH SPINACH PESTO

LINGUINE WITH WALNUT SAUCE

LINGUINE WITH BACON AND PROSCIUTTO

FETTUCCINE WITH SALAMI AND MUSHROOMS

RIGATONI WITH SAUSAGE CREAM SAUCE

FUSILLI WITH FOUR CHEESES

STRAW AND HAY

FETTUCCINE WITH ARTICHOKE HEARTS
Fettuccine con Carciofi

The very delicate flavor of artichoke hearts combined with fresh pasta makes a light but delicious Northern Italian dish.

SERVES 4—MAIN COURSE
SERVES 6—FIRST COURSE

2 packages (9 ounces each) frozen artichoke hearts
3 Tablespoons olive oil
2 Tablespoons unsalted butter
2 cloves garlic, split in half
1 cup thinly sliced scallions
⅓ cup chicken broth
1 teaspoon salt
½ teaspoon freshly milled white pepper
½ cup heavy cream

1 pound fettuccine, preferably homemade (page 36)
1 Tablespoon salt
1 Tablespoon unsalted butter, softened
½ cup freshly grated Parmigiano cheese
2 Tablespoons minced Italian parsley leaves (garnish)
Freshly grated Parmigiano cheese (for serving)

1. Rinse frozen artichokes under warm water and very carefully separate. Cut each artichoke heart into ½-inch wedges and place in a strainer to drain (artichokes will be easier to slice if partially frozen).
2. In a large sauté pan, heat olive oil over medium heat until haze forms, then add 2 Tablespoons butter. Sauté garlic, stirring constantly, until very lightly golden; remove garlic with a slotted spoon and discard. Add scallions and cook, stirring constantly, until barely tender, about 1 minute. Add artichoke wedges and continue cooking, stirring constantly, until tender-crisp when tested with a fork, about 3 minutes. Stir in chicken broth, 1 teaspoon salt and pepper and mix well to incorporate; cook an additional minute. Stir in heavy cream, turn heat down to low, and cook, stirring constantly, until sauce thickens slightly, about 2 minutes. Remove from heat and set aside.
3. Cook pasta in 6 quarts boiling water with 1 Tablespoon salt until al dente. Drain in a colander, transfer to a bowl containing 1 Tablespoon softened butter and toss quickly. Mix pasta with ¾ of the sauce and Parmigiano cheese; toss well. Spoon remaining sauce on top and garnish with minced parsley. Serve with additional freshly grated Parmigiano cheese.

Note: If you do not have chicken broth, dissolve ½ chicken bouillon cube in ⅓ cup hot water. Omit salt from recipe.

LINGUINE WITH BROCCOLI
Linguine alla Maria Angela

For all you broccoli lovers, this is one of the fastest pasta dishes to pre-pare—and one of the tastiest!

SERVES 4—MAIN COURSE
SERVES 6—FIRST COURSE

1 large bunch broccoli (about 1½ pounds)
1 Tablespoon salt
6 Tablespoons olive oil
4 ounces pancetta or very lean salt pork, finely diced
1½ cups thinly sliced scallions
1 teaspoon salt
½ teaspoon freshly milled black pepper
1 pound linguine
1 Tablespoon olive oil
½ cup freshly grated Parmigiano cheese
Freshly grated Parmigiano cheese (for serving)

1. Remove florets from broccoli, leaving about ½ inch of stems. Cut or break florets into 1-inch pieces. Wash in cold water, drain and set aside. Remove and discard the large coarse leaves from stems and cut off about ½ inch of tough lower part of stalk. Wash thoroughly and peel stalks with a vegetable peeler. Cut larger stalks in half lengthwise. If stalks are extremely large, cut into quarters. Cut stalks into 1-inch pieces.
2. Bring 6 quarts of water to a boil with 1 Tablespoon salt. Add broccoli stalks and cook until barely tender when tested with a fork, about 5 minutes. Add florets and continue cooking until barely tender when tested with fork, about 3 minutes. With a skimmer, transfer broccoli to a colander, rinse under cold water and set aside to drain. Reserve liquid for cooking pasta.
3. In a large sauté pan, heat 6 Tablespoons olive oil over medium heat until haze forms. Add pancetta or salt pork and cook, stirring constantly, until slightly crispy, about 2 minutes. Add scallions and continue cooking, stirring constantly, until barely tender, about 1 minute. Add broccoli, turn heat to low and cook, stirring constantly, until well incorporated, about 2 minutes. Season with 1 teaspoon salt and pepper and remove from heat.
4. Return water in which broccoli was cooked to a boil. Add pasta and cook until al dente. Before draining pasta, remove about ½ cup of pasta water and set aside. Drain pasta in colander, transfer to a bowl containing 1 Tablespoon olive oil and toss quickly. Add half of the vegetable mixture and Parmigiano cheese to pasta and toss well. Add about 6 Tablespoons of pasta water and toss quickly to loosen. Spoon remaining vegetable mixture on top and serve with additional Parmigiano cheese.

MARGHERITA WITH FRIED CAULIFLOWER
Margherita all'Elvira

The crispness of the fried cauliflower and garlic with the rippled noodles makes an unforgettable dish for late fall or winter. Easy to prepare and satisfying for the heartiest appetite!

SERVES 4—MAIN COURSE

SERVES 6—FIRST COURSE

1 large or 2 small heads cauliflower (about 3 pounds)
1 Tablespoon salt
½ cup Wondra flour
½ cup dry breadcrumbs
1 teaspoon salt
½ teaspoon freshly milled black pepper
½ cup olive oil
4 cloves garlic, thinly sliced

1 pound margherita (narrow rippled noodles)
1 Tablespoon olive oil
½ cup chicken broth, heated (see note)
½ cup freshly grated Romano cheese
2 teaspoons minced Italian parsley leaves (garnish)
Freshly grated Romano cheese (for serving)

1. Remove florets from cauliflower, including about 1 inch of stem. Break or cut into 1-inch pieces. Wash thoroughly in lukewarm water, drain in colander and set aside.
2. Bring 6 quarts of water to a boil. Add 1 Tablespoon salt and the cauliflower florets. Boil until barely tender when tested with a fork, about 5 minutes. With a skimmer or slotted spoon, transfer florets to a colander, rinse under cold water and drain well. Reserve liquid for cooking pasta.
3. In a shallow bowl, combine flour, breadcrumbs, 1 teaspoon salt and pepper. Dredge florets in flour mixture, being sure each piece is well coated. Arrange in a single layer on a large platter.
4. In a 12-inch skillet, heat ½ cup olive oil over medium heat until haze forms. Add garlic, turn heat to low and sauté until lightly golden, pressing the garlic flat in pan with the back of a wooden spoon. With a slotted spoon, remove garlic and drain on paper towel; set aside. (If you are not a garlic lover, discard.) Place florets in pan and sauté over medium heat, turning with spatula, until golden and crisp on all sides; don't be concerned if florets break apart while frying.
5. Meanwhile, return water in which cauliflower was cooked to a boil. Add pasta and cook until al dente; the cauliflower and pasta must be done at the same time so that the florets will still be crispy when tossed with the

pasta. Drain pasta in a large colander, transfer to a bowl containing 1 Tablespoon olive oil and toss quickly.

6. Mix half of the cauliflower and any of the browned fragments stuck to the bottom of the pan with the pasta. Add sautéed garlic, heated chicken broth, and Romano cheese; toss well again. Spoon remaining cauliflower on top and garnish with minced parsley. Serve immediately with additional grated Romano cheese.

Note: If you do not have chicken broth, remove ½ cup of the pasta water before draining and substitute for broth.

CONCHIGLIE WITH BROCCOLI, CAULIFLOWER AND ANCHOVIES
Conchiglie al Giardino con Acciughe

A truly elegant combination with a slight hint of anchovy. If you want a stronger flavor of anchovy, add another 2-ounce can and omit salt from recipe. Do not serve cheese with this sauce; you don't want to mask the piquant flavor of anchovy.

SERVES 4—MAIN COURSE
SERVES 6—FIRST COURSE

1 large head cauliflower (about 1½ pounds)
1 large bunch broccoli (about 1½ pounds)
1 Tablespoon salt
3 large cloves garlic, thinly sliced
½ cup olive oil
1 can (2 ounces) anchovy fillets, well drained and finely chopped
½ teaspoon salt
½ teaspoon freshly milled black pepper
1 pound conchiglie (medium-size shells)
1 Tablespoon olive oil

1. Remove florets from cauliflower, including about ½ inch of stem. Break or cut into ½-inch pieces. Wash thoroughly in lukewarm water, drain in a colander and set aside. Remove florets from broccoli, including about 1 inch of stem. Cut into 1-inch pieces. Wash thoroughly in lukewarm water, drain in colander and set aside.

2. Bring 6 quarts of water to a boil with 1 Tablespoon salt. Add cauliflower florets and cook for 5 minutes. Add broccoli florets and continue to cook until florets are tender when pierced with a fork, about 6 minutes. With a skimmer or slotted spoon, transfer florets to colander, rinse under cold water and set aside. Reserve liquid for cooking pasta.

3. In a large sauté pan, heat ½ cup olive oil over medium-high heat until haze forms. Add garlic and sauté, stirring constantly, until lightly golden. With a slotted spoon, remove garlic and reserve. Remove pan from heat and add anchovies. Mash anchovies with the back of a wooden spoon until they dissolve into a paste. Add florets and turn heat to medium. Cook, stirring constantly, until florets are well coated with anchovy sauce, about 4 minutes. Add ½ teaspoon salt, pepper and reserved garlic; mix well to incorporate.

4. Return water in which florets were cooked to a boil. Cook pasta until al dente. Drain pasta in colander, transfer to a bowl containing 1 Tablespoon olive oil and toss quickly. Add ¾ of the vegetable mixture to pasta and toss well. Spoon remaining vegetable mixture on top and serve immediately.

GREEN NOODLES WITH CARROTS AND MUSHROOMS
Pasta Verde con Carote e Funghi

A very light dish, this makes for a stimulating presentation because of the beautiful contrast in color.

SERVES 4—MAIN COURSE
SERVES 6—FIRST COURSE

1 pound carrots, peeled and cut into 2 × ¼-inch julienne strips
3 Tablespoons olive oil
3 Tablespoons unsalted butter
4 ounces pancetta or prosciutto, finely diced
1½ cups thinly sliced scallions
8 ounces mushrooms, trimmed, wiped and thinly sliced
1 teaspoon salt
½ teaspoon freshly milled black pepper
2 Tablespoons minced Italian parsley leaves
1 pound green noodles, preferably homemade (page 44)
1 Tablespoon salt
1 Tablespoon unsalted butter, softened
Freshly grated Parmigiano cheese (for serving)

1. Cook carrots in 2 quarts boiling water just until barely tender when tested with a fork, about 3 minutes. Drain in a strainer and set aside.
2. In large sauté pan, heat olive oil over medium heat until haze forms, then add 3 Tablespoons butter. Add pancetta or prosciutto and cook, stirring constantly, until soft but not brown, about 2 minutes. Add scallions and cook, stirring constantly, until barely tender, about 1 minute. Add carrots and cook, stirring constantly, until tender when pierced with a fork, about 2 minutes. Add mushrooms, turn heat to medium-high and cook, stirring constantly, just until they start to exude juices, about 1 minute. Season with 1 teaspoon salt and pepper and remove from heat. Add minced parsley and mix thoroughly.
3. Cook pasta in 6 quarts boiling water with 1 Tablespoon salt until al dente. Drain pasta in a colander, transfer to a bowl containing 1 Tablespoon softened butter and toss quickly. Mix ¾ of the vegetable mixture with pasta and spoon remaining mixture on top. Serve with freshly grated Parmigiano cheese.

ZITI WITH EGGPLANT AND ROASTED PEPPERS
Ziti con Melanzana e Peperoncini Arrostiti

A colorful, appetizing, robust pasta dish. Select a very firm, glossy eggplant, so that when sauce is finished eggplant will be tender but not soggy.

SERVES 4—MAIN COURSE
SERVES 6—FIRST COURSE

½ cup olive oil
1 cup thinly sliced scallions
2 teaspoons finely minced garlic
1 large firm eggplant (2 pounds), washed, ends trimmed, peeled and cut into ½-inch cubes
1 can (35 ounces) Italian plum tomatoes, well drained and coarsely chopped (can be chopped in food processor fitted with metal blade)
2 Tablespoons minced fresh basil or 2 teaspoons crumbled dried basil
1 teaspoon salt
½ teaspoon freshly milled black pepper

½ teaspoon sugar
3 large red bell peppers (1½ pounds), roasted, peeled and sliced into ½-inch strips (see procedure for roasting peppers on page 8), or 2 jars (7 ounces each) roasted peppers, well drained
3 Tablespoons minced Italian parsley leaves
1 pound ziti (or any large tubular pasta)
1 Tablespoon salt
1 Tablespoon olive oil
½ cup freshly grated Romano cheese
Freshly grated Romano cheese (for serving)

1. In a large sauté pan, heat ½ cup olive oil over medium heat until haze forms. Add scallions and sauté, stirring constantly, until tender, about 2 minutes. Add garlic and cook, stirring constantly, until slightly softened but not brown, about 2 minutes. Add eggplant and sauté, stirring constantly, until barely tender-crisp when tested with fork, about 2 minutes. Stir in tomatoes, basil, 1 teaspoon salt, pepper and sugar; mix well to incorporate. Cook uncovered, stirring frequently, for 10 minutes. Add roasted peppers and continue to cook until sauce is slightly thickened, about 10 minutes. Remove from heat and add minced parsley.

2. Cook pasta in 6 quarts boiling water with 1 Tablespoon salt until al dente. Drain in colander, transfer to a bowl containing 1 Tablespoon olive oil and toss quickly. Mix ¾ of the sauce and grated Romano cheese with pasta. Spoon remaining sauce on top and serve with additional freshly grated Romano cheese.

SPAGHETTI WITH LIMA BEANS, ARTICHOKE HEARTS AND PEAS
Spaghetti con Fritteda

You don't have to be from Palermo to enjoy this Sicilian favorite. It is traditionally made with the tops of very tender fresh fennel fronds, fresh fava beans, baby artichokes and tiny fresh peas. Since these vegetables are seasonal, I have improvised using frozen lima beans, artichoke hearts and peas so that the dish can be made any time.

SERVES 4—MAIN COURSE
SERVES 6—FIRST COURSE

½ cup olive oil
1 cup finely chopped yellow onion
1 package (10 ounces) frozen baby lima beans, defrosted and well drained
1 package (9 ounces) frozen artichoke hearts, defrosted and well drained
1 package (9 ounces) frozen tiny peas, defrosted and well drained

¼ cup minced fresh fennel fronds or 1½ teaspoon fennel seed
1 teaspoon salt
½ teaspoon freshly milled black pepper
1 pound spaghetti
1 Tablespoon salt
1 Tablespoon olive oil
Freshly grated Romano cheese (for serving)

1. In a large sauté pan, heat ½ cup olive oil over medium heat until haze forms. Add onion, turn heat to low and cook, stirring constantly, until soft but not brown, about 4 minutes. Add lima beans and mix with onion to incorporate. Cover pan and cook until beans are barely tender when tested with a fork, about 5 to 7 minutes. Stir in artichoke hearts, cover pan and cook until tender when tested with a fork, about 5 minutes. Stir in peas and fennel and continue to cook, covered, until tender, about 5 minutes. Season with 1 teaspoon salt and pepper and remove from heat.
2. Cook pasta in 6 quarts boiling water with 1 Tablespoon salt until al dente. Drain in a colander, transfer to a bowl containing 1 Tablespoon olive oil and toss quickly. Mix ¾ of the vegetable mixture with pasta and spoon remainder on top. Serve with freshly grated Romano cheese.

PENNE WITH MUSHROOMS AND PROSCIUTTO
Penne con Funghi e Prosciutto

Sautéed mushrooms, prosciutto and a light white sauce make a creamy, delicate Tuscan trio.

SERVES 4—MAIN COURSE

SERVES 6—FIRST COURSE

1 Tablespoon unsalted butter
1 Tablespoon flour
1 cup chicken broth
½ teaspoon salt
½ teaspoon freshly milled black pepper
½ teaspoon freshly grated nutmeg
2 Tablespoons olive oil
2 Tablespoons unsalted butter
1 cup thinly sliced scallions
4 ounces thinly sliced prosciutto, finely diced
1 pound medium mushrooms, trimmed, wiped and thinly sliced

1 teaspoon salt
½ teaspoon freshly milled black pepper
1 pound penne (or any short tubular pasta)
1 Tablespoon salt
1 Tablespoon unsalted butter, softened
½ cup freshly grated Parmigiano cheese
2 Tablespoons minced Italian parsley leaves (garnish)
Freshly grated Parmigiano cheese (for serving)

1. In a 1½ quart saucepan, melt 1 Tablespoon butter over low heat. When butter begins to froth, add the flour. Mix well with a wire whisk and cook over medium heat, stirring constantly, until lightly golden. Add chicken broth, ½ teaspoon salt, ½ teaspoon pepper and nutmeg. Turn heat to low and cook, whisking constantly, until slightly thickened, about 2 minutes. Cover saucepan and set white sauce aside.

2. In a large sauté pan, heat olive oil over medium heat until haze forms, then add 2 Tablespoons butter. Add scallions and cook, stirring constantly, until barely tender, about 1 minute. Stir in prosciutto and cook, stirring constantly, until softened but not brown, about 1 minute. Add mushrooms, turn heat to medium-high and cook, stirring constantly, until mushrooms just begin to exude their juices, about 1 minute. Season with remaining salt and pepper. Pour white sauce over mushroom mixture and blend well. Turn heat to low and cook, stirring constantly, until mixture is well incorporated, about 2 minutes. Remove from heat.

3. Cook pasta in 6 quarts boiling water with 1 Tablespoon salt until al dente. Drain in a colander, transfer to a bowl containing 1 Tablespoon softened butter and toss quickly. Mix ¾ of the sauce and Parmigiano cheese with pasta. Spoon remaining sauce over pasta and garnish with minced parsley. Serve with additional freshly grated Parmigiano cheese.

TAGLIATELLE WITH ZUCCHINI AND MUSHROOMS
Tagliatelle con Zucchini e Funghi

A very quick-to-prepare sauce with a delicate flavor.

SERVES 4—MAIN COURSE
SERVES 6—FIRST COURSE

1 pound medium zucchini
1 pound medium mushrooms
3 Tablespoons olive oil
3 Tablespoons unsalted
　butter
1 cup thinly sliced scallions
1 Tablespoon finely minced
　garlic
1 Tablespoon minced fresh
　basil or 1 teaspoon
　crumbled dried basil
1½ teaspoons salt
½ teaspoon freshly milled
　black pepper

1 pound tagliatelle,
　preferably homemade (page
　36)
1 Tablespoon salt
1 Tablespoon unsalted butter,
　softened
½ cup chicken broth, heated
2 Tablespoons finely minced
　Italian parsley leaves
　(garnish)
　Freshly grated Romano
　cheese (for serving)

1. Scrub zucchini well and blot dry with paper towel. Trim ends and cut zucchini into 2-inch lengths. Slice each piece in half lengthwise and slice into ¼-inch julienne strips.
2. Wipe mushrooms with damp cloth, trim ends and slice thinly.
3. In a 12-inch skillet, heat olive oil over medium heat until haze forms, then add 3 Tablespoons butter. Add scallions and sauté, stirring constantly, until barely tender, about 1 minute. Add garlic and sauté until soft but not brown, stirring constantly, about 30 seconds. Add zucchini and cook until tender-crisp, stirring once or twice, about 2 minutes. Stir in mushrooms and sauté, stirring constantly, until barely tender when tested with fork,

about 1 minute. Add basil, 1½ teaspoons salt and pepper; mix well and remove from heat.

4. Cook pasta in 6 quarts boiling water with 1 Tablespoon salt until al dente. Drain pasta in a colander, transfer to a bowl containing 1 Tablespoon softened butter and toss quickly. Add half of the vegetable sauce with chicken broth to pasta and toss well. Spoon remaining sauce on top of pasta and garnish with minced parsley. Serve with additional freshly grated Romano cheese.

LINGUINE WITH FRIED ZUCCHINI AND RICOTTA
Linguine alla Lorenza

Make this Sicilian specialty when you can find small, tender zucchini, about 1½ inches in diameter.

SERVES 4—MAIN COURSE
SERVES 6—FIRST COURSE

2 pounds small zucchini
½ cup olive oil
4 cloves garlic, thinly sliced
1 teaspoon salt
½ teaspoon freshly milled
  black pepper
1 pound linguine

1 Tablespoon salt
½ cup freshly grated Romano
  cheese
8 ounces whole milk ricotta
  cheese
Freshly grated Romano
  cheese (for serving)

1. Scrub zucchini and blot dry with paper towel. Trim both ends and cut into 2-inch lengths. Slice again lengthwise into ½-inch widths. Layer zucchini slices on a platter with paper towels between layers to absorb moisture. (This is done so that zucchini will not absorb too much olive oil when frying.)

2. In a large skillet, heat olive oil over medium-high heat until haze forms. Add garlic and sauté, stirring constantly, until very lightly golden. With a slotted spoon, remove garlic and reserve. Fry zucchini in two or three batches until golden on both sides. Transfer to a platter lined with paper towel. Season with 1 teaspoon salt and pepper. Remove pan from heat and let oil cool a little; return garlic to pan. Set aside.

3. Cook pasta in 6 quarts boiling water with 1 Tablespoon salt until al dente. Drain pasta in colander and transfer to a bowl; very quickly toss with oil-garlic mixture. Toss pasta again with half of the fried zucchini and Romano cheese. Place individual servings of pasta in bowls and place 3 or 4 slices of fried zucchini on top of each. Spoon 2 heaping Tablespoons of ricotta on top of zucchini. Serve with remaining ricotta and additional grated Romano cheese.

PASTA PRIMAVERA

There are many different vegetable combinations for Pasta Primavera. Since Primavera means spring, my version of this delightful melody is orchestrated for very small zucchini and thin tender asparagus.

SERVES 4—MAIN COURSE
SERVES 6—FIRST COURSE

1½ pounds asparagus
1 pound zucchini
3 Tablespoons olive oil
3 Tablespoons unsalted butter
2 large cloves garlic, thinly sliced
1 cup thinly sliced scallions
1 teaspoon salt
½ teaspoon freshly milled black pepper

1 pound gemelli (twists)
1 Tablespoon salt
1 Tablespoon unsalted butter, softened
1 cup chicken broth, heated
½ cup freshly grated Parmigiano cheese
Freshly grated Parmigiano cheese (for serving)

1. Wash asparagus several times in lukewarm water to remove sand. Refresh in cold water, drain well in a strainer and blot dry with paper towel. Slice off tough ends. If asparagus are thin they will not have to be peeled; if larger, peel lower portion with a vegetable peeler. Slice diagonally into 1-inch lengths and place tips in a separate bowl.
2. Scrub zucchini and blot dry with paper towel. Trim both ends and cut into 2-inch lengths. Slice each piece into ½-inch strips.
3. In a large sauté pan, heat olive oil over medium heat until haze forms, then add 3 Tablespoons butter. Stir in garlic and sauté until lightly golden; dis-

card with a slotted spoon. Add scallions and cook until tender-crisp, about 2 minutes. Add the bottoms of the asparagus and cook until barely tender when tested with a fork, about 2 minutes. Add zucchini and cook, stirring constantly with wooden spoon until tender, about 2 minutes. Stir in asparagus tips, 1 teaspoon salt and pepper; continue stirring and cook until tips are barely tender when tested with fork, about 2 minutes (do not overcook tips or they will fall apart when tossed with pasta).

4. While you are cooking vegetables, cook pasta in 6 quarts boiling water with 1 Tablespoon salt until al dente. Drain pasta in a colander, transfer to a bowl containing 1 Tablespoon softened butter and toss quickly.

5. Mix half of the vegetables, heated broth and Parmigiano cheese with pasta; toss well. Spoon remaining vegetable mixture on top and serve with additional freshly grated Parmigiano cheese.

TAGLIARINI WITH BASIL PESTO SAUCE
Tagliarini con Pesto alla Genovese

When I was a little girl, my Nonno Donato prepared this classic Ligurian dish the hard way, by making a paste of the ingredients in a mortar with a pestle (this is how it got its name). Today, with the aid of a food processor, it can be done in less than 5 minutes. Make batches of the paste when fresh basil is plentiful. Pack in jars and cover it with ½ inch of olive oil. It will keep in the refrigerator for 4 to 5 months, though it will definitely darken in color. When ready to use, return to room temperature and blend in the cheese.

SERVES 4—MAIN COURSE
SERVES 6—FIRST COURSE

¼ cup pine nuts (pignoli)
2 cups tightly packed fresh basil leaves
½ cup olive oil
1 teaspoon salt
½ teaspoon freshly milled black pepper
1 large clove garlic, split in half
1 cup freshly grated Sardo cheese or ⅔ cup freshly grated Parmigiano cheese and ⅓ cup freshly grated Romano cheese

1 pound tagliarini (thin noodles), preferably homemade (page 36)
1 Tablespoon salt
2 teaspoons vegetable or olive oil
1 Tablespoon olive oil
Freshly grated Sardo or combined Parmigiano and Romano cheese (for serving)

1. Toast pine nuts in a small skillet over medium heat, swirling pan around until nuts are lightly golden. Transfer to a small bowl and set aside (nuts will continue to toast if left in heated pan).
2. Wash basil leaves in cold water, drain well and blot thoroughly dry with paper towel.
3. In food processor fitted with metal blade, place basil, ½ cup olive oil, 1 teaspoon salt and pepper. Turn machine on and drop garlic through the feed tube. Stop machine once or twice and scrape down inside of work bowl with a rubber spatula. Run machine until you have a smooth, thick paste. Transfer paste to a medium bowl. Blend in the Sardo or Parmigiano-Romano mixture with a fork.
4. Cook pasta in 6 quarts boiling water with 1 Tablespoon salt and 2 teaspoons oil until al dente. Before draining pasta, remove about ½ cup of the pasta water and set aside. Drain pasta in a colander, transfer to a bowl con-

taining 1 Tablespoon olive oil and toss quickly. Toss half of the pesto sauce with pasta. Add about 6 Tablespoons of the pasta water and toss again to loosen. Add remaining pesto and toss well again. Garnish with toasted pine nuts and serve with additional freshly grated cheese.

FARFALLE WITH SPINACH PESTO
Farfalle con Pesto di Spinaci

While the authentic pesto sauce depends on the availability of fresh basil, this classic dish can be made and enjoyed year round.

SERVES 4—MAIN COURSE
SERVES 6—FIRST COURSE

⅓ cup blanched almonds
8 ounces fresh spinach
3 Tablespoons unsalted
butter
4 large scallions, cut into
1-inch lengths
2 medium cloves garlic, split
in half
⅓ cup tightly packed Italian
parsley leaves
½ cup olive oil
½ teaspoon salt
½ teaspoon freshly milled
black pepper

1 cup freshly grated Sardo
cheese or ½ cup Romano
and ½ cup Parmigiano
cheese
1 pound farfalle (bows)
1 Tablespoon salt
1 Tablespoon unsalted butter,
softened
Freshly grated Sardo
cheese or Romano-
Parmigiano mixture (for
serving)

1. To toast almonds, place on a cookie sheet and toast on center rack of preheated 350°F oven for 5 to 7 minutes. Remove from oven and let cool to room temperature. Place in food processor fitted with metal blade. Run machine nonstop until coarsely chopped. Set aside.
2. Wash spinach several times in lukewarm water to remove sand. Remove stems and discard. Blot leaves dry with paper towel and snip into 1-inch pieces; set aside.
3. In a small saucepan, melt 3 Tablespoons butter over low heat. Add scallions and garlic and cook, covered, until tender, about 3 minutes.

4. Place scallion-garlic mixture in food processor fitted with metal blade. Add spinach, parsley, olive oil, ½ teaspoon salt and pepper. Turn machine on and run nonstop for 30 seconds. Stop machine once or twice and scrape down inside of work bowl with a rubber spatula. Run machine until you have a smooth, thick paste. Transfer to a bowl and blend in Sardo cheese or Romano-Parmigiano mixture with a fork.

5. Cook pasta in 6 quarts boiling water with 1 Tablespoon salt until al dente. Before draining pasta, take about ½ cup of the pasta water and set aside. Drain pasta in a colander, transfer to a bowl containing 1 Tablespoon softened butter and toss quickly. Toss half of the pesto sauce and half of the almonds with pasta. Add about 6 Tablespoons of the pasta water and toss. Add remaining pesto sauce and toss well again. Garnish with remaining almonds and serve with additional freshly grated cheese.

LINGUINE WITH WALNUT SAUCE
Linguine con Salsa di Noce

A very rich and satisfying combination. A word of warning—keep the portions small!

SERVES 6—MAIN COURSE
SERVES 8—FIRST COURSE

1 cup whole milk ricotta cheese
½ cup heavy cream
½ cup freshly grated Parmigiano cheese
3 Tablespoons olive oil
2 Tablespoons unsalted butter
3 large cloves garlic, split in half
1 cup coarsely chopped walnuts
3 Tablespoons minced fresh basil or 1 Tablespoon crumbled dried basil
1 pound linguine
1 Tablespoon salt
1 Tablespoon unsalted butter, softened
Freshly grated Parmigiano cheese (for serving)

1. In a small bowl, combine ricotta, heavy cream and Parmigiano cheese. Mix well with a fork and set aside.

2. In a medium skillet, heat olive oil over medium heat until haze forms, then add 2 Tablespoons butter. Sauté garlic, stirring constantly, until lightly golden. Discard with a slotted spoon. Add walnuts, turn heat to low and sauté, stirring constantly, until lightly toasted, about 1 minute. Stir in basil and mix well; remove from heat.

3. Cook pasta in 6 quarts boiling water with 1 Tablespoon salt until al dente. Drain in a colander, transfer to a bowl containing 1 Tablespoon softened butter and toss quickly. Toss all the cheese mixture and half of the walnut-basil mixture with pasta. Spoon remaining walnut-basil mixture on top and serve with freshly grated Parmigiano cheese.

LINGUINE WITH BACON AND PROSCIUTTO
Linguine alla Carbonara

There are many different ways of preparing this Roman classic of bacon and eggs. My version derives its zip from the addition of prosciutto and scallions.

SERVES 4—MAIN COURSE
SERVES 6—FIRST COURSE

2 Tablespoons olive oil
4 ounces pancetta or very lean bacon, sliced into 2 × ¼-inch strips
3 ounces prosciutto, sliced into 2 × ½-inch strips
1 cup thinly sliced scallions
3 large egg yolks
¼ cup heavy cream
½ cup freshly grated Parmigiano cheese
1 teaspoon freshly milled black pepper
1 pound linguine
1 Tablespoon salt
1 Tablespoon unsalted butter, softened
2 Tablespoons minced Italian parsley leaves (garnish)
Freshly grated Parmigiano cheese (for serving)

1. In a large skillet, heat olive oil over medium heat until haze forms. Add pancetta or bacon and sauté, stirring constantly, until lightly golden and slightly crispy. Add prosciutto and continue to sauté until softened, about 1 minute. With a slotted spoon, transfer mixture to paper towel to drain.

2. Pour off all but about 2 Tablespoons of the pan drippings. Add scallions

and sauté, stirring constantly, over medium heat until tender-crisp, about 2 minutes; as scallions are cooking, scrape bottom of pan with wooden spoon to loosen any fragments. Return pancetta and prosciutto to pan, mix well and set aside.

3. In a small bowl, using a wire whisk, beat egg yolks and heavy cream. Add Parmigiano cheese and black pepper; whisk again until smooth.

4. Cook pasta in 6 quarts boiling water with 1 Tablespoon salt until al dente. Drain in a colander, transfer to a bowl containing 1 Tablespoon softened butter and toss quickly. Toss half of the pancetta-scallion mixture with pasta. Immediately toss with egg-cheese mixture. Spoon remaining pancetta-scallion mixture on top and garnish with minced parsley. Serve with additional freshly grated Parmigiano cheese.

FETTUCCINE WITH SALAMI AND MUSHROOMS
Fettuccine alla Giovanni "A"

The highly seasoned flavor of salami makes a savory combination with mushrooms, eggs and cream. This is definitely a one-dish meal. A green salad with mustard vinaigrette would be a perfect accompaniment, and a light bodied white wine such as Frascati would complement both.

SERVES 4—MAIN COURSE

½ cup (1 stick) unsalted butter, cut into 8 pieces

1 pound mushrooms, trimmed, wiped and thinly sliced

6 ounces thinly sliced soprassata or Genoa salami, cut into ¼-inch-thick strips

¾ cup thinly sliced scallions

½ teaspoon salt

½ teaspoon freshly milled black pepper

3 large egg yolks

½ cup heavy cream

½ cup freshly grated Parmigiano cheese

1 pound fettuccine, preferably homemade (page 36)

1 Tablespoon salt

2 teaspoons vegetable or olive oil

1 Tablespoon unsalted butter, softened

¼ cup thinly sliced scallions (garnish)

Freshly grated Parmigiano cheese (for serving)

1. In a large sauté pan, melt ½ cup butter over medium-high heat. Add mushrooms and quickly toss with a wooden spoon until they are well coated with butter. Cook, stirring constantly, just until they begin to exude their juices, about 1 minute. Very quickly stir in salami and scallions; mix well. Cook, stirring constantly, until scallions are barely tender when tested with fork, about 30 seconds. Season with ½ teaspoon salt and pepper; set aside.
2. In a small bowl, using a wire whisk, beat egg yolks and cream. Add Parmigiano cheese and whisk again until you have a thick, smooth paste.
3. Cook pasta in 6 quarts boiling water with 1 Tablespoon salt and 2 teaspoons oil until al dente. Drain in a colander, transfer to a bowl containing 1 Tablespoon softened butter and toss quickly. Very quickly toss pasta with egg-cheese mixture. Toss again with half of the salami-mushroom mixture; spoon remaining mixture on top. Garnish with sliced scallions and serve with additional freshly grated Parmigiano cheese.

RIGATONI WITH SAUSAGE CREAM SAUCE
Rigatoni con Salsiccia alla Crema

A real quickie to make. The sausage can be cooked and chopped several hours ahead of time and the sauce can be prepared while water is boiling for pasta.

SERVES 4—MAIN COURSE
SERVES 6—FIRST COURSE

1 pound sweet Italian sausage (with fennel)	1 cup freshly grated Parmigiano cheese
½ cup (1 stick) unsalted butter	1 pound rigatoni
1 cup heavy cream	1 Tablespoon salt
¼ teaspoon freshly grated nutmeg	1 Tablespoon unsalted butter, softened
½ teaspoon salt	2 Tablespoons minced Italian parsley leaves (garnish)
½ teaspoon freshly milled black pepper	Freshly grated Parmigiano cheese (for serving)

1. Place sausage in a 2-quart saucepan with 1½ cups water. Cover, bring to a boil and turn heat down to low. Simmer, covered, for 10 minutes. Remove from heat and let sausage cool to room temperature in cooking liquid. Dis-

card liquid, remove casings from sausage and chop finely (can be chopped in food processor fitted with metal blade).

2. In a medium skillet, melt ½ cup butter over medium heat. Add heavy cream, turn heat to low and cook until mixture is well blended and slightly thickened, stirring once or twice with wooden spoon. Stir in sausage, nutmeg, ½ teaspoon salt and pepper; cook for 1 minute. Stir in Parmigiano cheese and remove from heat.

3. Cook pasta in 6 quarts boiling water with 1 Tablespoon salt until al dente. Drain in a colander, transfer to a bowl containing 1 Tablespoon softened butter and toss quickly. Mix ¾ of the sauce with pasta and spoon remaining sauce on top. Garnish with minced parsley and serve with additional freshly grated Parmigiano cheese.

FUSILLI WITH FOUR CHEESES
Fusilli con Quattro Formaggi

A northern Italian favorite with several of my students; the only reservation is that you must be a cheese lover. Make the sauce just before you cook the pasta. If it is made too far in advance, the oils from the cheese will separate and rise to the top of the pot, and you will have to cook it again to blend.

SERVES 4—MAIN COURSE
SERVES 6—FIRST COURSE

½ cup (1 stick) unsalted butter	1 cup heavy cream
4 ounces ricotta salata cheese (semi-soft variety), grated on the coarse holes of grater	1 teaspoon freshly milled white pepper
4 ounces Gorgonzola cheese, crumbled	1 pound fusilli (twists)
4 ounces Fontina cheese, cut into ½-inch cubes	1 Tablespoon salt
1 cup freshly grated Asiago or Parmigiano cheese	1 Tablespoon unsalted butter, softened
	2 Tablespoons minced Italian parsley leaves (garnish)

1. Melt ½ cup butter in a heavy 3-quart saucepan over low heat. Add ricotta salata, Gorgonzola and Fontina cheese and stir constantly with a wire

whisk until melted. Stir in the Asiago or Parmigiano cheese, cream and pepper. Cook, whisking constantly, until all the cheeses are completely blended. Remove from heat and set aside.

2. Cook pasta in 6 quarts boiling water with 1 Tablespoon salt until al dente. Drain pasta in a colander, transfer to a bowl containing 1 Tablespoon softened butter and toss quickly. Toss with half of the sauce and toss again with remaining sauce. Garnish with minced parsley and serve immediately.

STRAW AND HAY
Paglia e Fieno

The green noodles represent hay; the yellow stand for straw. A showy display of color and ever so tasty when egg yolks, cream, prosciutto and peas are added. You can use all green or yellow noodles for this sauce; the dish is not as colorful, but just as good. If using homemade pasta recipes from this book, you can cook both pastas together. If you are purchasing pasta, however, I would suggest cooking them separately, as cooking times may vary.

SERVES 4—MAIN COURSE
SERVES 6—FIRST COURSE

¼ cup unsalted butter, cut into 8 pieces
1 cup thinly sliced scallions
4 ounces prosciutto, finely diced
1 package (9 ounces) frozen tiny peas, defrosted and well drained
1 teaspoon salt
½ teaspoon freshly milled white pepper
2 extra large egg yolks
1 cup heavy cream
½ cup freshly grated Parmigiano cheese

⅛ teaspoon freshly grated nutmeg
8 ounces green noodles, preferably homemade (page 44)
8 ounces yellow noodles, preferably homemade (page 36)
1 Tablespoon salt
2 teaspoons vegetable or olive oil
1 Tablespoon unsalted butter, softened
Freshly grated Parmigiano cheese (for serving)

1. Melt ¼ cup butter in a large skillet over medium heat. Add scallions and sauté, stirring constantly, until barely tender, about 1 minute. Stir in prosciutto and cook, stirring constantly, until soft but not brown, about 1 min-

ute. Stir in peas, 1 teaspoon salt and pepper. Continue to cook, stirring constantly, until peas are tender-crisp (test by tasting), about 3 minutes. Set aside.

2. In a small bowl, using a wire whisk, beat together egg yolks and cream. Add Parmigiano cheese and nutmeg; whisk again until smooth.

3. Cook pasta in 6 quarts boiling water with 1 Tablespoon salt and 2 teaspoons oil until al dente. Drain in a colander, transfer to a bowl containing 1 Tablespoon softened butter and toss quickly. Very quickly toss pasta with egg-cheese mixture. Toss again with half of the pea-prosciutto mixture and spoon remainder on top. Serve with additional freshly grated Parmigiano cheese.

Seafood Sauces

CONCHIGLIE WITH WHITE CLAM SAUCE

SPAGHETTINI WITH CRABMEAT

FETTUCCINE WITH LOBSTER SAUCE

GREEN TAGLIATELLE WITH SCALLOPS

LINGUINE WITH SHRIMP

ORECCHIETTE WITH SHRIMP AND SCALLOPS

CONCHIGLIE WITH WHITE CLAM SAUCE
Conchiglie con Vongole al Bianco

Fresh or canned clams provide succulent flavor in this sauce, which is very quick to make. If fresh clams are unavailable, you can substitute two 6½-ounce cans of chopped or minced clams. After draining canned clams, make up the difference in liquid needed with dry white wine.

SERVES 4—MAIN COURSE
SERVES 6—FIRST COURSE

3 dozen shucked cherrystone clams (including liquid)
6 Tablespoons olive oil
½ cup thinly sliced scallions
1 Tablespoon finely minced garlic
1 teaspoon salt
½ teaspoon freshly milled white pepper

2 Tablespoons minced Italian parsley leaves
1 pound conchiglie (medium-size shells)
1 Tablespoon salt
1 Tablespoon olive oil

1. Drain shucked clams in a strainer set over a bowl. Wash clams thoroughly to get rid of any sand. Drain well and chop coarsely. Set aside. Strain liquid from clams through a strainer set over a bowl lined with a triple layer of dampened cheesecloth. Measure out 1½ cups of the strained liquid and reserve.
2. In a 2-quart saucepan, heat 6 Tablespoons olive oil over medium heat until haze forms. Add scallions and sauté, stirring constantly, until tender, about 2 minutes. Turn heat to low, add garlic and sauté until soft but not brown, about 2 minutes. Pour in the strained clam liquid or combined liquid and wine. Raise the heat to high and bring to a boil. Turn heat down to medium and cook until liquid is slightly reduced, about 5 minutes. Add clams and turn heat down to low, stirring once or twice; continue to cook for an additional 2 minutes. Season with 1 teaspoon salt and pepper. Stir in parsley and remove from heat.
3. Boil pasta in 6 quarts boiling water with 1 Tablespoon salt until al dente. Drain in a colander, transfer to a bowl containing 1 Tablespoon olive oil and toss quickly. Add ¾ of the clam sauce and toss well. Spoon remaining sauce on top and serve immediately.

SPAGHETTINI WITH CRABMEAT
Spaghettini con Granchio

Here is a very sweet-tasting sauce with just a tingle of hotness; for crab lovers it's a definite favorite. This is one Sicilian seafood sauce that can be prepared up to 4 hours before serving. Cover pan and reheat sauce over very low heat while pasta is cooking.

SERVES 4—MAIN COURSE
SERVES 6—FIRST COURSE

1 pound fresh jumbo lump crabmeat
¼ cup olive oil
1½ cups finely chopped yellow onion
1 can (28 ounces) concentrated crushed tomatoes (see note)
2 Tablespoons minced fresh basil or 2 teaspoons crumbled dried basil
1 teaspoon salt
½ teaspoon red pepper flakes
½ teaspoon sugar
1 pound spaghettini
1 Tablespoon salt
1 Tablespoon olive oil
2 Tablespoons minced Italian parsley leaves (garnish)

1. Using your fingertips, pick over crabmeat to remove any bits of shell or cartilage. Set crab aside.
2. In a large sauté pan, heat ¼ cup olive oil over medium heat until haze forms. Add onion, turn heat to low and sauté, stirring frequently, until soft but not brown, about 5 minutes. Stir in tomatoes, basil, salt, red pepper and sugar. Increase heat to high and bring sauce to a boil. Turn heat to low and cook sauce uncovered, stirring frequently, until slightly thickened, about 20 minutes. Stir in crabmeat and continue to cook, stirring constantly, for 5 minutes. Remove from heat.
3. Cook pasta in 6 quarts boiling water with 1 Tablespoon salt until al dente. Drain in a colander, transfer to a bowl containing 1 Tablespoon olive oil and toss quickly. Mix half of the crabmeat sauce with pasta and spoon remaining sauce on top. Garnish with minced parsley and serve immediately.

Note: If concentrated crushed tomatoes are unavailable, use a 35-ounce can of Italian plum tomatoes, coarsely chopped, juice included (can be chopped in food processor fitted with metal blade). Increase cooking time by 10 minutes.

FETTUCCINE WITH LOBSTER SAUCE
Fettuccine con Aragosta

Frozen lobster tails tend to be rather tough when cooked too long. The timing given in this recipe is for 6-ounce tails. If using smaller lobster tails, reduce cooking time to 1 minute. When slicing, the lobster meat should still be slightly raw in center. The addition of sun-dried tomatoes will give this Northern Italian sauce a very pale pink, speckled appearance. If using tomato paste, your sauce will be a deeper pink.

SERVES 4—MAIN COURSE
SERVES 6—FIRST COURSE

4 frozen lobster tails (6 ounces each; 1½ pounds total weight), defrosted and well drained
1½ Tablespoons unsalted butter
1½ Tablespoons flour
1½ cups milk
½ teaspoon salt
½ teaspoon freshly milled black pepper
1 Tablespoon minced sun-dried tomatoes, well drained or 1 Tablespoon tomato paste (see note)
2 medium zucchini (8 ounces)
¼ cup unsalted butter

1 cup thinly sliced scallions
½ teaspoon salt
½ teaspoon freshly milled black pepper
1 pound fettuccine, preferably homemade (page 36)
1 Tablespoon salt
2 teaspoons vegetable or olive oil
1 Tablespoon unsalted butter, softened
1 Tablespoon minced Italian parsley leaves (garnish)
Freshly grated Parmigiano cheese (for serving)

1. In a 6-quart pot, bring 4 quarts of water to a boil. Add lobster tails, cover pot and bring to a boil. As soon as water returns to a boil, uncover and cook just until the tails start to curl and turn pink, about 2 minutes. Using tongs, transfer tails to a colander and quickly rinse under cold water. With a pair of kitchen shears, snip shell lengthwise along the underside and top side of tail. Remove the tail meat and cut into ½-inch slices. Set aside.

2. In a 2½-quart saucepan, melt 1½ Tablespoons butter over low heat. When butter begins to froth, add the flour. Mix well with a wire whisk and cook over medium heat, whisking constantly, until lightly golden. Add milk, ½ teaspoon salt and ½ teaspoon pepper; turn heat to low. Cook over low heat, whisking constantly, until slightly thickened, about 2 minutes. Add minced

dried tomatoes or tomato paste and cook, stirring constantly with whisk, for another 30 seconds. Cover pan and set tomato bechamel sauce aside.

3. Scrub zucchini well and blot dry with paper towel. Trim ends and cut into 1½-inch lengths. Halve each piece lengthwise and slice into ¼-inch strips.

4. In a 12-inch skillet, melt ¼ cup butter over low heat. Add scallions, turn heat to medium and sauté, stirring constantly, until tender-crisp, about 1 minute. Add zucchini and sauté, stirring constantly, until barely tender when tested with a fork, about 2 minutes. Add lobster meat and cook, stirring constantly, for another minute. Season with ½ teaspoon each salt and pepper. Stir in tomato bechamel sauce and mix well. Turn heat to low and cook, stirring constantly, until heated through, about 1 minute.

5. Cook pasta in 6 quarts rapidly boiling water with 1 Tablespoon salt and 2 teaspoons oil until al dente. Drain pasta in a colander, transfer to a bowl containing 1 Tablespoon softened butter and toss quickly. Add half of the lobster sauce to pasta and toss well. Spoon remaining sauce on top of pasta and garnish with minced parsley. Serve with freshly grated Parmigiano cheese.

Note: Sun-dried tomatoes are available in gourmet or Italian specialty shops. They come packed in jars, covered with olive oil. Drain well and scrape out seeds before using.

GREEN TAGLIATELLE WITH SCALLOPS
Tagliatelle Verdi con Pettine

Green noodles paired with creamy scallop sauce and topped with fresh parsley are not only mouthwatering for seafood lovers, but spectacular in presentation as well. The sauce may seem a little thin when first tossed with pasta—but don't despair, it will thicken by the time you get it to the table. A true Northern Italian favorite.

SERVES 4—MAIN COURSE
SERVES 6—FIRST COURSE

1½ pounds sea or bay scallops
¼ cup unsalted butter
1 cup thinly sliced scallions
1 teaspoon finely minced garlic
½ cup dry vermouth
½ cup heavy cream
2 Tablespoons minced Italian parsley leaves
1 cup freshly grated Parmigiano cheese
¼ teaspoon freshly grated nutmeg
1 teaspoon salt

½ teaspoon freshly milled white pepper
1 pound green tagliatelle, preferably homemade (page 44)
1 Tablespoon salt
2 teaspoons vegetable or olive oil
1 Tablespoon unsalted butter, softened
2 Tablespoons minced Italian parsley leaves (garnish)
Freshly grated Parmigiano cheese (for serving)

1. Wash scallops several times in cold water to remove sand. Place in a strainer and blot dry with paper towel. If using tiny bay scallops, leave whole; if using sea scallops, cut horizontally into ½-inch slices.
2. In a large sauté pan, melt ¼ cup butter over medium heat. Add scallions and sauté, stirring constantly, until barely tender, about 2 minutes. Add garlic and sauté until soft but not brown, about 2 minutes. Turn heat to high, add vermouth and cook, stirring once or twice, until liquid is reduced a little, about 3 minutes. Turn heat down to medium, stir in scallops and cook for 1 minute. Turn heat to low, stir in heavy cream and cook mixture, stirring constantly, until well combined, about 2 minutes. Stir in 2 Tablespoons parsley, Parmigiano cheese, nutmeg, 1 teaspoon salt and pepper. Mix well and remove from heat.
3. Cook pasta in 6 quarts boiling water with 1 Tablespoon salt and 2 tea-

spoons oil until al dente. Drain pasta in a colander, transfer to a bowl containing 1 Tablespoon softened butter and toss quickly. Mix ¾ of the sauce with pasta and toss well. Spoon remaining sauce on top and garnish with 2 Tablespoons parsley. Serve with freshly grated Parmigiano cheese.

LINGUINE WITH SHRIMP
Linguine con Gamberi

The subtle flavor of lemon mixed with shrimp and herbs is truly memorable. This piquant Ligurian sauce is ready in minutes and is guaranteed to please.

SERVES 4—MAIN COURSE
SERVES 6—FIRST COURSE

1½ pounds medium shrimp
¼ cup olive oil
¼ cup unsalted butter
1 cup thinly sliced scallions
1 teaspoon finely minced garlic
¼ cup fresh lemon juice
2 Tablespoons minced fresh basil or 2 teaspoons crumbled dried basil

1 teaspoon salt
½ teaspoon freshly milled white pepper
¼ cup minced Italian parsley leaves
1 pound linguine
1 Tablespoon salt
1 Tablespoon unsalted butter, softened

1. Peel and devein shrimp. Wash thoroughly under cold water and blot dry with paper towel. Set aside.
2. In a large sauté pan, heat olive oil over medium heat until haze forms, then add ¼ cup butter. Add scallions and cook, stirring constantly, until barely tender, about 2 minutes. Add garlic and cook, stirring constantly, until soft but not brown, about 2 minutes. Add shrimp, turn heat to medium-high and cook, stirring constantly, just until shrimp turn pink, about 2 to 3 minutes. Add lemon juice and basil, turn heat to low and cook, stirring constantly, until well incorporated, about 30 seconds. Season with 1 teaspoon salt and pepper. Stir in parsley and remove from heat.
3. Cook pasta in 6 quarts boiling water with 1 Tablespoon salt until al dente. Drain in a colander, transfer to a bowl containing 1 Tablespoon softened butter and toss quickly. Add half of the shrimp mixture to pasta and toss well. Spoon remaining shrimp mixture on top and serve immediately.

ORECCHIETTE WITH SHRIMP AND SCALLOPS
Orecchiette con Gamberi e Pettine

The shrimp and scallops lodge in each pasta cavity, making this Neapoli-
tan sauce doubly delicious. The sauce can be made earlier in the day, but
omit adding shrimp and scallops. While pasta is cooking, reheat sauce;
add seafood and cook about 2 minutes or just until shrimp turn pink.

SERVES 4—MAIN COURSE
SERVES 6—FIRST COURSE

1 pound medium-size fresh
shrimp
1 pound bay or sea scallops
2 Tablespoons olive oil
2 Tablespoons unsalted
butter
2 large cloves garlic, split in
half
1 cup thinly sliced scallions
1 can (35 ounces) Italian
plum tomatoes, strained
through a food mill, juice
included
2 Tablespoons minced fresh
basil or 2 teaspoons
crumbled dried basil

1 teaspoon salt
½ teaspoon freshly milled
black pepper
½ teaspoon sugar
1 pound orecchiette or any
shell-type pasta
1 Tablespoon salt
1 Tablespoon unsalted butter,
softened
2 Tablespoons minced Italian
parsley leaves (garnish)

1. Clean and devein shrimp. Wash in cold water, place in a strainer and blot
dry with paper towels. Cut shrimp into ½-inch slices and set aside. Wash
scallops several times in cold water to remove sand. Place in strainer and
blot dry with paper towels. If using tiny bay scallops, leave whole; if using
sea scallops, cut horizontally into ½-inch slices. Combine with shrimp. Set
aside.

2. In a large sauté pan, heat olive oil over medium heat until haze forms, then
add 2 Tablespoons butter. Add garlic and sauté until lightly golden. Using
a slotted spoon, remove garlic and discard. Add scallions and cook, stirring
constantly, until barely tender, about 2 minutes. Add strained tomatoes,
basil, 1 teaspoon salt, pepper and sugar; mix well. Bring sauce to a boil
over high heat, then turn heat to low. Simmer uncovered, stirring frequently, until sauce is slightly thickened, about 15 minutes. Stir in shrimp and
scallops and continue to cook, stirring constantly, just until shrimp turn
pink, about 2 minutes. Remove from heat.

3. Meanwhile, cook pasta in 6 quarts boiling water with 1 Tablespoon salt until al dente. Drain in a colander, transfer to a bowl containing 1 Tablespoon softened butter and toss quickly. Mix half of the seafood sauce with pasta and toss well. Spoon remaining sauce on top and garnish with minced parsley. Serve immediately.

Pasta Specialties

BAKED ZITI

LASAGNE

RAVIOLI

SPINACH–RICOTTA DUMPLINGS

FIVE-LAYER PASTA PIE

PASTA ROLL

BAKED ZITI
Ziti al Forno

This robust sauce combined with the creamy flavor of ricotta cheese and pasta makes a delectable Neapolitan dish. It can be completely assembled a day ahead, covered with plastic wrap and refrigerated. Return to room temperature before baking.

SERVES 8—MAIN COURSE
SERVES 10—FIRST COURSE

TOMATO SAUCE

1 pound Italian sweet sausage with fennel seed (see note)
3 Tablespoons dry red wine
¼ cup olive oil
1 cup finely chopped yellow onion
1½ teaspoons finely minced garlic
2 cans (28 ounces each) concentrated crushed tomatoes (see note)
2 Tablespoons minced fresh basil or 2 teaspoons crumbled dried basil
¼ teaspoon freshly grated nutmeg
1 teaspoon sugar
2 teaspoons salt
1 teaspoon freshly milled black pepper

1. Remove casings from sausage. Crumble sausage and combine in a 1½-quart saucepan with red wine. Cook, covered, over medium heat until most of the wine is evaporated, about 15 minutes. Transfer sausage to a strainer and let any drippings drain off for at least 15 minutes.
2. In a large sauté pan, heat olive oil over medium heat until haze forms. Add onion, turn heat to low and sauté, stirring constantly, until soft but not brown, about 5 minutes. Add minced garlic and continue to sauté until garlic is soft but not brown, about 2 minutes. Add remaining ingredients including sausage and turn heat to high. Bring to a boil, stirring constantly, then turn heat down to low. Cook sauce partially covered, stirring frequently, until slightly thickened, about 40 minutes.

Note: If sausage with fennel is not available, add ½ teaspoon fennel seed to sausage when cooking with wine.

If crushed tomatoes are unavailable, use 2 cans (35 ounces each) of Italian plum tomatoes, coarsely chopped, juice included (can be chopped in food processor fitted with metal blade). Increase cooking time by 20 minutes.

FILLING

1 pound whole milk ricotta
cheese
2 extra large eggs, lightly
beaten
½ cup freshly grated Romano
cheese
½ teaspoon salt
½ teaspoon freshly milled
black pepper
2 Tablespoons minced Italian
parsley leaves

In a medium bowl, combine ricotta and eggs with a fork. Add remaining ingredients and blend well with fork. Set aside.

TO ASSEMBLE AND COOK

1 pound ziti
1 Tablespoon salt
1 Tablespoon unsalted butter,
softened
½ cup freshly grated Romano
cheese
Freshly grated Romano
cheese (for serving)

1. Cook ziti in 6 quarts boiling water with 1 Tablespoon salt until barely tender when tested with a fork, about 4 minutes after water returns to a boil. Drain pasta in a colander and transfer to a bowl containing softened butter; toss quickly. In same bowl, divide ziti into 3 portions.
2. In a 13 × 9 × 2-inch ovenproof casserole, spread a very thin layer of sauce. Arrange one portion of ziti in a single layer. Spoon half of the ricotta filling over pasta and very carefully spread with a metal spatula to completely cover pasta. Spoon a thin layer of sauce over filling and sprinkle with ⅓ of the Romano cheese. Repeat with another layer of ziti, ricotta filling, sauce and Romano cheese. Cover top layer with remaining ziti. Spread with a thin layer of sauce and sprinkle with remaining Romano cheese.
3. Adjust rack to center of oven and preheat to 350°F. Bake ziti uncovered until lightly crusty on top, about 40 to 50 minutes. Remove from oven and allow to rest for at least 10 minutes before serving.
4. To serve, cut into squares and lift out with a metal spatula. Serve with remaining sauce and additional Romano cheese.

LASAGNE

Once you have learned to make pasta, this is a great dish for entertaining because it can be completely assembled a day in advance. Cover with plastic wrap and refrigerate, then return to room temperature before baking. You will receive endless compliments for your efforts. I always serve this Ligurian lasagne as a first course for Easter.

SERVES 8—MAIN COURSE
SERVES 10 TO 12—FIRST COURSE

PASTA

Prepare 1½ batches of homemade pasta (page 36).

If mixing dough in food processor, it will be easier if you make two single batches and reserve half of one batch for tagliarini or tagliatelle.

While dough is resting, make meat sauce, bechamel sauce and cheese filling.

MEAT SAUCE

2 Tablespoons olive oil	8 ounces ground veal
2 Tablespoons unsalted butter	1 cup dry red wine
4 ounces pancetta, finely diced	2 cups canned Italian plum tomatoes, strained though a food mill, juice included
1 cup finely chopped yellow onion	1½ cups beef broth
1 cup finely chopped celery, strings removed	1 teaspoon salt
1 cup finely chopped carrot	½ teaspoon freshly milled black pepper
8 ounces very lean ground round steak	½ teaspoon freshly grated nutmeg
8 ounces very lean ground pork	

In a 5-quart Dutch oven, heat olive oil and butter together over medium heat. Add pancetta and cook, stirring constantly, until soft but not brown, about 1 minute. Add onion, celery and carrot and cook, stirring constantly, until soft, about 5 minutes. Stir in the ground beef, pork and veal. Turn heat to low and cook, stirring constantly, just until meat begins to lose its pinkness, about 5 minutes. Stir in wine and raise heat to high. Cook, stirring frequently, until wine is reduced a little and sauce begins to thicken slightly, about 10 minutes. Add tomatoes, beef broth, salt, pepper and nutmeg. Bring sauce to a boil, then reduce heat to low. Simmer sauce uncovered, stirring frequently, until cooking liquids have reduced and sauce is thick, about 1 hour. Remove from heat, cover pan and cool to room temperature. Skim off any surface fat with a metal spoon.

BECHAMEL SAUCE

6 Tablespoons unsalted butter	3 cups milk
	½ teaspoon salt
½ cup flour	⅓ teaspoon freshly grated nutmeg

In a 2-quart saucepan, melt butter over low heat. When butter begins to froth, add the flour. Mix well with a wire whisk and cook over medium heat, whisking constantly, until lightly golden. Add milk, salt and nutmeg; turn heat to low. Cook over low heat, stirring constantly with whisk, until thick and creamy, about 5 minutes. Cover saucepan and set aside.

CHEESE FILLING

8 ounces whole milk Mozzarella cheese, coarsely grated	1½ cups freshly grated Parmigiano cheese

Combine cheeses in a large shallow bowl, cover with plastic wrap and refrigerate until needed.

TO ROLL PASTA BY HAND

1. Divide pasta dough into 4 equal pieces. Remove 1 piece of dough and keep the remaining dough covered to prevent drying.
2. On a lightly floured board, roll each piece of dough evenly into a ⅛-inch-thick rectangle about 13½ × 14 inches. Cut each strip lengthwise into 3 pieces and trim ends (you will need a total of 12 strips of pasta). Lay strips on lightly floured kitchen towels, making sure they do not touch.

TO ROLL USING PASTA MACHINE

1. Divide dough into 6 even pieces. Remove 1 piece and keep the remaining dough covered to prevent drying.
2. Follow directions for pasta machine rolling, page 39, until you have a strip of dough at least 4½ inches wide and 25 inches long. Cut strip in half horizontally and trim off ends. You will have 12 strips of dough when finished, each approximately 12 inches in length. Lay strips on lightly floured kitchen towels, making sure they do not touch.

TO ASSEMBLE AND COOK

2 teaspoons salt

½ teaspoon vegetable or olive
  oil

¼ cup unsalted butter

½ cup freshly grated
  Parmigiano cheese

1. Lay some clean dry towels on your counter or work surface.
2. In a 5-quart sauté pan or large, deep skillet, bring 3½ quarts of water to a boil with salt and oil.
3. Cook 2 strips of pasta at a time for just 10 seconds after the water returns to a boil. Remove pasta with two wooden forks. Lay strips flat on towels. Cook remaining pasta in the same manner.
4. Grease the bottom and sides of a 14 × 9 × 2½-inch baking dish with 1 Tablespoon butter.
5. Reserve ¾ cup of bechamel sauce for topping.
6. In bottom of casserole, spread an even layer of bechamel sauce using a metal spatula. Place 2 strips of pasta in pan, overlapping the strips no more than ½ inch. Spoon another layer of bechamel over pasta and spread evenly with metal spatula. Spoon a thin layer of meat sauce over bechamel and spread evenly with spatula. Sprinkle cheese filling over meat sauce. Make 4 more layers using the ingredients in this order: pasta, bechamel, meat sauce and cheese filling. Cover top layer with last 2 strips of pasta. Tuck the corners of pasta down into the sides of pan so that they will not burn in baking. Spread reserved bechamel sauce evenly over top layer of pasta. Dot with remaining 3 Tablespoons butter and sprinkle with Parmigiano cheese.
7. Adjust oven rack to center of oven and preheat to 350°F. Bake until top layer is lightly golden and crispy, about 50 minutes. Remove from oven and allow to rest for at least 15 minutes before serving.
8. To serve, cut into squares and lift out with a metal spatula. Serve immediately.

RAVIOLI

When making ravioli, prepare the whole recipe; eat some and freeze the rest. This dish is popular in Liguria, Tuscany and Naples.

YIELDS 96 2-INCH SQUARES

PASTA
Make two batches of homemade pasta, page 36.
While pasta is resting, prepare the filling.

FILLING

1 package (10 ounces) frozen leaf spinach, defrosted and well drained
1 whole chicken breast (1½ pounds), cooked, boned and skinned
¼ cup unsalted butter
½ cup finely minced yellow onion
4 ounces lean prosciutto, finely chopped

½ teaspoon salt
½ teaspoon freshly milled black pepper
½ teaspoon freshly grated nutmeg
3 extra large eggs
¼ cup heavy cream
¾ cup freshly grated Parmigiano cheese

1. Chop spinach very finely, place in a strainer and squeeze thoroughly dry with your hands (can be chopped in food processor fitted with metal blade). Set aside.
2. Chop cooked chicken to a very fine consistency (can be chopped in food processor fitted with metal blade; cut chicken into 1-inch chunks before placing in processor). Set aside.
3. In a medium skillet, melt butter over low heat. Add onion and cook, stirring frequently, until soft but not brown, about 2 minutes. Stir in prosciutto and cook until soft, about 1 minute. Add spinach and cook, stirring constantly, until there is no more liquid left in pan and spinach starts to stick to bottom of pan, about 2 minutes. Add chicken and mix well with a wooden spoon. Season with salt, pepper and nutmeg; remove from heat. Transfer mixture to a shallow bowl and let cool slightly (stir with a fork occasionally to hasten cooling).
4. While mixture is cooling, beat eggs with heavy cream. Add cheese and blend thoroughly with fork. Blend egg mixture into spinach mixture with fork.

TO ROLL USING PASTA MACHINE

1. Divide each batch of dough into 4
   pieces (8 total). Remove 1 piece
   and keep the remaining dough
   covered to prevent drying.

2. Follow pasta machine method for
   rolling dough; try to keep the
   dough the exact width of rollers.
   Each strip of dough should be at
   least 5 inches wide by 32 inches
   long. With ravioli cutter or pastry
   wheel, cut dough in half
   horizontally and trim ends evenly.
   After trimming, each sheet should
   be 5 inches wide and 15 inches
   long.

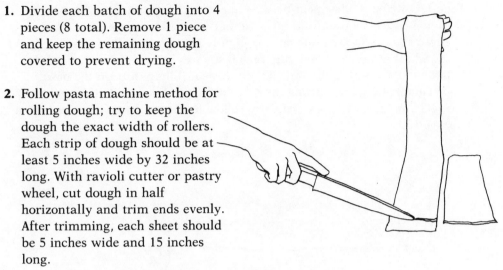

TO ASSEMBLE AND COOK

Place 1 teaspoon of filling every 2½ inches across and down the sheet of
pasta (you should have 12 mounds). Fill a small bowl with warm water. Dip
a pastry brush in water and make vertical and horizontal lines between
mounds of filling (the water acts as a seal to bond the dough strips
together). Place second sheet of pasta evenly over the first sheet. With your

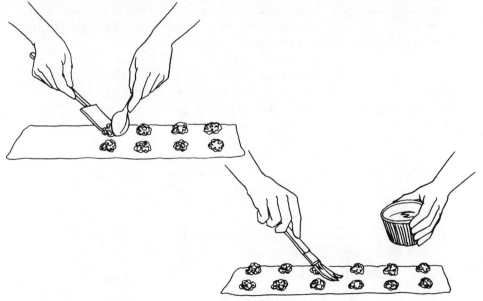

index fingers, press dough firmly between mounds to seal. With a ravioli cutter or pastry wheel, cut between mounds to form squares. (If using a ravioli cutter, trim outside edges so that you will have a perfect zigzag-edged square. To facilitate cutting, lightly brush a little flour on the edge of the wheel as needed.) Separate ravioli squares and set them on a lightly floured dishtowel to dry out slightly. Repeat rolling through the pasta machine, filling and cutting the other portions of dough. At this point, ravioli are ready to cook or freeze. Follow directions for cooking ravioli on page 58.

To freeze ravioli: Arrange 12 ravioli in a single layer between lightly floured sheets of waxed paper. Place in a plastic bag and tie ends of bag with a twist tie. Freeze on a cookie sheet. Remove sheet when frozen. Cook ravioli right from freezer. Can be kept frozen up to 3 months.

Note: There is a ravioli plate on sale at gourmet shops and department stores which makes ravioli shaping very easy. Called the Ravioli Maker No. 512, by Vitantonio Mfg. Company, it makes 12 perfect 2-inch squares.

TO ROLL BY HAND

1. Divide each batch of pasta dough into 4 pieces (8 total). Remove 1 piece and keep the remaining dough covered to prevent drying.

2. On a well floured board, roll dough into a thin rectangular sheet approximately 11 inches wide and 16 inches long. Cover the rolled pasta with a dampened towel to prevent drying out while rolling second piece.

3. Place 1 teaspoon of filling every 2½ inches across and down the sheet of pasta (you should have 24 mounds). Follow procedure given for assembling, page 99.

SPINACH–RICOTTA DUMPLINGS
Gnocchi Verdi

I prefer serving this Ligurian dish as an accompaniment to the entree rather than as a first course.

SERVES 6 TO 8
YIELDS 30 DUMPLINGS

1½ pounds fresh spinach
¼ cup unsalted butter
1 cup whole milk ricotta
 cheese
2 large eggs, lightly beaten
6 Tablespoons unbleached
 flour
1 cup freshly grated
 Parmigiano cheese
½ teaspoon salt
½ teaspoon freshly milled
 black pepper

⅛ teaspoon freshly grated
 nutmeg
1 Tablespoon salt
½ cup unbleached flour (for
 hands)
6 Tablespoons unsalted
 butter, melted
½ cup freshly grated
 Parmigiano cheese (for
 topping)

1. Stem spinach and wash several times in warm water to remove sand. Place spinach in a 4-quart pot (do not add water; the final rinse water clinging to leaves will be sufficient to steam them). Cook, covered, over medium heat just until leaves are wilted, about 3 minutes. Transfer to a colander, refresh under cold water and drain. Squeeze spinach dry in cheesecloth or towel. Finely mince spinach and squeeze dry again in cheesecloth or towel (can also be minced in food processor fitted with metal blade).
2. In a medium skillet, melt ¼ cup butter over medium-high heat. Add spinach and sauté, stirring constantly, until it begins to stick lightly to skillet, about 2 to 3 minutes. Turn heat down to medium and stir in ricotta. Cook, stirring constantly, for 3 to 4 minutes (at this point, mixture should be a little on the dry side). Transfer mixture to a bowl and let cool about 10 minutes (stir with a spoon occasionally to hasten cooling).
3. Stir in eggs, flour, 1 cup Parmigiano cheese, ½ teaspoon salt, pepper and nutmeg; blend well with a fork. Refrigerate, covered, for at least 1 hour or until gnocchi mixture is quite firm.
4. Bring 6 quarts of water to a rolling boil and add 1 Tablespoon salt.
5. Place remaining flour in a shallow bowl. Flour your hands lightly and pick up 1 Tablespoon of the chilled mixture at a time. Shape into balls about 1½

inches in diameter and arrange in a single layer on a platter. Keep flouring your hands with each ball you make.

6. Gently drop half of the balls into boiling water and cook uncovered until they puff lightly and rise to the surface, about 5 to 8 minutes. Lift the balls out gently with a slotted spoon or small strainer and arrange in a single layer on a platter lined with paper towel to drain. Repeat with second batch of gnocchi.

7. Adjust oven rack to 6 inches from broiler and preheat oven to broil setting.

8. Pour 2 Tablespoons of the melted butter into a shallow flameproof serving dish and swirl the butter around until bottom of dish is evenly coated. Arrange gnocchi in a single layer and drizzle with remaining butter. Sprinkle with remaining ½ cup Parmigiano cheese. Place serving dish on rack and broil until cheese is melted and lightly golden on top, about 3 to 5 minutes (watch carefully so gnocchi don't burn). Serve at once.

Note: Gnocchi can be made up to 5 hours before serving. After they are well drained on paper towel, remove paper, cover with plastic wrap and refrigerate. Arrange in flameproof dish and finish off with butter and cheese just before serving.

FIVE-LAYER PASTA PIE
Timballo di Capellini

This presentation always reminds me of a birthday cake. Once sliced, the beautiful layers of zucchini, pasta and chicken striped with the tomato sauce are ever so colorful. All you need is a lovely salad to accompany this very filling Tuscan entree.

SERVES 8 TO 10

CHICKEN–TOMATO SAUCE

3 Tablespoons olive oil
2 Tablespoons unsalted butter
3 whole chicken breasts (2½ pounds), washed, dried and split in half
½ cup finely chopped yellow onion
½ cup finely chopped carrot
1 teaspoon finely minced garlic

2 cans (35 ounces each) Italian plum tomatoes, strained through a food mill, juice included
1 teaspoon sugar
2 teaspoons salt
1 teaspoon freshly milled black pepper
¼ cup minced fresh basil or 4 teaspoons crumbled dried basil

1. In a 5-quart sauté pan or Dutch oven, heat olive oil over medium-high heat until haze forms, then add butter. Sauté chicken, skin side down first, on both sides until lightly golden. Transfer chicken to a platter lined with paper towel.
2. Turn heat down to medium and sauté onion and carrot, stirring constantly, until tender-crisp, scraping up any fragments left in bottom of pan with wooden spoon, about 3 minutes. Add garlic and sauté until soft but not brown, stirring constantly, for an additional minute. Add tomatoes, sugar, salt, pepper and basil; mix well with a wooden spoon. Return chicken to pan, skin side down. Cook sauce uncovered over medium heat, stirring frequently, until slightly thickened, about 30 minutes.
3. Remove chicken from sauce; cool slightly, skin and bone. Cut chicken into ¼-inch cubes and set aside in bowl.
4. Let sauce rest for at least 30 minutes. Skim off any surface fat with a metal spoon.

BECHAMEL SAUCE

¼ cup unsalted butter
¼ cup flour

2 cups milk
1 teaspoon salt

In a 1½-quart saucepan, melt butter over low heat. When butter begins to froth, add the flour. Mix well with a wire whisk and cook over medium heat, whisking constantly, until lightly golden. Add milk and salt; turn heat to low. Cook over low heat, stirring constantly with whisk, until very thick and creamy, about 4 minutes. Pour bechamel sauce into tomato sauce and whisk thoroughly. Cover pan and set aside.

TO ASSEMBLE AND COOK

3 medium zucchini (1½ pounds), well scrubbed, ends trimmed

1 teaspoon salt

1 pound capellini (very thin spaghetti)

1 Tablespoon salt

3 Tablespoons unsalted butter, softened

1½ cups freshly grated Parmigiano cheese

3 extra large eggs, lightly beaten

1 Tablespoon unsalted butter

2 Tablespoons dry breadcrumbs

½ cup freshly grated Parmigiano cheese

1 bunch curly parsley sprigs (garnish)

Freshly grated Parmigiano cheese (for serving)

1. Cook whole zucchini in 2 quarts boiling water with 1 teaspoon salt until barely tender when tested with a fork. Drain well and blot dry with paper towel. Let cool slightly and slice zucchini into ¼-inch round slices; set aside.
2. Break pasta in half and cook in 6 quarts boiling water with 1 Tablespoon salt until barely tender, about 3 minutes. Drain pasta in a colander and transfer to a large bowl dotted with 3 Tablespoons softened butter; toss well. Add 1½ cups Parmigiano cheese and toss well again. Let pasta cool slightly, about 15 minutes; add beaten eggs and mix well with two wooden forks (the texture will be a little pasty). In same bowl, divide pasta into 5 portions.
3. Grease the bottom and sides of a 10-inch springform pan with 1 Tablespoon butter. Coat bottom and sides of pan with breadcrumbs.
4. Spread 1 portion of pasta evenly in bottom of prepared pan. Arrange half of the cubed chicken in an even layer on top and press chicken down into pasta with the back of a spoon. Coat with a thin layer of sauce (about 9 Tablespoons). Spread another layer of pasta on top of the chicken layer. Arrange half of the sliced zucchini evenly over pasta and again press down with the back of a spoon. Coat with another thin layer of sauce. Make 2 more layers using ingredients in this order: pasta, chicken, sauce, pasta, zucchini, sauce. Cover top layer with last portion of pasta. Sprinkle remaining Parmigiano cheese over top layer.

5. Adjust rack to center of oven and preheat to 350°F. Bake pie until nice and crusty on top, about 50 minutes. Remove from oven and let stand for at least 10 to 15 minutes before unmolding.
6. Place a folded piece of dampened paper towel in the center of a serving platter to prevent bottom of spring-form pan from sliding when ready to slice.
7. Place timballo on platter and run a knife around side. Carefully release ring and remove. Garnish platter with parsley sprigs.
8. Slice into 2-inch wedges and serve with remaining sauce and additional Parmigiano cheese.

Note: The timballo can be completely assembled 1 day ahead, covered with plastic wrap and refrigerated. Return to room temperature for 3 hours before baking.

PASTA ROLL
Rotolo di Pasta

This is a luscious presentation topped with a delicate tomato bechamel sauce. My students agree that this elegant Northern Italian creation looks like a strudel when rolled. It's well worth the time it takes to make. If serving as a main course, nothing more than a lovely tossed salad is needed for accompaniment.

SERVES 6—MAIN COURSE
SERVES 8—FIRST COURSE

PASTA

Make 1 recipe of homemade pasta, page 36. While dough is resting, prepare sauces and filling.

TOMATO SAUCE

2 Tablespoons olive oil
2 Tablespoons unsalted butter
½ cup finely chopped yellow onion
½ cup finely chopped carrot
1 can (35 ounces) Italian plum tomatoes, strained through a food mill, juice included

1 teaspoon salt
½ teaspoon freshly milled black pepper
½ teaspoon sugar
2 Tablespoons minced fresh basil or 2 teaspoons crumbled dried basil

In a large skillet, heat olive oil and butter over medium heat. Add onion and carrot, turn heat to low and cook, stirring constantly with a wooden spoon, until soft but not brown, about 5 minutes. Add tomatoes, salt, pepper, sugar and basil; mix well with wooden spoon. Cook sauce uncovered over medium heat, stirring frequently, until slightly thickened, about 20 minutes. Remove from heat, cover pan and set aside.

BECHAMEL SAUCE

2 Tablespoons unsalted
  butter
2 Tablespoons flour

1 cup milk
½ teaspoon salt

1. In a 2½-quart saucepan, melt butter over low heat. When butter begins to froth, add the flour. Mix well with a wire whisk and cook over medium heat, whisking constantly, until lightly golden. Add milk and salt; turn heat to low. Cook over low heat, stirring constantly with whisk, until thick and creamy, about 3 minutes.
2. Pour tomato sauce into bechamel sauce and mix thoroughly with whisk. Cover saucepan and set aside.

FILLING

2 pounds fresh spinach
½ teaspoon salt
5 Tablespoons unsalted
  butter
½ cup finely chopped yellow
  onion
4 ounces prosciutto, finely
  diced
1½ cups whole milk ricotta
  cheese

1¼ cups freshly grated
  Parmigiano cheese
½ teaspoon salt
½ teaspoon freshly milled
  black pepper
2 large egg yolks, lightly
  beaten

1. Stem spinach and wash several times in warm water. Place spinach in a 4-quart pot with ½ teaspoon salt and cover (do not add water; the final rinse water clinging to leaves will be sufficient to steam them). Cook over medium heat until spinach is limp, about 3 minutes. Transfer to a colander, refresh under cold water and squeeze out excess moisture with your hands. Place spinach in a piece of cheesecloth or towel and squeeze again until there is not a drop of moisture left. Finely chop spinach and set aside (can be chopped in food processor fitted with metal blade).
2. In a 10-inch skillet, melt butter over medium heat. Add onion and sauté until lightly golden, stirring constantly, about 2 minutes. Add prosciutto and cook until softened, stirring constantly, about 30 seconds. Add spinach

and continue to cook, stirring constantly, until there is no liquid left in pan, about 2 minutes.

3. Transfer spinach mixture to a bowl and add ricotta, Parmigiano cheese, salt and pepper. Mix well with a wooden spoon. Add lightly beaten egg yolks and mix well with a fork.

4. Divide filling in half. Set aside.

TO ROLL BY HAND

1. Divide dough in half. Make sure you keep one half covered to prevent drying.

2. On a well-floured board, roll out half of dough into a thin sheet approximately 12 to 14 inches wide by 24 to 26 inches long.

3. Follow directions for filling and then prepare second batch of dough.

TO ROLL USING PASTA MACHINE

1. Divide dough into 6 even pieces. You will need 3 pieces of dough for each pasta roll.

2. Follow directions for pasta machine rolling, page 39, until you have a sheet of dough approximately 4½ inches wide and 26 inches long. Place sheet of dough on lightly floured pastry cloth or linen towel. Work 2 more pieces of dough as you did first sheet.

3. Lay the 3 sheets of pasta side by side lengthwise. Lightly brush ½ inch of side edges of center sheet with water. Place the 2 outer sheets over the moistened edges of center sheet to overlap by ½ inch.

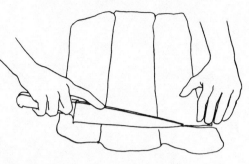

Press along seams so sheets stick together (you can also seal by rolling over seams lightly with a rolling pin). Trim top and bottom ends with a sharp knife so that you have a rectangular sheet approximately 12 inches wide by 26 inches long.

4. Follow directions for filling, then prepare second batch of dough (this must be done in two batches so that dough will still be moist when rolled with filling).

TO ASSEMBLE AND COOK

1 Tablespoon salt
½ cup freshly grated Parmigiano cheese (approximately)

Freshly grated Parmigiano cheese (for serving)

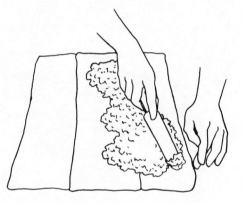

1. Cut 2 pieces of cheesecloth approximately 8 inches wide and 30 inches long. Dip in water and wring out tightly so that cheesecloth is just damp to the touch.

2. Position sheet of pasta on pastry cloth or towel with narrow end facing you. Leaving a 3-inch margin at edge nearest you and a ½-inch margin at other 3 sides, spread dough with filling using a metal spatula. Fold the 3-inch border up over filling and roll up like a jelly roll. Wrap pasta roll in damp cheesecloth and tie both ends securely with kitchen twine.

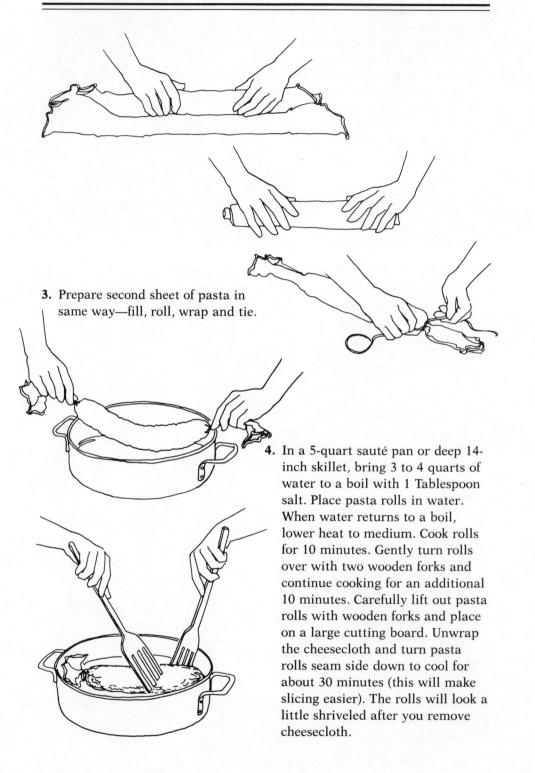

3. Prepare second sheet of pasta in same way—fill, roll, wrap and tie.

4. In a 5-quart sauté pan or deep 14-inch skillet, bring 3 to 4 quarts of water to a boil with 1 Tablespoon salt. Place pasta rolls in water. When water returns to a boil, lower heat to medium. Cook rolls for 10 minutes. Gently turn rolls over with two wooden forks and continue cooking for an additional 10 minutes. Carefully lift out pasta rolls with wooden forks and place on a large cutting board. Unwrap the cheesecloth and turn pasta rolls seam side down to cool for about 30 minutes (this will make slicing easier). The rolls will look a little shriveled after you remove cheesecloth.

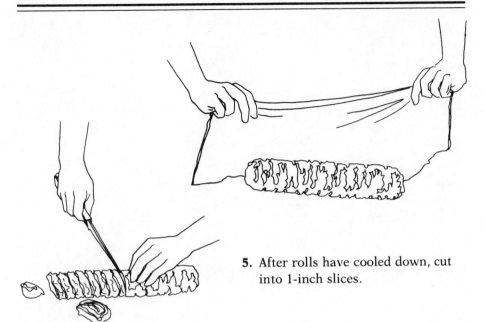

5. After rolls have cooled down, cut into 1-inch slices.

6. Spread bottom of a large ovenproof platter with about 7 Tablespoons of tomato bechamel sauce. Arrange slices in a slightly overlapping pattern and spoon about 1 Tablespoon of sauce over each slice. Sprinkle about 1 teaspoon Parmigiano cheese on top of each slice.

7. Adjust rack to upper third of oven and preheat to 350°F. Bake until cheese has melted and turned very lightly golden, about 20 minutes.
Remove from oven and let rest for about 3 minutes before serving. Serve with remaining sauce and additional freshly grated Parmigiano cheese.

Note: Pasta rolls can be made up to 2 days before serving. After the rolls are sliced, place in a single layer on a jelly roll pan lined with waxed paper. Cover with plastic wrap and refrigerate. Arrange on a platter and finish with sauce up to 2 hours before serving. Pasta rolls can also be frozen up to one month. Cover with aluminum foil over plastic wrap before freezing. Allow to defrost 2 hours before arranging on platter and finishing off with sauce. The sauce must be made the same day as serving the pasta roll.

POLENTA

BASIC RECIPE FOR POLENTA
BAKED POLENTA WITH TOMATO AND DRIED MUSHROOM SAUCE
POLENTA WITH FONTINA CHEESE

Polenta, cooked yellow cornmeal, is a hearty dish that is usually served from late fall through the cold winter months. Traditionally, polenta is made with a coarse-grained meal. It is not always available, however, so for the recipe in this book I have used the regular, enriched cornmeal found in almost any supermarket.

I can remember asking Mamma, after I was married, how many portions her basic recipe served. Her answer to me was, "Well, Anna, it depends on how hungry you are" (her recipe generously serves eight people).

My parents always teased each other as to whose method of cooking produced fewer lumps in the polenta. My father would take a fistful of cornmeal and very slowly pour it through his fingers into the simmering water, stirring continuously with a long wooden spoon. Mamma always mixed the cornmeal with cold water to produce a paste before adding it to the boiling water. After testing both methods I found that Mamma's produced fewer lumps, so her procedure will be given.

Polenta was served at least once a week in our household during the winter months. It was not only the evening meal, but there was always an ample amount left over for breakfast the next morning. Mamma would slice it into slabs about 1 inch thick, then into 3-inch strips. Each strip would be lightly dredged in about ½ cup unbleached flour and then fried in about ¼ cup unsalted butter over medium heat until lightly toasted on both sides. She would then serve it with a little maple syrup or homemade jam on top. To me, this was better than French toast. I would be just as excited about breakfast as I was about the evening's meal. So, when making polenta, make the full batch and save some for breakfast.

BASIC RECIPE FOR POLENTA

YIELDS ABOUT 6 CUPS COOKED POLENTA

2 cups enriched yellow cornmeal
2 cups cold water

6 cups water
1 Tablespoon salt

1. In a medium bowl, mix cornmeal and 2 cups cold water with a fork until you have a smooth paste.
2. In a heavy 5-quart saucepan, bring 6 cups water to a boil, then add the salt.
3. Add the cornmeal paste to the boiling water, stirring constantly with a long wooden spoon. Bring mixture to a boil, then turn heat to low. Cook the polenta, stirring frequently to keep the mixture smooth, until very thick, about 30 minutes; if some lumps form in cooking, push them against the sides of the pan with the wooden spoon to dissolve them. When polenta is cooked, the mixture will come away from the sides of the pan and should be so thick that a 6-inch wooden spoon will stand up unsupported in the middle.
4. Cooked polenta can be poured onto a buttered platter and served immediately with a tomato-based sauce (it is especially good with Tomato–Chicken Sauce, page 56).
5. Alternatively, pour cooked polenta into a well-buttered bowl (a 3-quart soufflé dish works very well), cover with plastic wrap and allow to cool to room temperature or refrigerate overnight.
6. When polenta is cooled, unmold it onto a wooden cutting board and slice. (Polenta is traditionally sliced with a long piece of linen thread. Fit the thread under the polenta and draw it through the top surface into ½-inch slices. If you are going to use this method, watch carefully as you pull up with the string to keep both sides even). If polenta is well chilled, it can also be sliced with a long, thin knife.
7. Polenta is now ready to be baked, fried or broiled.

BAKED POLENTA WITH TOMATO
AND DRIED MUSHROOM SAUCE
Polenta al Forno

Baked Polenta with Tomato and Dried Mushroom Sauce can be completely assembled the day before serving, covered with plastic wrap and refrigerated overnight. Return to room temperature and bake just before serving.

SERVES 8

Double recipe of Tomato
and Dried Mushroom
sauce, page 51
1 basic recipe for polenta,
chilled and cut into long 1-
inch slices

1 cup freshly grated
Parmigiano cheese
Freshly grated Parmigiano
cheese (for serving)

1. Adjust rack to center of oven and preheat to 375°F.
2. Lightly butter a 9 × 13-inch baking dish. Arrange a single layer of polenta slices in casserole and spread an even layer of tomato sauce on top. Sprinkle with half of the Parmigiano cheese. Place another layer of polenta on top. Spread with another even layer of sauce and the remaining cheese.
3. Bake until cheese is thoroughly melted and top forms a light crust, about 35 minutes.
4. Remove from oven and let rest for 10 minutes before serving.
5. To serve, cut into squares and lift out with a metal spatula onto individual plates. Serve with remaining sauce and additional freshly grated Parmigiano cheese.

POLENTA WITH FONTINA CHEESE
Polenta con Fontina

Broiled polenta topped with Fontina or Swiss cheese is excellent when served with Sautéed Sausage with Spinach, page 173.

SERVES 6

1 basic recipe for polenta, chilled and cut into ½-inch × 5-inch serving pieces
2 Tablespoons unsalted butter
8 ounces thinly sliced Fontina or imported Swiss cheese

1 cup freshly grated Parmigiano cheese
Freshly milled black pepper to taste (optional)

1. Adjust oven rack to 6 inches from broiler and preheat oven to broil setting. Butter a large jelly roll pan.
2. Arrange sliced polenta in a single layer in pan and broil until lightly golden on both sides.
3. Remove from oven and cover each slice with a thin layer of Fontina or Swiss cheese. Sprinkle Parmigiano on top and return to oven just until cheese is melted. Transfer to a platter and sprinkle with freshly milled black pepper. Serve immediately.

RICE

BASIC RISOTTO

RISOTTO WITH MUSHROOMS

RISOTTO WITH SCALLOPS

RICE WITH CARROTS

RICE WITH PEAS

RICE WITH ZUCCHINI

RICE WITH EGGS AND CHEESE

BAKED RICE WITH RICOTTA

RICE SALAD

STUFFED RICE BALLS

Mamma served rice so often and in so many different ways that I think there were times when she preferred it to pasta!

Rice, like pasta, is considered one of the most versatile foods in an Italian household. In many parts of Northern Italy, it takes the place of pasta and is served as a first course in the dish called risotto, which is made by a special method of preparing the rice.

For most of the recipes in this chapter, I recommend using imported Italian Arborio rice, which is available in Italian specialty and gourmet shops. It is a short-grain variety grown in the Po Valley. When properly cooked, this type of rice is very moist and tender, with grains that have a tendency to cling together more than those of the long-grain rice available in this country. It also has a nuttier flavor than the common long-grain type.

For risotto I am a purist, and insist upon using Arborio rice. For the other recipes, converted natural long-grain rice may be substituted for Arborio.

BASIC RISOTTO

There are many variations of this classic Northern Italian dish. It can be served plain, with a little freshly grated Parmigiano cheese on top of each portion. A simple risotto can become quite an elegant and substantial main course when sautéed vegetables or seafood are added. A word of warning: the broth must be added a little at a time, allowing the hot rice to absorb each addition. Simmering and constant stirring are necessary to prepare this dish properly. The rice in risotto should be al dente when served, and the consistency should be very creamy.

SERVES 4—MAIN COURSE
SERVES 6 TO 8—SIDE DISH

¼ teaspoon saffron threads
1 cup dry white wine
5 cups chicken broth
5 Tablespoons unsalted butter
¾ cup finely chopped yellow onion
2 cups Arborio rice, picked over to remove any dark grains

½ teaspoon salt
½ teaspoon freshly milled white pepper
1 cup freshly grated Parmigiano cheese
2 Tablespoons finely minced Italian parsley leaves
Freshly grated Parmigiano cheese (for serving)

1. Combine saffron and wine in a small saucepan. Place over very low heat and bring to a gentle simmer, stirring occasionally, until most of the threads dissolve in the wine, about 5 minutes. Set aside.
2. In a 4-quart saucepan, bring broth to a boil. As soon as the broth comes to a boil, turn heat to low and keep it barely simmering over low heat.
3. In a heavy 5-quart saucepan, melt butter over medium heat. Add onion and cook until soft but not brown, about 5 minutes. Add rice and stir with wooden spoon until opaque and well coated with butter, about 2 minutes. Add saffron-wine mixture to rice and cook, stirring constantly with wooden spoon over low heat until all the liquid has been absorbed, about 3 minutes (if some of the juices from saffron have coated inside of small pan, add about 2 Tablespoons of the chicken broth to pan, swirl around and pour into rice). Add 1 cup of the simmering broth to the rice and cook over low heat, stirring constantly with wooden spoon, until all the liquid has been absorbed, about 3 to 5 minutes; watch carefully so that rice does not stick to bottom of pan. Continue adding broth 1 cup at a time, stirring constantly and waiting until each addition has been absorbed before adding more. When rice has finished cooking, the risotto should have a very creamy con-

sistency. Test by tasting a few grains; it should be soft on the outside and just a little bit chewy on the inside. Total cooking time will be approximately 30 to 35 minutes. Season with salt and pepper.

4. Add Parmigiano cheese and 1 Tablespoon minced Italian parsley; mix well with wooden spoon.

5. To serve, transfer to a heated bowl, garnish with remaining parsley and serve immediately with additional freshly grated Parmigiano cheese.

RISOTTO WITH MUSHROOMS
Risotto con Funghi

You can substitute any vegetable of your choice for the mushrooms—try asparagus tips, thinly sliced zucchini or peas.

SERVES 4—MAIN COURSE
SERVES 6 TO 8—SIDE DISH

Single recipe of Basic
Risotto through step 3
(page 121)
¼ cup unsalted butter
1 pound small white
mushrooms, trimmed,
wiped and thinly sliced
¾ cup freshly grated
Parmigiano cheese

1 Tablespoon minced Italian
parsley leaves (garnish)
Freshly grated Parmigiano
cheese (for serving)

1. As soon as the risotto is finished cooking, melt butter in a 10-inch skillet over medium-high heat. Add mushrooms and sauté briefly just until they start to exude their juices, about 2 minutes. Stir mushrooms (including liquid) into risotto. Cook uncovered over low heat, stirring constantly, until mushrooms and liquid are completely incorporated into rice, about 30 seconds. Remove from heat and stir in freshly grated Parmigiano cheese.

2. To serve, transfer to a heated bowl and garnish with minced parsley; serve with additional freshly grated Parmigiano cheese.

RISOTTO WITH SCALLOPS
Risotto con Pettine

Risotto with sea or bay scallops can be an elegant main course or a first-rate starter. You can substitute shrimp for the scallops, or use a combination of both (if substituting shrimp, sauté just until they turn pink, about 2 minutes). Wash scallops or devein shrimp before making basic risotto. The seafood must be sautéed as soon as the risotto is finished, so that when you add it to the pot the consistency of the risotto will still be creamy when served.

SERVES 4—MAIN COURSE
SERVES 6—FIRST COURSE

Single recipe of Basic
Risotto through step 3
(page 121)
1½ pounds sea or bay scallops
¼ cup unsalted butter
1 cup thinly sliced scallions
½ teaspoon salt
½ teaspoon freshly milled
white pepper

1 Tablespoon grated lemon
rind
2 Tablespoons finely minced
Italian parsley leaves
Freshly grated Parmigiano
cheese (for serving)

1. Wash scallops several times in cold water to remove sand. Place in a strainer and blot dry with paper towel. If using tiny bay scallops, leave whole; if using sea scallops, cut horizontally into ½-inch slices.
2. In a large sauté pan, melt butter over medium heat. Add scallions and sauté, stirring constantly, until barely tender, about 2 minutes. Add scallops and cook, stirring constantly, for 2 minutes. Add salt, pepper and lemon rind; mix well and remove from heat.
3. Stir scallops into risotto. Cook uncovered over low heat, stirring constantly, until juices from scallops are completely absorbed into rice, about 1 to 2 minutes. Remove from heat and stir in parsley.
4. Transfer to a heated bowl and serve with freshly grated Parmigiano cheese.

RICE WITH CARROTS
Riso con Carote

This should stir up a lot of culinary excitement for an old standby!

SERVES 8

3 Tablespoons unsalted
butter
½ cup finely chopped yellow
onion
1½ cups Arborio or converted
long-grain rice, picked over
to remove any dark grains
4 cups chicken broth, heated
3 Tablespoons unsalted
butter

1½ cups finely diced carrot
1 Tablespoon minced fresh
tarragon or 1 teaspoon
crumbled dried tarragon
1 teaspoon salt
½ teaspoon freshly milled
white pepper
1 Tablespoon finely minced
Italian parsley leaves
(garnish)

1. In a heavy 5-quart saucepan, melt 3 Tablespoons butter over medium heat. Add onion and cook until soft but not brown, about 5 minutes. Add rice and stir until opaque and well coated with butter. Add heated broth, turn heat to high and bring to a boil, stirring once or twice with a wooden spoon. Cover pan, turn heat to low and cook undisturbed for about 25 minutes. At this point, the liquid should be completely absorbed into rice; if it isn't, cover pan and continue to cook for an additional minute or two.
2. While rice is cooking, melt 3 Tablespoons butter in a small saucepan over low heat. Add carrots and cook, covered, until tender, about 6 minutes. Add tarragon and mix well. Stir carrots into cooked rice and season with salt and pepper. Cover pan and let rice rest for 5 minutes before serving so that all the flavors meld together.
3. Transfer rice to a serving bowl and garnish with parsley. Serve immediately.

RICE WITH PEAS
Riso con Piselli

Not quite as creamy as Risotto, but just as flavorful and a lot easier to make!

SERVES 6

3 Tablespoons unsalted butter
½ cup finely chopped yellow onion
½ cup finely diced celery, strings removed
1 cup Arborio or converted long-grain rice, picked over to remove any dark grains

3 cups chicken broth, heated
1 package (9 ounces) tiny frozen peas, defrosted and well drained
1 teaspoon salt
½ teaspoon freshly milled white pepper
¾ cup freshly grated Parmigiano cheese

1. In a heavy 5-quart saucepan, melt butter over medium heat. Add onion and celery; cook until soft but not brown, stirring constantly with a wooden spoon, about 3 minutes. Add rice and stir constantly until opaque and well coated with butter. Add heated broth and stir to incorporate. Cover pan, turn heat to low and cook undisturbed for 20 minutes.
2. Stir peas into rice mixture. Cover pan and continue to cook over low heat for another 5 minutes. At this point, the liquid should be completely absorbed into the rice; if it isn't, cover pan and continue to cook for another minute or two. Season with salt and pepper.
3. Remove from heat, stir in Parmigiano cheese, transfer to a bowl and serve immediately.

Note: If you don't have chicken broth on hand, substitute 2 chicken bouillon cubes dissolved in 3 cups boiling water. Omit salt from recipe.

RICE WITH ZUCCHINI
Riso con Zucchini

The crunchy texture of barely-cooked zucchini with rice makes this a delicious partner for any of the veal or chicken scaloppine dishes.

SERVES 6

2 Tablespoons unsalted butter

1 cup Arborio or converted long-grain rice, picked over to remove any dark grains

3 cups chicken broth, heated

3 Tablespoons olive oil

2 cloves garlic, split in half

2 medium zucchini (1 pound), well scrubbed, trimmed and sliced into 1 × ½-inch strips

½ teaspoon salt

½ teaspoon freshly milled black pepper

½ cup freshly grated Asiago or Parmigiano cheese

1. In a heavy 5-quart saucepan, melt butter over medium heat. Add rice and stir until opaque and well coated with butter.
2. Add heated broth and stir with a wooden spoon once or twice. Cover pan, turn heat to low and cook undisturbed for 20 minutes, or until the liquid is completely absorbed and rice is tender. Test by tasting a few grains.
3. While rice is cooking, heat olive oil in a medium skillet over medium-high heat until haze forms. Sauté garlic until lightly golden, then discard with a slotted spoon. Add zucchini, turn heat down to medium and sauté, stirring constantly, until barely tender when tested with fork, about 2 minutes. Remove from heat and season with salt and pepper.
4. Mix zucchini with cooked rice. Stir in freshly grated Asiago or Parmigiano cheese. Transfer to a bowl and serve immediately.

RICE WITH EGGS AND CHEESE
Riso alla Mamma

The addition of eggs and Parmigiano cheese makes this a rich, yet light and tangy rice dish. Mamma's foolproof technique calls for the rice to be boiled in lots of water.

SERVES 8

1 Tablespoon salt
1½ cups Arborio or converted
  long-grain rice, picked over
  to remove any dark grains
3 large eggs
½ teaspoon freshly milled
  white pepper

1 cup freshly grated
  Parmigiano cheese
3 Tablespoons unsalted
  butter
¼ cup finely minced Italian
  parsley leaves

1. In a large pot, bring 6 quarts of water to a rolling boil over high heat; add 1 Tablespoon salt. Bring water back to a boil and pour in rice in a slow steady stream so that the water never stops boiling. Stir rice with a wooden spoon once or twice. Reduce heat to medium. Boil, uncovered and undisturbed, until tender, about 15 minutes. Test by tasting a few grains; it should be soft on the outside and very slightly chewy on the inside. Transfer rice to a strainer and quickly refresh under cold water.
2. In a small bowl, beat eggs and pepper with a fork. Beat in the cheese a little at a time until completely blended.
3. In a 5-quart Dutch oven, melt butter over low heat. Stir in rice and fluff with a fork. Stir in egg-cheese mixture with fork and cook, stirring gently with fork until mixture is creamy, about 2 minutes. Turn off heat, cover pot and let rice rest for 5 minutes before serving. Add parsley and mix well. Transfer to a bowl and serve immediately.

BAKED RICE WITH RICOTTA
Riso con Ricotta al Forno

One of the specialties that Mamma served quite often instead of pasta. This is a great do-ahead dish; it can be completely assembled up to 6 hours before baking, covered with plastic wrap and refrigerated. Remove from refrigerator 1 hour before baking.

SERVES 8

1½ Tablespoons unsalted butter, softened
2 Tablespoons unsalted butter
1 cup Arborio or converted long-grain rice, picked over to remove any dark grains
2½ cups chicken broth, heated
2 large eggs

3 Tablespoons freshly grated Romano cheese
2 cups whole milk ricotta cheese
¼ cup finely minced Italian parsley leaves
½ teaspoon salt
½ teaspoon freshly milled white pepper

1. Generously grease a 9 × 11-inch baking dish with 1½ Tablespoons softened butter. Set aside.
2. In a heavy 5-quart saucepan, melt 2 Tablespoons butter over medium heat. Add rice and stir until opaque and well coated with butter. Add heated broth and stir once or twice with a wooden spoon. Cover pan, turn heat to low and cook undisturbed for 12 minutes. Taste a few grains; it should be a little soft on the outside and somewhat chewy on the inside (do not worry if all the liquid is not absorbed). Set rice aside and let cool to almost room temperature.
3. While rice is cooling, beat eggs with a wire whisk. Add Romano cheese and whisk again until well combined. Beat in the ricotta cheese a little at a time until completely blended. Add parsley, salt and pepper; mix again until well combined. Add the egg-ricotta mixture to the cooled rice and mix well. Pour rice mixture into prepared casserole and smooth the top surface with a metal spatula.
4. When ready to bake, adjust rack to center of oven and preheat to 350°F.
5. Bake rice until lightly golden on top, about 40 minutes. Remove from oven and let rest for 10 minutes before serving.
6. To serve, cut into squares and lift out with a metal spatula.

RICE SALAD
Insalata di Riso

This dish always reminds me of the Italian flag, with its broad stripes of red, white and green. A lovely composition to serve during the summer months.

SERVES 8 TO 10

1 Tablespoon salt
1½ cups Arborio or converted long-grain rice, picked over to remove any dark grains
3 Tablespoons olive oil
1 cup thinly sliced scallions
3 medium zucchini (1½ pounds), well scrubbed, trimmed and coarsely grated (can be grated in food processor fitted with shredding disc)
2 jars (7 ounces each) pimientos, well drained, blotted dry and sliced into ½-inch strips

1. In a 6-quart pot, bring 4 quarts of water to a rolling boil over high heat; add 1 Tablespoon salt. Pour in rice in a slow, steady stream so that the water never stops boiling. Stir rice with a wooden spoon once or twice. Lower heat to medium and boil rice, uncovered, until tender, about 15 minutes (test by tasting a few grains). Transfer rice to a strainer and quickly refresh under cold water. Drain well and set aside.
2. In a 10-inch skillet, heat olive oil over medium heat until haze forms. Add scallions and cook, stirring constantly, until barely tender, about 1 minute. Add zucchini and cook, stirring constantly, until tender-crisp when tested with fork, about 2 minutes.
3. Transfer rice to a serving bowl. Add zucchini mixture and sliced pimientos. Toss well with two wooden forks.

DRESSING

3 Tablespoons olive oil
3 Tablespoons imported white wine vinegar
1 teaspoon salt
½ teaspoon freshly milled black pepper
3 Tablespoons minced Italian parsley leaves
2 Tablespoons minced fresh basil or 2 teaspoons crumbled dried basil
½ cup pine nuts (pignoli), toasted (optional garnish; see note)

1. Combine all the ingredients except pine nuts in a small bowl and blend thoroughly with a wire whisk. Pour dressing over salad and toss gently

with two forks. Cover and refrigerate for at least 4 hours or overnight.

2. Just before serving, add half of the pine nuts and toss well. Sprinkle the rest on top for garnish and serve.

Note: See procedure for toasting pine nuts under Basil Pesto Sauce, page 74, step 1.

STUFFED RICE BALLS
Arancini di Riso

This family favorite was created by Papa Casale. It has long been a tradition to have these orange-shaped surprise packages served on Christmas Eve. The holiday always provides the opportunity for new members of the family—nieces, grand-nieces, daughters, cousins, and even an occasional son-in-law—to learn Papa's technique and to carry on the heritage.

YIELDS 24
SERVES 8 TO 10

FILLING

2 Tablespoons olive oil
1 Tablespoon unsalted butter
½ cup finely chopped yellow onion
½ cup finely chopped carrot
8 ounces very lean ground round steak
4 ounces very lean ground pork
2 ounces soprassata sausage (casing removed), finely diced (½ cup)

1 Tablespoon tomato paste
1 Tablespoon water
½ teaspoon salt
¼ teaspoon freshly milled black pepper
1 Tablespoon finely minced fresh basil or 1 teaspoon crumbled dried basil
½ cup freshly grated Asiago or Provolone cheese
2 Tablespoons finely minced Italian parsley leaves

1. In a large skillet, heat olive oil over medium heat until haze forms, then add butter. Add onion and carrot; sauté, stirring constantly, until tender, about 3 minutes. Stir in ground steak and pork. Turn heat to low and cook, stirring constantly, until meat turns pale pink, about 3 minutes. Stir in so-

prassata and mix well. Mix tomato paste with water and stir into meat. Add salt, pepper and basil. Continue to cook filling over medium heat, stirring frequently, until thick, about 10 minutes. Remove from heat and add cheese and parsley; mix well. Transfer to a platter and cool to room temperature. (The filling can be made one day ahead, covered and refrigerated until needed.)

TO PREPARE

2 teaspoons salt
1 pound Carolina long-grain rice, picked over to remove any dark grains

2 extra large eggs
½ cup freshly grated Romano cheese

1. In a heavy 7-quart pot, bring 5 cups water to a boil. Add 2 teaspoons salt and stir in rice. Cover pan, turn heat to low and cook undisturbed until all the liquid is absorbed, about 20 minutes.
2. Transfer rice to a large, shallow bowl and cool to almost room temperature, stirring frequently with a large spoon to hasten cooling.
3. In a small bowl, beat eggs and Romano cheese with a fork. Add to cooled rice and mix thoroughly with fork.

TO ASSEMBLE AND FRY

5 extra large eggs
1 teaspoon salt
3½ cups fine dry breadcrumbs

1½ quarts vegetable oil, preferably corn
Several curly parsley sprigs (garnish)

1. In a shallow bowl, beat eggs and salt. Place breadcrumbs in another shallow bowl.

2. Have a bowl of warm water ready for wetting hands. The rice balls will be easier to shape if you dip your hands in water each time you measure out the rice mixture.

3. Scoop out ¼ cup of rice and place it in the cupped palm of your hand. Using the three middle

fingers of your other hand, shape
rice into a well resembling a bird's
nest. With thumb, make a light
indentation in the center of nest.
Place 1 heaping Tablespoon of
filling in the indentation. Bring
rice from the outer rim of nest up
and over filling to form a ball. In
forming ball, make sure the filling
is completely and evenly covered
with rice so it won't crack open in
frying.

4. Roll balls in breadcrumbs, then in
   beaten eggs. Roll again in
   breadcrumbs. Arrange in a single
   layer on a large platter lined with
   waxed paper. Refrigerate for at
   least 1 hour to set the coating.

5. In a 5½-quart fryer, heat the oil to
   350°F. Fry rice balls 4 at a time
   until golden on all sides. Transfer
   to trays lined with paper towels.

6. To serve, pile in three layers
   (pyramid fashion) on a large
   platter. Garnish with parsley
   sprigs.

Note: Arancini can be made up to 2 days ahead of time, arranged on cookie sheets in single layers, covered with plastic wrap and refrigerated. Return to room temperature before reheating. Reheat on center rack of preheated 350°F oven for 30 minutes. Arancini can also be frozen up to 3 months. Wrap cookie sheets with plastic wrap and then a layer of aluminum foil before freezing. Allow 3 hours to defrost completely before reheating in oven.

MEATS

BEEF

VEAL

PORK

LAMB

Trips to the butcher shop with my father were as informative and educational as an afternoon at a museum. I recall the fascination with which I looked through the glass cases at all the different cuts of meat. Every time we went there would be new lessons to learn.

When he selected beef, he would instruct, "See, Anna, all the marbling of fat through the steak? That means it is tender. The fat will make it juicer. But not a lot of fat, just a light marbling."

Lessons at the butcher shop were not always learned directly. I often picked up pointers through observation rather than instruction; for instance:

- □ *when my father chose a pork roast, he would always specify "center cut."*
- □ *when he ordered a roast or rack of lamb, it was only young spring lamb.*
- □ *if Italian pot roast was on the menu, my father would peruse both the chuck and rump roasts. Whichever one "looked best," or had better marbling, was the one he purchased.*

Whenever veal was being selected, instruction once again became formal. A stool would be pulled up to the counter for me to observe and learn, as first the color test was applied. "Look, Anna, for the meat to be a very pale pink color. This shows that the calf was on a milk-based diet. The fat, too, has a special color. It must be creamy white." From my vantage point, I would watch the cutting of veal scallops or boned veal cutlets with awe. I held my breath as the butcher placed his hand on the tender inner leg and practically shaved away the thin scallops. "Will he remove a layer of his palm this time?" I would wonder.

It is not my intention to teach you how to butcher meat, but rather, I want to emphasize the importance of meeting a good butcher. Don't be afraid to shop around until you find a butcher you like. Once you have found him, treat him well—he could turn out to be a very good friend.

Beef

BREADED STEAK

FILET MIGNON WITH WINE AND CAPER SAUCE

BRAISED BEEF WITH WINE AND MUSHROOM SAUCE

STUFFED FLANK STEAK

PREPARING ROUND STEAK FOR STUFFING

STUFFED BEEF ROLLS

BEEF ROLLS WITH TOMATO SAUCE

BREADED STEAKS
Bistecca alla Papa

The breadcrumb coating makes the steaks crusty on the outside and helps hold in the juices during pan-frying.

SERVES 6

6 individual boneless rib-eye or top loin steaks, 6 ounces each and ½ inch thick, well trimmed
1 large clove garlic, split in half
3 Tablespoons (approx.) olive oil
1½ cups dry breadcrumbs
2 teaspoons finely minced Italian parsley leaves

1 Tablespoon finely minced fresh oregano or 1 teaspoon crumbled dried oregano
1 teaspoon salt
½ teaspoon freshly milled black pepper
2 Tablespoons olive oil
2 Tablespoons unsalted butter

1. Rub steaks on both sides with garlic; discard garlic.
2. Place 3 Tablespoons olive oil in a shallow bowl. In another shallow bowl, combine breadcrumbs, parsley, oregano, salt and pepper
3. Brush both sides of steaks with olive oil. Firmly press steaks into breadcrumb mixture on both sides and shake off excess. Arrange steaks on a platter in a single layer and chill for at least 1 hour (chilling will prevent breadcrumb coating from coming off during frying).
4. Use two skillets large enough to hold all the steaks in a single layer (do not crowd or steaks will not cook properly). Heat 1 Tablespoon olive oil and 1 Tablespoon butter in each skillet over medium-high heat. Cook steaks just until the blood starts to surface to the top of the breadcrumb mixture, about 2 minutes. Turn and cook for an additional 2 minutes for medium-rare. For medium steaks, cook 3 minutes on each side.
5. Transfer to a platter and serve immediately.

FILET MIGNON WITH WINE AND CAPER SAUCE
Bistecca all'Anna

This presentation with a zesty wine and caper sauce is top-drawer for those special guests.

SERVES 6

2½ pounds filet mignon, cut into 6 slices, each approximately 1 inch thick
1 large clove garlic, split in half
1 Tablespoon (approximately) olive oil
2 Tablespoons olive oil or just enough to coat the pan used for cooking
Salt and freshly milled black pepper to taste

¼ cup unsalted butter
5 Tablespoons finely minced shallots
3 Tablespoons capers, rinsed and well drained
½ cup Barolo or any good dry red wine
1 teaspoon arrowroot
2 teaspoons cold water
⅓ cup minced Italian parsley leaves (garnish)

1. Rub each filet mignon on both sides with split garlic; discard garlic. Brush both sides of steaks with olive oil (the oil tenderizes the meat). Arrange steaks in a single layer on a platter, cover with plastic wrap and refrigerate for at least 1 hour.

2. Choose a large skillet or sauté pan that can hold all the steaks without crowding. Pour enough oil into pan to make a thin film on the bottom. Heat over medium-high heat until haze forms. Arrange steaks in pan. Raise heat to high and sear the steaks until the bottoms are moderately brown, about 2 minutes. Turn steaks with a pair of tongs; if steaks are sticking to the pan, loosen with a metal spatula. Lower heat to medium. About 1 minute after turning, begin testing for doneness by pressing center of steak with finger; the softer the meat, the rarer it is. Approximate cooking time after turning is 2 to 3 minutes for medium-rare and 5 to 6 minutes for well-done. Salt and pepper steaks and transfer to a heated platter.

3. Discard oil from pan. Add butter, stirring and scraping any fragments left in the bottom of pan with a wooden spoon. Add shallots and sauté over medium heat, stirring constantly, until lightly golden, about 1 minute. Stir in capers and wine; cook sauce for another minute. Dissolve arrowroot in water and stir into sauce; cook until slightly thickened, about 20 seconds. Add juices that have accumulated on steak platter. Arrange steaks on a large platter. Spoon sauce over meat and garnish with parsley. Serve immediately.

BRAISED BEEF WITH WINE
AND MUSHROOM SAUCE
Manzo con Salsa di Vino
e Funghi

The wine in which the beef is braised is important to the full-bodied flavor of this dish. My choice is a dry, light-bodied red wine such as Valpolicella. Buy several bottles and use the rest for serving with the meal.

SERVES 6

1 4-pound boneless chuck
 roast, trimmed and tied
 with kitchen twine in 2 or 3
 places
¼ cup vegetable oil,
 preferably corn
1 cup coarsely chopped
 yellow onion
1 cup coarsely chopped
 carrot
½ cup coarsely chopped
 celery, strings removed

2 cups dry red wine
1 cup beef broth
2 bay leaves
1 teaspoon minced fresh
 thyme or ½ teaspoon
 crumbled dried thyme
1 teaspoon salt
1 teaspoon freshly milled
 black pepper

1. Adjust rack to center of oven and preheat to 350°F.
2. In a heavy 5-quart Dutch oven, heat oil over medium-high heat until haze forms. Brown meat on all sides and transfer to a platter. Discard most of the pan drippings, leaving about 2 Tablespoons.
3. Add onion, carrot and celery. Turn heat to medium and cook, stirring constantly, until soft but not brown, about 5 minutes. Add wine and turn heat to high, scraping up any browned fragments that cling to the bottom of pan. Remove from heat and place roast in pan. Add broth, bay leaves, thyme, salt and pepper. Place over high heat and bring to a boil.
4. Cover pan and place in oven. Braise the beef, turning it 2 or 3 times in cooking liquid, until very tender when pierced with the tip of a knife, about 1 hour and 15 minutes. Transfer meat to platter and cover with foil.
5. Using a metal spoon, remove any surface fat from sauce. Remove bay leaves and transfer sauce to food processor fitted with metal blade. Run machine nonstop until you have a smooth puree. (If you do not have a food processor, strain sauce through a food mill.) Set aside.

MUSHROOM SAUCE

3 Tablespoons unsalted butter	2 teaspoons arrowroot
8 ounces medium mushrooms, trimmed, wiped and thinly sliced	3 Tablespoons dry red wine

1. In a 2-quart saucepan, melt butter over low heat. Add mushrooms, turn heat to medium-high and sauté, stirring constantly, just until mushrooms start to exude their liquid, about 1 minute. Add pureed sauce to pan and continue to cook, stirring constantly, for an additional minute.
2. Dissolve arrowroot in wine and add to sauce. Turn heat to low and cook, stirring constantly, until slightly thickened, about 5 minutes. Taste sauce and season with additional salt and pepper if needed.
3. Cut the meat into ½-inch slices and arrange, slightly overlapping, down the middle of a platter. Spoon a little of the hot sauce over the meat. Serve the remaining sauce separately.

STUFFED FLANK STEAK
Bistecca Imbottita

A broad spectrum of color, flavor and texture, this dish is also excellent served cold without the sauce. If serving cold, save the sauce and mix it with 8 ounces of cooked pasta for another meal.

SERVES 8 TO 10

1 flank steak (about 2 pounds), well trimmed

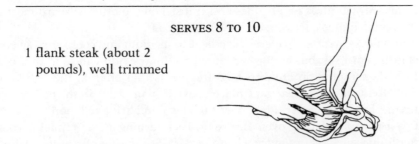

With a small, sharp paring knife, cut a pocket into flank steak lengthwise, leaving a 1-inch border of solid meat on 3 sides. If by accident you should cut through the top of the meat, slice a thin piece off the narrow end and use it as a patch to plug up the hole where you goofed. The stuffing will hold the patch in place.

STUFFING

¼ cup unsalted butter
½ cup finely chopped yellow
   onion
½ cup finely chopped carrot
1½ cups fresh breadcrumbs
8 ounces lean ground pork
8 ounces ground veal
4 ounces spinach, washed,
   dried, stemmed and
   coarsely chopped (1 cup
   well packed)
6 ounces capocolla or
   imported ham, finely diced

1 cup freshly grated
   Fontinella or imported
   Swiss cheese
1 teaspoon salt
½ teaspoon freshly milled
   black pepper
2 Tablespoons minced fresh
   basil or 2 teaspoons
   crumbled dried basil
2 large eggs, lightly beaten

1. In a medium skillet, melt butter over medium heat and sauté onion and carrot together until barely tender, about 2 minutes. Stir in breadcrumbs and remove from heat. Transfer to a large bowl. Add remaining ingredients except eggs and mix well with a wooden spoon. Add beaten eggs and mix well with a fork until completely incorporated.

2. Fill pocket of steak with stuffing, using a wooden spoon to press stuffing into all the corners.

3. Bring the lower lip of flank steak against the stuffing. Then bring the upper lip down on top to form a loaf. Tie crosswise at 1-inch intervals and twice around lengthwise. Make sure both ends are tied securely.

TO COOK

3 Tablespoons Wondra flour
5 Tablespoons olive oil
½ cup finely chopped yellow
  onion
½ cup finely chopped carrot
2 cups canned Italian plum
  tomatoes, coarsely
  chopped, juice included
  (can be chopped in food
  processor fitted with metal
  blade)

1½ cups beef broth
1 cup dry red wine
3 bay leaves
1 teaspoon salt
½ teaspoon freshly milled
  black pepper
1 bunch curly parsley sprigs
  (garnish)

1. Adjust rack to center of oven and preheat to 350°F.
2. Dredge stuffed meat in flour and shake off excess (dredge just before browning or flour coating will get gummy).
3. In a large Dutch oven, heat olive oil over medium-high heat until haze forms. Brown the steak on all sides. Transfer steak to a platter and pour off most of the pan drippings, leaving about 2 Tablespoons. Add onion and carrot to pan and sauté over medium heat until barely tender, about 3 minutes, scraping up any browned fragments left in bottom of pan with a wooden spoon. Stir in remaining ingredients; bring to a boil over high heat. Turn heat down to medium and cook sauce uncovered, stirring frequently, for 5 minutes.
4. Return meat to pan, spoon some of the sauce on top and bake, covered, for 1 hour and 15 minutes, basting every 20 minutes with sauce.
5. Transfer steak to platter, cover with foil and let rest for 30 minutes before slicing.
6. Remove bay leaves, transfer sauce to small saucepan and keep warm over very low heat.
7. Remove twine from steak. Cut meat into ½-inch slices at a 20° angle (slicing at this angle and thickness, you will be cutting against the grain and meat will be tender).
8. To serve, arrange slices on a large platter in a slightly overlapping pattern. Garnish platter with parsley sprigs. Serve sauce separately.

To Prepare Round Steak for Stuffing

Try to select or ask the butcher for boneless round steak cut from the top round. This portion of the rump is more tender than steaks cut from the bottom round.

Trim most of the fat from the edges of meat. Cut each steak in half horizontally. Place slices between sheets of waxed paper and pound each slice with a flat mallet; each slice should be slightly less than ¼ inch thick when finished. (I always have to work on the steaks after purchasing, because they are never pounded thin enough for me even from an excellent butcher.)

Make sure you pound the edges well, so that when you go to roll and tuck the ends in, they will stay in place and none of the filling will come out in cooking. Arrange meat slices on a work surface with ends facing you. In this way you will be rolling with the grain, and cooked beef rolls will be easier to slice.

STUFFED BEEF ROLLS
Rollatini di Manzo

Mincing most of the ingredients in a food processor fitted with the metal blade makes this beef dish a breeze to prepare. For a beautiful presentation, arrange beef rolls in the center of a large platter and serve with border of Rice with Carrots, page 124.

SERVES 8

4 large slices top round steak,
    ¼ inch thick (about 2
    pounds)

Follow procedure for preparing round steak. Line pounded slices of round steak on work surface with ends of meat facing you.

STUFFING

2 Tablespoons unsalted
butter
½ cup finely chopped yellow
onion
½ cup fresh breadcrumbs
½ cup freshly grated
Parmigiano cheese
8 ounces soprassata dried
sausage, casing removed
(can be minced in
processor; cut into 1-inch
cubes before placing in
work bowl)

3 extra large eggs, hard
cooked and minced
½ cup raisins, plumped in hot
water, well drained and
finely minced
½ teaspoon salt
½ teaspoon freshly milled
black pepper

1. In a medium skillet, melt butter over low heat. Add onion and cook, stir-ring constantly, until soft but not brown, about 5 minutes. Remove from heat, add remaining ingredients and mix well with a fork. In same skillet, divide filling into 8 portions.
2. Spread filling over beef slices, leaving a ¼-inch border of meat on all 4 sides. Starting from the end of the steak, carefully roll up like a jelly roll and tuck ends in. Tie each roll with kitchen twine at 1-inch intervals; tie lengthwise once. Do not tie too tightly or the twine will cut into the meat during cooking.

TO COOK

½ cup Wondra flour
1 teaspoon salt
½ teaspoon freshly milled
black pepper
3 Tablespoons olive oil
2 Tablespoons unsalted
butter

½ cup dry red wine
1½ cups beef broth
3 bay leaves
1½ teaspoons arrowroot
¼ cup cold water
1 bunch curly parsley
(garnish)

1. Adjust rack to center of oven and preheat to 350°F.
2. In a shallow bowl, combine flour, salt and pepper. Dredge rolls in flour mixture and shake off excess (dredge just before browning or beef rolls will become gummy).
3. In a large ovenproof sauté pan, heat olive oil over medium heat until haze forms, then add butter. Lightly brown rolls on all sides in two batches. Transfer rolls to a platter. Pour off almost all of the pan drippings, leaving just a thin film on the bottom (about 1 Tablespoon). Deglaze pan with red

wine, scraping up any browned fragments that cling to bottom of pan. Add beef broth, turn heat to high and cook sauce uncovered for 2 minutes. Add bay leaves and remove from heat.

4. Arrange rolls in a single layer in pan and spoon some of the sauce on top of each. Bake covered in preheated oven, turning rolls and basting frequently, until meat is tender when pierced with the tip of a knife, about 40 minutes. Transfer rolls to a platter and cover with foil.

5. Using a metal spoon, skim off any surface fat from sauce. Remove bay leaves and strain sauce through a strainer set over a 1½-quart saucepan.

6. Dissolve arrowroot in water and add to sauce. Cook over medium heat, stirring constantly, until slightly thickened, about 5 minutes.

7. Clip and discard twine. Arrange rolls on platter and garnish with a border of curly parsley sprigs. Spoon a little sauce over rolls. Serve the remaining sauce separately.

BEEF ROLLS WITH TOMATO SAUCE
Braciole con Salsa di Pomodoro

The braciole can be completely cooked up to 3 hours before serving. Just keep the beef rolls in the tomato sauce and baste frequently so that the meat does not dry out. Reheat over low heat and finish off sauce just before serving.

SERVES 8 TO 10

4 large slices top round steak,
¼ inch thick (about 2¼
pounds)

Follow procedure for preparing round steak, page 145. Line pounded slices of round steak on work surface with ends of meat facing you.

STUFFING

1 cup fresh breadcrumbs
3 Tablespoons freshly grated
Romano cheese
2 Tablespoons finely minced
Italian parsley leaves
½ teaspoon salt
½ teaspoon freshly milled
black pepper
1 large egg

2 large egg yolks
8 ounces ground veal
4 ounces thinly sliced
soprassata or Genoa
salami, cut into 2 × ½-inch
strips
4 ounces Asiago or Provolone
cheese, cut into 1-inch × ¼-
inch strips

1. In a medium bowl, combine breadcrumbs, Romano cheese, parsley, salt and pepper. In another bowl, place whole egg and yolks; beat lightly with a fork. Add to breadcrumb mixture and mix well with fork. Add ground veal and mix well with your hands. Divide stuffing into 8 portions.

2. With a metal spatula, spread stuffing over slices of round steak, leaving a ¼-inch border of meat on all 4 sides. Arrange strips of salami and cheese horizontally over stuffing; press them lightly into place with your fingers. Starting from ends of steak, carefully roll up like a jelly roll and tuck ends in. Tie each roll with kitchen twine at 1-inch intervals; tie lengthwise once. Do not tie too tightly or the twine will cut into the meat during cooking.

TO COOK

½ cup Wondra flour
1 teaspoon salt
½ teaspoon freshly milled
black pepper
½ cup olive oil
½ cup finely chopped yellow
onion
1 Tablespoon finely minced
garlic
1 cup dry red wine

1 can (35 ounces) Italian
plum tomatoes, coarsely
chopped, including juice
(can be chopped in food
processor fitted with metal
blade)
1 Tablespoon finely minced
fresh basil or 1 teaspoon
crumbled dried basil
1 bunch curly parsley sprigs
(garnish)

1. Adjust rack to center of oven and preheat to 350°F.

2. In a shallow bowl, combine flour, salt and pepper. Dredge beef rolls in flour mixture and shake off excess (dredge just before browning or beef rolls will become gummy).

3. In a large ovenproof sauté pan, heat olive oil over medium heat until haze forms. Lightly brown rolls on all sides in two batches. Transfer rolls to a platter and pour off most of the pan drippings, leaving about 2 Table-

spoons. Add onion and sauté until lightly golden, stirring constantly, about 5 minutes. Add garlic and continue to cook, stirring constantly, until soft but not brown, about 1 minute. Add wine, turn heat to high and bring to a boil, scraping up any browned fragments that cling to bottom of pan, about 2 minutes. Add tomatoes and basil; turn heat down to medium and cook sauce, stirring constantly, for 5 minutes. Remove from heat.

4. Arrange rolls in a single layer in pan and spoon some of the sauce on top of each. Bake covered in preheated oven, basting frequently with sauce, until meat is very tender when pierced with the tip of a knife, about 45 minutes. Transfer rolls to a platter and cover with foil.

5. Using a metal spoon, skim off any surface fat from pan. Transfer sauce to food processor fitted with metal blade and run machine nonstop until smooth (if you do not have a food processor, strain through a food mill). Transfer sauce to a 2-quart saucepan and cook over medium heat, stirring constantly, until slightly reduced, about 10 minutes.

6. Snip the twine from beef rolls and cut rolls at a 20° angle into 1-inch slices. Arrange slices in a slightly overlapping pattern on a large platter. Surround with parsley sprigs. Spoon a little sauce over the meat and serve the remaining sauce separately.

Veal

VEAL SCALLOPS WITH CARROTS AND DRIED SAUSAGE

VEAL SCALLOPS WITH MUSHROOMS AND MARSALA

VEAL SCALLOPS WITH PROSCIUTTO AND PEAS

VEAL WITH TOMATO—LEMON SAUCE

VEAL BIRDS

BAKED VEAL CHOPS WITH POTATOES

STUFFED VEAL CHOPS

ROAST VEAL AMADEO

VEAL SHANKS, MILANESE STYLE

VEAL STEW

VEAL SCALLOPS WITH CARROTS
AND DRIED SAUSAGE
Scaloppine alla Siciliano

This is a Sicilian-style scaloppine that can be made up to 2 hours before serving. Spoon most of the vegetable-sausage mixture on top of veal to keep it moist, and cover. When ready to serve, reheat uncovered over low heat. If it seems a little dry when reheating, just add a bit more vermouth.

SERVES 8

1½ pounds veal scallops, sliced ¼ inch thick
½ cup Wondra flour
1 teaspoon salt
½ teaspoon freshly milled black pepper
¼ cup olive oil
¼ cup unsalted butter
2 cups scallions sliced into ½-inch lengths
2 cups carrots peeled and cut into ¼-inch cubes

4 ounces soprassata sausage (casing removed), finely diced
2 Tablespoons minced fresh basil or 2 teaspoons crumbled dried basil
½ cup dry vermouth
2 Tablespoons minced Italian parsley leaves (garnish)

1. Cut each veal scallop horizontally into 3-inch widths.
2. In a shallow bowl, combine flour, salt and pepper. Dredge each piece of veal in flour mixture and shake off excess (dredge just before sautéing or the flour coating will become gummy).
3. In a large sauté pan, heat olive oil over medium-high heat until haze forms, then add butter. Sauté veal in two batches on both sides until lightly golden. Remove veal and set aside.
4. Turn heat down to medium-low and add scallions and carrots; cook until tender-crisp, scraping up any browned fragments in bottom of pan with a wooden spoon, about 5 minutes. Add diced soprassata and sauté until softened, stirring constantly, about 1 minute. Add basil and mix well.
5. Return veal to pan and mix with scallion-carrot mixture. Pour in dry vermouth, turn heat to high and cook uncovered, stirring constantly, for another 2 minutes. Taste and season with additional salt and pepper if needed.
6. To serve, arrange veal on a large platter; spoon vegetable-sausage mixture on top. Garnish with minced parsley.

Note: Instead of veal, you can use chicken suprêmes (see page 183) made from 2 large whole chicken breasts (2½ pounds total weight before boning).

VEAL SCALLOPS WITH MUSHROOMS AND MARSALA
Scaloppine con Funghi e Marsala

For authentic flavor, you must use dry Marsala in this dish.

SERVES 6 TO 8

1½ pounds veal scallops, sliced ¼ inch thick
½ cup Wondra flour
1 teaspoon salt
½ teaspoon freshly milled black pepper
¼ cup olive oil
¼ cup unsalted butter
1 cup scallions sliced into ½-inch lengths
4 ounces thinly sliced capocolla or imported ham, sliced into 2 × ½-inch strips
1 pound medium mushrooms, trimmed, wiped and thinly sliced
½ cup dry Marsala
2 Tablespoons minced Italian parsley leaves (garnish)

1. Cut each veal scallop horizontally into 2-inch widths.
2. In a shallow bowl, combine flour, salt and pepper. Dredge each piece of veal in flour mixture and shake off excess (dredge just before sautéing or the flour coating will become gummy).
3. In a large sauté pan, heat olive oil over medium-high heat until haze forms, then add butter. Sauté veal in two batches until lightly golden on both sides. Remove veal and set aside.
4. Turn heat down to medium, add scallions and cook until tender-crisp, scraping up any browned fragments left in bottom of pan with a wooden spoon. Add capocolla and sauté until softened, stirring constantly, about 1 minute. Stir in mushrooms and sauté, stirring constantly, just until they begin to exude their juices, about 1 minute.
5. Return veal to pan and spoon most of the mushroom mixture on top. Pour in Marsala, turn heat to high and cook uncovered, stirring constantly, until wine is slightly reduced, about 2 minutes.
6. To serve, arrange veal on a large platter; spoon mushroom-wine sauce on top. Garnish with minced parsley and serve immediately.

Note: Instead of veal, you can use chicken suprêmes (see page 183) made from 2 large whole chicken breasts (2½ pounds total weight before boning).

VEAL SCALLOPS WITH PROSCIUTTO AND PEAS
Scaloppine di Vitello alla Toscana

This Tuscan specialty is fast and simple to prepare. The tiny peas and prosciutto add color and delicate flavor.

SERVES 8

1½ pounds veal scallops, sliced ¼ inch thick
½ cup Wondra flour
1 teaspoon salt
½ teaspoon freshly milled black pepper
¼ cup olive oil
¼ cup unsalted butter
1½ cups thinly sliced scallions
4 ounces thinly sliced prosciutto, cut into thin 2½ × ½-inch strips

1 package (10 ounces) tiny frozen peas, defrosted and well drained
4 canned Italian plum tomatoes, drained, halved, seeded and coarsely chopped
½ cup dry vermouth

1. Cut each veal scallop horizontally into 2-inch widths.
2. In a shallow bowl, combine flour, salt and pepper. Dredge each piece of veal in flour mixture and shake off excess (dredge just before sautéing or the flour coating will become gummy).
3. In a large sauté pan, heat olive oil over medium-high heat until haze forms, then add butter. Sauté veal in two batches on both sides until lightly golden. Remove veal and set aside. Turn heat down to medium, add scallions and cook until tender-crisp, scraping up any browned fragments in bottom of pan with a wooden spoon, about 2 minutes. Add prosciutto and sauté until softened but not brown, stirring constantly, about 1 minute. Stir in peas and tomatoes; cook for another minute just to incorporate. Return veal to pan and spoon most of the sauce on top. Pour in vermouth, turn heat to high and cook uncovered, stirring once or twice, until peas are tender (test by tasting), about 2 minutes.
4. To serve, arrange veal on a large platter; spoon sauce and peas on top. Serve immediately.

Note: Instead of veal, you can use chicken suprêmes (see page 183) made from 2 large whole chicken breasts (2½ pounds total weight before boning).

VEAL WITH TOMATO–LEMON SAUCE
Cotoletti alla Mamma

Mamma was always praised by family and guests when she made this dish. The slight hint of lemon blended with the tomato sauce brings out a distinctive savory taste.

SERVES 6 TO 8

½ cup Wondra flour
3 large eggs
½ teaspoon salt
¼ teaspoon freshly milled black pepper
1½ cups fine dry breadcrumbs

2 Tablespoons minced Italian parsley leaves
½ cup freshly grated Romano cheese
1½ pounds thinly sliced veal cutlet (12 slices)

Place flour in a shallow bowl. In another shallow bowl, beat eggs with salt and pepper. In third shallow bowl, combine breadcrumbs, parsley and Romano cheese. Dredge veal in flour, dip in beaten eggs and then coat with breadcrumb mixture. Refrigerate cutlets in a single layer on a platter lined with waxed paper for at least 1 hour (chilling prevents coating from coming off during frying). While veal is chilling, prepare tomato sauce.

TOMATO SAUCE

2 Tablespoons olive oil
2 Tablespoons unsalted butter
1 cup finely chopped yellow onion
½ cup finely chopped carrot
1 can (35 ounces) Italian plum tomatoes, strained through a food mill, juice included
1 Tablespoon minced fresh sage or 1 teaspoon crumbled dried sage

1 teaspoon salt
½ teaspoon freshly milled black pepper
½ teaspoon sugar
1 Tablespoon finely grated lemon rind
2 Tablespoons minced Italian parsley leaves

In a large sauté pan, heat olive oil over medium heat until haze forms, then add butter. Turn heat to low, add onion and carrot and sauté, stirring constantly, until soft but not brown, about 5 minutes. Stir in tomatoes, sage, salt, pepper and sugar and bring to a boil. Lower heat to medium and cook sauce uncovered, stirring frequently, until slightly thickened, about 20 minutes. Remove pan from heat and add lemon rind and parsley.

TO ASSEMBLE AND COOK

1½ cups vegetable oil,   1 bunch curly parsley sprigs
     preferably corn   (garnish)

1. In a large skillet, heat vegetable oil over medium heat until haze forms. Fry cutlets on both sides until golden. Transfer cutlets to a platter lined with paper towel.
2. Adjust rack to center of oven and preheat to 350°F.
3. Coat the bottom of a large jelly roll pan with a thin layer of sauce. Place veal cutlets in a single layer in prepared pan. Top each cutlet with 2 heaping Tablespoons of sauce, spreading evenly with a spatula over entire cutlet. Bake for 25 minutes.
4. Transfer to a large platter and garnish with a border of curly parsley sprigs. Serve immediately.

Note: Instead of veal, you can use chicken suprêmes (see page 183) made from 2 large whole chicken breasts (2½ pounds total weight before boning).

VEAL BIRDS
Spiedini alla Papa

These little veal birds are alive with the flavor of lemon. Another one of Papa Casale's creations.

SERVES 6

1½ pounds veal cutlet, thinly sliced

4 ounces very lean bacon, thinly sliced

5 Tablespoons unsalted butter

1 cup finely chopped yellow onion

2 Tablespoons finely minced Italian parsley leaves

1 Tablespoon grated lemon rind

½ teaspoon salt

½ teaspoon freshly milled black pepper

1 cup fresh breadcrumbs, well packed

1 extra large egg, lightly beaten

¼ cup olive oil

2 ounces Asiago or Provolone cheese, sliced into julienne strips 1½ inches long × ¼ inch wide

10 bay leaves, broken into pieces

½ cup fresh lemon juice

1 bunch curly parsley sprigs (garnish)

1. Place each veal cutlet between pieces of waxed paper and lightly pound to about ⅛ inch thickness. Slice each into pieces about 4 inches long. Place cutlets on work surface. Slice bacon into 3-inch strips. Place one strip in center of each cutlet.

2. Adjust rack to center of oven and preheat to 375°F.

3. In a 10-inch skillet, melt butter over low heat. Sauté onion, stirring frequently, until soft, about 5 minutes. Add parsley, lemon rind, salt and pepper. Add breadcrumbs, turn heat up to medium and cook, stirring constantly, until crumbs are lightly toasted. Remove from heat and let mixture cool slightly. Add lightly beaten egg and mix well.

4. Using a metal spatula, spread about 2 heaping Tablespoons of filling over each cutlet. Place one strip of cheese horizontally across end facing you. Starting at this end, roll up veal and secure with 2 toothpicks.

5. Brush the bottom of a large baking pan with 2 Tablespoons olive oil. Arrange veal rolls in a single layer in pan, seam side down. Insert pieces of bay leaf between veal rolls. Drizzle remaining olive oil on top and pour lemon juice over veal. Bake uncovered, basting frequently with pan juices, until veal is a light golden color on top, about 35 minutes. Transfer veal birds to a cutting board and remove toothpicks.

6. Using a pair of kitchen tongs, remove all the pieces of bay leaf and discard.
7. To serve, arrange veal birds on a large platter and garnish with a border of curly parsley. Pour some of the pan juices over veal and serve immediately.

BAKED VEAL CHOPS WITH POTATOES
Vitello e Patate Pizzaiola

A great one-dish meal for those busy days when you don't feel like fussing in the kitchen. Split chicken breasts (with skin left on) or well-trimmed pork chops are just as succulent.

SERVES 6

¼ cup olive oil
6 loin or rib veal chops, 1 inch thick (about 2½ pounds)
4 medium Idaho or Russet potatoes (about 1¾ pounds), peeled, halved lengthwise and cut into 1-inch wedges
1 large yellow onion (10 ounces), halved and thinly sliced
2 cups canned Italian plum tomatoes, well drained and coarsely chopped

2 Tablespoons finely minced fresh oregano or 2 teaspoons crumbled dried oregano
1 teaspoon salt
½ teaspoon freshly milled black pepper
2 Tablespoons minced Italian parsley leaves (garnish)

1. Adjust rack to center of oven and preheat to 350°F.
2. Brush the bottom of a large baking pan with 2 Tablespoons olive oil. Arrange veal chops in pan in a single layer. Arrange potatoes between and around chops. Place a single layer of onion slices over chops and potatoes. Spoon tomatoes over onions. Sprinkle oregano on top; season with salt and pepper. Drizzle remaining olive oil over.
3. Cover pan with foil and bake for 30 minutes. Remove foil and baste with pan juices. Return to oven and continue cooking uncovered, basting frequently with pan juices, until veal is very tender and potatoes are done

when tested with a fork, about 25 minutes; total cooking time will be about 55 to 65 minutes.

4. To serve, transfer veal and potatoes to a platter and spoon tomatoes and onions on top. Pour some of the pan juices over and garnish with parsley. Serve immediately.

STUFFED VEAL CHOPS
Coste di Vitello all'Anna

An enchanting and novel taste awaits anyone who makes this family favorite.

SERVES 6

6 large loin or rib veal chops
(1¼ inches thick), trimmed
(about 3 pounds)

To make pockets for stuffing, cut a slit down the center and full length of each chop right to the bone (or have this done by the butcher). Place chops on a flat surface and open up the pockets. Set aside.

STUFFING

3 Tablespoons unsalted
butter
1 cup finely chopped yellow
onion
4 ounces prosciutto, finely
chopped
3 Tablespoons minced Italian
parsley leaves

2 Tablespoons grated orange
rind
1 teaspoon salt
½ teaspoon freshly milled
black pepper
1 cup fresh breadcrumbs
¼ cup freshly grated
Parmigiano cheese

1. In a large skillet, melt butter over medium heat. Sauté onion, stirring constantly, until soft but not brown, about 3 minutes. Add prosciutto and sauté, stirring constantly, until soft, about 1 minute. Stir in parsley, orange rind, salt and pepper; mix well. Remove from heat and add breadcrumbs and cheese; mix again. Divide stuffing into 6 portions in the pan and let cool slightly.

2. Stuff each chop, bringing flaps together to enclose stuffing. Fasten the edges with toothpicks.

TO COOK

½ cup Wondra flour
½ teaspoon salt
¼ teaspoon freshly milled
  black pepper
2 Tablespoons olive oil

2 Tablespoons unsalted
  butter
1 cup orange juice
½ to 1 cup dry white wine
1 bunch curly parsley sprigs
  (garnish)

1. In a shallow bowl, combine flour, salt and pepper. Dredge each chop in flour mixture and shake off excess (dredge just before browning or flour coating will become gummy).
2. In a large sauté pan, heat olive oil over medium heat until haze forms, then add butter. Add chops and brown lightly on both sides. Transfer chops to plate and pour off most of the pan drippings, leaving about 1 Tablespoon. Turn heat to high and deglaze pan with orange juice and ½ cup white wine, scraping the bottom of pan to loosen any fragments that might be stuck. Return chops to pan and cook covered over medium heat, basting frequently with pan juices, until very tender when pierced with the tip of a knife, about 40 minutes; if juices evaporate during cooking, add a little more wine.
3. To serve, place chops on a platter and remove toothpicks. Pour pan juices over chops and garnish platter with curly parsley.

ROAST VEAL AMADEO
Vitello all'Amadeo

My father was an expert at preparing veal roasts. His technique of cooking the roast in cheesecloth not only added moisture to the veal, but helped hold it together. If there is any left over, it is delicious served cold, topped with homemade mayonnaise (see page 269).

SERVES 8

1 3-pound boned shoulder of veal, well trimmed of fat	2 Tablespoons grated lemon rind
6 Tablespoons unsalted butter	1 teaspoon salt
½ cup finely chopped onion	½ teaspoon freshly milled black pepper
½ cup finely chopped carrot	1½ cups fresh breadcrumbs
3 Tablespoons minced Italian parsley leaves	1 egg yolk, lightly beaten
3 Tablespoons capers, rinsed and well drained	

1. Place boned shoulder of veal on a board or work surface with skin side down. Set aside.
2. Melt butter in a medium skillet over medium heat. Add onion and carrot and sauté, stirring constantly, until soft but not brown, about 3 minutes. Add parsley, capers, lemon rind, salt and pepper; continue cooking, stirring constantly, for an additional 30 seconds. Add breadcrumbs and blend thoroughly. Remove from heat and let mixture cool slightly. Add lightly beaten egg yolk and mix well with a fork. Let cool to room temperature.

TO ASSEMBLE AND COOK

4 ounces thinly sliced lean pancetta or imported ham	1 cup finely chopped onion
¼ cup olive oil	½ cup finely chopped carrot
3 Tablespoons unsalted butter	½ cup fresh lemon juice
	1½ cups dry white wine (or more)

1. Cut a piece of cheesecloth about 14 × 20 inches. Wet cheesecloth with water and squeeze dry. Set aside.
2. Arrange pancetta or ham on veal in a slightly overlapping pattern. With a metal spatula, spread stuffing evenly over pancetta. Roll into a jelly roll

shape and tie with kitchen twine at 2-inch intervals. With your hands, rub 1 Tablespoon olive oil all over roast. Wrap cheesecloth around roast and tie with kitchen twine at 3-inch intervals. Tie both ends securely with kitchen twine.

3. In a large Dutch oven, heat remaining 3 Tablespoons olive oil over medium heat until haze forms, then add butter. Brown the veal roast on all sides (it will brown through the cheesecloth). Remove roast and set aside.

4. Add onion and carrot, turn heat to low and sauté, stirring constantly, until soft but not brown, about 5 minutes. Return roast to pan; add lemon juice and 1½ cups wine. Bring to a boil over high heat. Turn heat to low and cook covered, basting and turning roast in cooking liquid every 20 minutes, for about 1½ hours or until meat is extremely tender when pierced through cheesecloth with the tip of a knife; if pan juices evaporate during cooking, add a little more wine.

5. Transfer roast to platter and immediately remove cheesecloth (you must do this quickly or cheesecloth will stick to roast). Cover with foil and let roast rest for 15 minutes before slicing.

6. To serve, cut veal into ½-inch slices and arrange in a slightly overlapping pattern on a large platter. Heat pan juices and spoon a little over sliced veal; serve remaining sauce separately.

VEAL SHANKS, MILANESE STYLE
Ossobuco alla Milanese

This dish is traditionally served with a topping called gremolata, *which consists of minced parsley, garlic and grated lemon rind. I find it even more flavorful to add the lemon and garlic to the sauce and just top it off with minced parsley. Veal shanks are usually served with risotto. I also love serving them with Fluffy Potato Pie, page 249.*

SERVES 6

2 large veal shanks, cut into cross sections 2 inches thick (about 6 pounds)
½ cup Wondra flour
½ teaspoon salt
½ teaspoon freshly milled black pepper
¼ cup olive oil
¼ cup unsalted butter
1 cup finely chopped onion
1 cup finely chopped carrots
1 cup finely chopped celery
1 Tablespoon minced garlic
1 Tablespoon grated lemon rind

1 cup dry white wine
1½ cups coarsely chopped Italian plum tomatoes, including juice
1 cup beef broth
1 Tablespoon minced fresh basil or 1 teaspoon crumbled dried basil
1 Tablespoon minced fresh thyme or 1 teaspoon crumbled dried thyme
2 large bay leaves
¼ cup minced Italian parsley leaves (garnish)

1. Adjust rack to center of oven and preheat to 350°F.
2. Tie kitchen twine around circumference of veal to prevent bone from popping out while cooking.
3. In a shallow bowl, combine flour, salt and pepper. Dredge veal shanks in flour mixture (dredge just before sautéing or flour coating will become gummy).
4. Use a large ovenproof sauté pan or Dutch oven that can hold the veal in a single layer without crowding. Heat olive oil in pan over medium-high heat until haze forms, then add butter. Sauté veal shanks on all sides in two batches until lightly golden. Remove veal and set aside.
5. Turn heat down to medium and add onion, carrots and celery. Sauté, stirring constantly, until soft but not brown, scraping bottom of pan to loosen any fragments that might be stuck, about 5 minutes. Add garlic and lemon rind; mix well. Add wine, turn heat to high and cook, stirring constantly, until slightly reduced, about 5 minutes. Remove pan from heat and ar-

range veal shanks upright in pan (this will also prevent bone and marrow from popping out).

6. Add tomatoes, broth, basil, thyme and bay leaves to pan; bring to a boil over high heat.

7. Cover pan and bake for 30 minutes. Remove from oven and baste veal with pan juices. Continue to cook, basting frequently, until meat is very tender when pierced with a fork, about 1 hour; the meat is finished cooking when it almost falls from the bone.

8. Transfer veal shanks to a large platter and remove twine.

9. Discard bay leaves from sauce. Remove any surface fat with a large spoon. Ladle sauce over veal and garnish with minced parsley. Serve immediately.

Note: This dish can be made up to 2 hours before serving; keep pan covered. Reheat over low heat, basting frequently with sauce.

VEAL STEW
Spezzatino di Vitello

The fragrant combination of olives and capers adds an extra dimension of flavor and texture to this Neapolitan stew. Rice with peas or zucchini is an excellent side dish.

SERVES 6

3 Tablespoons olive oil
2 Tablespoons unsalted butter
2½ pounds boned shoulder of veal, well trimmed of fat, cut into 1½-inch cubes
1 large yellow onion (10 ounces), halved and thinly sliced
2 carrots (3 ounces), trimmed, peeled, halved and cut into 1-inch pieces
2 cups canned Italian plum tomatoes, coarsely chopped, including juice

1½ Tablespoons minced fresh sage or 1½ teaspoons crumbled dried sage
3 bay leaves
1 teaspoon salt
½ teaspoon freshly milled black pepper
1 can (6 ounces) small pitted California black olives, well drained
3 Tablespoons capers, rinsed and well drained
2 Tablespoons minced Italian parsley leaves (optional garnish)

1. In a 5-quart Dutch oven, heat olive oil over medium heat until haze forms, then add butter. Add meat in two batches and sauté, stirring constantly,

until lightly golden. Remove with a slotted spoon. Discard most of the pan drippings, leaving about 2 Tablespoons.

2. Add onion and carrot and sauté, stirring constantly to loosen any fragments that might be stuck to bottom of pan, until barely tender, about 2 minutes.

3. Add tomatoes, sage, bay leaves, salt and pepper. Return meat to pan and bring to a boil uncovered over high heat, stirring constantly. Turn heat down to low and cook partially covered, stirring frequently, until meat is extremely tender when pierced with the tip of a knife, about 1 hour. (Watch cooking liquid; if it starts to evaporate, add about ¼ cup hot water.)

4. Add olives and capers and continue to cook, partially covered, for an additional 5 minutes.

5. When ready to serve, remove bay leaves, transfer stew to a platter and garnish with minced parsley.

Note: Stew can be made up to 3 hours before serving and reheated over low heat.

Pork

PORK CHOPS WITH VINEGAR
HERB-STUFFED PORK CHOPS
ROLLED PORK CUTLETS
ROAST PORK WITH HERBED BUTTER
SAUTÉED SAUSAGE WITH SPINACH

PORK CHOPS WITH VINEGAR
Coste di Maiale con Aceto

The sweet taste of red peppers combined with colorful green peppers, black olives and vinegar adds a piquant touch to the pork.

SERVES 6

½ cup Wondra flour
1 teaspoon salt
½ teaspoon freshly milled black pepper
6 center cut pork chops, ¼ inch thick (about 1½ pounds), well trimmed
3 Tablespoons olive oil
3 Tablespoons unsalted butter
3 cloves garlic, split in half
½ large yellow onion (6 ounces), thinly sliced

2 large red bell peppers (1 pound), washed, dried, halved, cored and thinly sliced
1 large green bell pepper (8 ounces), washed, dried, halved, cored and thinly sliced
½ cup medium-size pitted California black olives (about 14), well drained and thinly sliced
½ cup imported white wine vinegar
1 Tablespoon sugar

1. In a shallow bowl, combine flour, salt and pepper. Dredge chops in flour mixture and shake off excess (dredge just before sautéing or they will become gummy).
2. In a large sauté pan, heat olive oil over medium heat until haze forms, then add butter. Sauté garlic until lightly golden; discard. Sauté chops in two batches until lightly browned on both sides. Remove and set aside.
3. Discard most of the pan drippings, leaving about 2 Tablespoons. Sauté onion and peppers over medium heat, stirring constantly and scraping up any browned fragments left in bottom of pan, until tender-crisp when tested with a fork, about 5 minutes. Set vegetables aside and remove pan from heat. Return chops to pan in a slightly overlapping pattern. Arrange vegetables over chops and sprinkle olives on top.
4. In a small bowl, combine vinegar and sugar. Stir mixture together until sugar is completely dissolved (this is best done with your index finger so that you can feel when sugar is dissolved). Spoon vinegar mixture on top of olive-vegetable mixture.
5. Cover pan and turn heat to low. Simmer, basting frequently with pan juices, until chops are extremely tender when tested with the tip of a knife, about 15 minutes. Season with additional salt and pepper if needed.
6. To serve, arrange chops on a platter with a border of vegetables and olives.

HERB-STUFFED PORK CHOPS
Involtini di Maiale

The savory blend of herbs and white wine gives this dish its full-bodied flavor. It is a favorite with my family, friends and students. The pork chops can be cooked up to 2 hours before serving; keep covered after cooking and baste frequently with pan juices. When ready to serve, reheat in 300°F oven for 20 minutes; check pan juices and add a little more white wine if needed.

SERVES 6

6 center cut pork chops, 1½ inches thick (about 3 pounds)
2 Tablespoons pine nuts (pignoli)
¼ cup unsalted butter
½ cup finely chopped celery, strings removed
¾ cup finely chopped yellow onion
1⅓ cups fine dry breadcrumbs
1 Tablespoon minced fresh basil or 1 teaspoon crumbled dried basil
1 Tablespoon minced fresh rosemary or ½ teaspoon powdered rosemary
1 Tablespoon minced fresh sage or 1 teaspoon crumbled dried sage
3 Tablespoons minced Italian parsley leaves
½ teaspoon salt
½ teaspoon freshly milled black pepper
Olive oil (if needed)

1. To make pockets in pork for stuffing, cut a slit down the center and full length of each chop right to the bone (or have this done by the butcher). Place chops on a flat surface and open up the pockets.

2. In a medium skillet, toast pine nuts over medium heat, swirling pan around until nuts are lightly golden. Transfer to a small bowl and set aside.

3. In same skillet, melt butter over low heat. Add celery and onion and cook, stirring constantly, until soft but not brown, about 5 minutes. Stir in breadcrumbs and mix well. Turn heat to high and stir breadcrumbs constantly until lightly toasted, about 1 minute. Remove from heat and stir in pine nuts and remaining ingredients. (At this point the mixture should still be a little moist; if it seems dry, moisten with a few drops of olive oil.) Divide stuffing into 6 portions in pan. Let cool to room temperature before stuffing.

4. Stuff each chop, bringing flaps together to enclose stuffing. Fasten the edges with 2 toothpicks.

TO COOK

½ cup Wondra flour
1 teaspoon salt
½ teaspoon freshly milled
  black pepper

2 Tablespoons olive oil
2 Tablespoons unsalted
  butter
1 cup dry white wine

1. Adjust rack to center of oven and preheat to 350°F.
2. In a shallow bowl, combine flour, salt and pepper. Dredge each chop in flour mixture and shake off excess (dredge just before browning or chops will get gummy).
3. In a large ovenproof sauté pan, heat olive oil over medium heat until haze forms, then add butter. Add pork chops and brown lightly on both sides. Remove chops and pour off most of drippings, leaving about 2 Tablespoons. Turn heat to high and deglaze pan with a little of the white wine, scraping the bottom of pan to loosen any fragments that might be stuck. Return chops to pan and add remaining wine. Cover pan and bake, basting every 15 minutes with pan juices, until chops are very tender when pierced with the tip of a knife, about 1 hour; if pan juices seem to be evaporating during baking, add a little water.
4. Transfer chops to a serving platter, remove toothpicks and pour pan juices over each chop. Serve immediately.

ROLLED PORK CUTLETS
Rollatini di Maiale

A very affordable main-course roll-up. Here's proof that good things come in small packages!

SERVES 8

3 pounds pork cutlet, ¼ inch
  thick (cut from boned loin
  of pork, well trimmed)

Place slices of pork between sheets of waxed paper and pound each slice with a flat mallet. Make sure you pound the edges well so that they will be easier to roll. When finished, each slice should be slightly less than ¼ inch thick. Line up cutlets on work surface in a single layer.

BECHAMEL SAUCE

3 Tablespoons unsalted butter	¼ teaspoon freshly milled white pepper
3 Tablespoons flour	6 Tablespoons freshly grated
1 cup milk	Parmigiano or Swiss cheese
½ teaspoon salt	

In a 1½-quart saucepan, melt butter over low heat. When butter begins to froth, add the flour. Mix well with a wire whisk and cook until lightly golden, whisking constantly. Stir in milk, salt and pepper. Cook over low heat, whisking constantly, until very thick, about 3 minutes. Add grated cheese to sauce and mix well. Set aside to cool to room temperature.

TO ASSEMBLE AND COOK

6 ounces prosciutto, thinly sliced	¼ cup olive oil
¼ cup minced Italian parsley leaves	¼ cup unsalted butter
	1 cup finely chopped yellow onion
3 extra large eggs	½ cup dry vermouth
½ teaspoon salt	2 Tablespoons minced Italian
3 cups fine dry breadcrumbs	parsley leaves (garnish)

1. Slice prosciutto to fit each cutlet, leaving about a ½-inch border of meat on all sides. Place sliced prosciutto on top of cutlets. Using a metal spatula, spread a thin layer of bechamel sauce over prosciutto. Sprinkle a little parsley over bechamel and press lightly with fingertips. Roll each cutlet and secure with 2 toothpicks.
2. In a shallow bowl, beat eggs lightly with salt. Place breadcrumbs in another shallow bowl. Dredge each roll in crumbs, dip in beaten egg and coat again with breadcrumbs; shake off excess. Arrange rolls on a platter lined with waxed paper and refrigerate for at least 1 hour (chilling prevents coating from coming off during cooking).
3. In a large sauté pan, heat olive oil over medium heat until haze forms, then add butter. Turn heat to low and sauté rolls, turning frequently with tongs, until lightly golden. Drain on paper towels.
4. Pour off most of the pan drippings, leaving about 2 Tablespoons. Add onion

and cook over low heat, stirring constantly, until soft but not brown, about 5 minutes. Return rolls to pan, add vermouth and cover. Cook, basting frequently with pan juices, until very tender when pierced with the tip of a knife, about 20 minutes.

5. Transfer rolls to platter and remove toothpicks. Top with sautéed onion and pan juices. Garnish with minced parsley and serve immediately.

ROAST PORK WITH HERBED BUTTER
Maiale alla Nonno Donato

One of Nonno Donato's Tuscan specialties was this self-basting, boned loin of pork studded with herb butter and roasted on a "rack" of bones and vegetables.

SERVES 6 TO 8

1 4-pound center cut loin of pork, boned (about 3 to 3½ pounds after boning)—reserve bones to use as a roasting rack

3 large carrots (8 ounces), peeled and sliced diagonally into 2-inch pieces

½ large yellow onion (6 ounces), cut into 8 chunks

3 Tablespoons unsalted butter, softened

1 teaspoon finely minced garlic

2 teaspoons minced Italian parsley leaves

1 teaspoon minced fresh thyme or ½ teaspoon crumbled dried thyme

1 teaspoon minced fresh rosemary or ¼ teaspoon powdered rosemary

½ teaspoon salt

½ teaspoon freshly milled black pepper

1 teaspoon arrowroot (optional)

1 bunch curly parsley sprigs (garnish)

1. Adjust rack to center of oven and preheat to 375°F.

2. Arrange bones in a single layer in the center of a roasting pan to form rack for roasting. Place onion and carrot pieces in between and around bones.

3. Trim top layer of fat from roast, leaving a ¼-inch layer. With a sharp knife, make a deep pocket between the meat and top layer of fat on both ends.

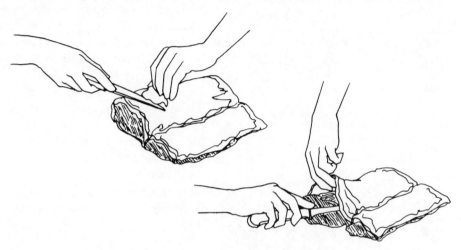

4. Blend butter, garlic, herbs, salt and pepper with mortar and pestle to form a smooth paste, or blend in a small bowl with the back of a wooden spoon.

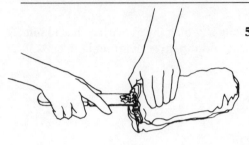

5. Place boned pork flat on a board with fat side facing down; spread ⅓ of the herbed butter inside roast. Shape into roll and spread another ⅓ of the herbed butter into both pockets. Tie roast at 2-inch intervals with kitchen twine. Lightly coat top and both ends with remaining herbed butter. Place roast on rack of bones in preheated oven for 30 minutes. Reduce heat to 350°F and bake until thermometer inserted in meat reaches 165°F, about 1½ to 2 hours, depending upon thickness of roast.

6. Transfer roast from pan to a platter and cover loosely with foil to keep warm. Let meat rest for at least 20 minutes before slicing.

7. Discard bones and vegetables from pan. Tilt pan and spoon off any fat. Add 6 Tablespoons water and place over medium heat, scraping up any fragments left in the bottom of pan with a wooden spoon. Transfer to a gravy boat. If you want a thicker gravy, dissolve arrowroot in 2 Tablespoons cold water; add to pan after scraping up fragments from bottom and cook sauce until slightly thickened.

8. Remove twine from roast and garnish platter with parsley sprigs. Slice at table; serve with gravy.

SAUTÉED SAUSAGE WITH SPINACH
Salsiccia e Spinaci Saltati

The red wine not only adds a wonderful flavor to the sausage, but also keeps it moist in cooking. The spinach is very quickly sautéed in the sausage drippings. A robust combination, especially when accompanied by broiled polenta.

SERVES 8

3½ pounds spinach
1 teaspoon salt
2½ pounds Italian sweet sausage with fennel (see note)
¾ cup dry red wine

2 large cloves garlic, split in half
2 Tablespoons olive oil (optional)
1 teaspoon salt
1 teaspoon freshly milled black pepper

1. Discard any spinach leaves that are not crisp and green. Wash spinach in clusters in lukewarm water several times to remove sand. Trim off about ½ inch from bottom of stems. Transfer spinach directly from final rinse water to a 5-quart pot. Add 1 teaspoon salt and cover pot. Cook spinach, covered, over high heat just until leaves are limp, about 3 minutes. Transfer to a colander and rinse under cold water. With your hands, squeeze out excess water. Set aside.

2. Preheat oven to 200°F. Cut sausage into 2½-inch lengths. In a 12-inch skillet, place sausage, red wine and garlic. Cover skillet and bring to a boil. Reduce heat to low and cook covered until sausage turns a deep pink, about 15 minutes. Uncover pan and remove garlic with a slotted spoon. Turn heat to high and fry sausage, turning frequently, until it is golden brown on all sides and all of the liquid has evaporated. Transfer sausage to the center of a large ovenproof platter; keep warm in oven while sautéing spinach.

3. Discard most of the pan drippings, leaving about 2 Tablespoons. If sausage is particularly lean and there are no pan drippings left, add 2 Tablespoons olive oil.

4. Add spinach, turn heat to medium-high and sauté, stirring constantly, scraping bottom of pan to loosen any fragments that might be stuck. Cook just until spinach is warmed through, about 3 minutes. Season with salt and pepper. Arrange spinach in a border around sausage and serve immediately.

Note: If you cannot find sausage with fennel, add 1 teaspoon fennel seed to skillet along with red wine and garlic.

Lamb

PAN-FRIED LAMB CHOPS

STUFFED BONED LEG OF LAMB

CRUSTY RACK OF LAMB

LAMB STEW

PAN-FRIED LAMB CHOPS
Agnello Fritto

One of the quickest and simplest methods of cooking either rib or loin chops. You can prepare the chops with breadcrumb coating up to 3 hours ahead. Just place in a single layer on a platter lined with waxed paper and refrigerate uncovered until ready to cook.

SERVES 6

12 rib or loin lamb chops, ½ inch thick (3 pounds), well trimmed of fat
2 cloves garlic, split in half
⅓ cup fresh lime or lemon juice
1½ cups dry breadcrumbs
2 teaspoons finely minced parsley

1 teaspoon finely minced garlic
1 teaspoon salt
½ teaspoon freshly milled black pepper
¼ cup olive oil
Lemon or lime wedges (optional garnish)

1. Rub each chop with garlic on both sides; discard garlic.
2. Place juice in a shallow bowl. In another shallow bowl, combine breadcrumbs, parsley, garlic, salt and pepper. Brush both sides of chops with juice. Firmly press both sides of chops into breadcrumb mixture; shake off excess. Arrange in a single layer on one large or two smaller platters lined with waxed paper and refrigerate for at least 1 hour (chilling will prevent breadcrumb coating from coming off during pan frying).
3. Use two skillets large enough to hold all the chops in a single layer. Heat two Tablespoons of olive oil in each skillet over medium heat until haze forms. Cook chops for 2 minutes on each side for rare, 4 minutes for medium, or five minutes on each side for well done.
4. Arrange chops in an overlapping pattern on a large platter. Garnish platter with lime or lemon wedges and serve immediately.

STUFFED BONED LEG OF LAMB
Arrosto d'Agnello

*Most Italians do not have a leg of lamb boned, nor do they marinate it.
They just stud it with sliced garlic, rub it all over with rosemary and bake
it with lots of lemon juice. I prefer having it boned, marinating it overnight and adding just a thin layer of stuffing. The marinade enhances the
flavor of the lamb and the stuffing makes for a beautiful presentation
when the meat is thinly sliced.*

SERVES 10

1 7-pound leg of lamb,
   trimmed and boned (about
   5½ pounds after boning)

MARINADE

4 cloves garlic, split in half
¼ cup olive oil
½ cup fresh lemon juice
1 Tablespoon Dijon mustard
2 Tablespoons minced fresh
   mint or 2 teaspoons
   crumbled dried mint

1 Tablespoon minced fresh
   rosemary or 1 teaspoon
   crumbled dried rosemary
   or ½ teaspoon powdered
   rosemary
1 teaspoon salt
½ teaspoon freshly milled
   black pepper

In a large, shallow bowl, combine all of the marinade ingredients. Place the
boned lamb flat in bowl and spoon some of the marinade over. Cover with
plastic wrap and refrigerate for at least 24 hours, turning lamb in marinade
every 3 to 4 hours.

STUFFING

2 Tablespoons grated lemon
   rind
2 teaspoons minced garlic
½ cup minced Italian parsley
   leaves

2 Tablespoons minced fresh
   mint or 2 teaspoons
   crumbled dried mint
1 cup fresh breadcrumbs,
   well packed
3 Tablespoons olive oil

In a bowl, combine all of the above ingredients except olive oil. Add the olive
oil and toss lightly with a fork to incorporate; the mixture should feel moist.

TO ASSEMBLE AND COOK

1. Adjust rack to center of oven and preheat to 350°F.
2. Remove lamb from marinade and place on work surface skin side down; blot dry with paper towel. Transfer marinade to a small bowl.
3. Using a metal spatula, spread stuffing over lamb. Starting at shank end (thickest part), fold ⅓ of the meat over, then fold leg portion over top. Tie with kitchen twine at 1-inch intervals, starting at thicker end of roll. Make sure you tuck in ends and tie lengthwise once.
4. Place meat on a rack in a shallow roasting pan with seam side down. Brush with some of the marinade. Roast meat for 1 hour, then start basting with remaining marinade every 20 minutes until thermometer inserted into thickest part of meat registers 130°F to 135°F for rare, about 2 hours. (For medium, the thermometer should register between 145°F and 150°F, about 2½ hours.
5. Transfer lamb to serving platter, cover with foil and let rest 15 to 20 minutes before carving.
6. Using a metal spoon, discard any surface fat from pan. Add ½ cup hot water to pan juices and place over medium heat. Scrape up any browned fragments that might be stuck to the bottom of pan and cook for about 3 minutes. Strain pan juices through a small strainer into a small saucepan. Keep warm over low heat.
7. Remove twine and thinly slice roast; arrange slices on a large platter in a slightly overlapping pattern. Spoon some pan juices on top of lamb. Serve the remaining juices separately.

CRUSTY RACK OF LAMB
Agnello Incrostati

The parsley-breadcrumb coating seals in the juices, while mustard adds additional flavor to this truly succulent meat.

SERVES 3 TO 4

1 rack of lamb, 8 ribs (about 2¼ pounds)
1 clove garlic, split in half
¼ cup fresh lemon juice
½ teaspoon salt
¼ teaspoon freshly milled black pepper
1 Tablespoon minced fresh thyme or 1 teaspoon crumbled dried thyme

½ cup fresh breadcrumbs
1 Tablespoon minced Italian parsley leaves
1 teaspoon Dijon mustard
1 small bunch curly parsley sprigs (garnish)
1 lemon, cut into wedges (garnish)

1. Ask your butcher to make a ½-inch cut between each rib so that carving will be easier. Have him also trim about 2 inches of fat and meat from between ribs to dress up the rack. Trim most of the fat from the top of the meat.
2. Adjust rack to center of oven and preheat to 375°F.
3. Rub the roast well with garlic, lemon juice, salt, pepper and thyme.
4. Wrap each exposed bone end of the chops with foil to prevent burning while baking.
5. Place lamb meat side down on a rack in a roasting pan. Cook until meat thermometer registers 140°F for medium-rare, about 35 minutes, or 145°F for medium, about 45 minutes.
6. While meat is roasting, combine breadcrumbs and parsley in a small bowl; set aside.
7. Remove lamb from oven and turn it over. Spread mustard over meat and firmly press breadcrumb mixture over top of lamb. Return to oven and bake until crumb mixture is lightly browned, about 10 minutes. Remove foil from bone ends and let rest for 10 minutes before serving (this will make carving easier).
8. Place rack on a large oval platter and garnish with a border of curly parsley sprigs and lemon wedges. Carve between ribs to serve.

LAMB STEW
Umido d'Agnello

To insure the greatest tenderness, use only boned leg of lamb for this Nea-politan stew. The dish can be prepared up to 4 hours before serving and reheated over very low heat. A nice bottle of Bardolino and a tossed salad will round out this hearty one-dish meal.

SERVES 6

5 Tablespoons olive oil
1 4-pound leg of lamb, boned (about 3 pounds after boning), well trimmed of fat and cut into 1½-inch cubes
1½ cups chopped yellow onion
1 teaspoon minced garlic
1½ cups coarsely chopped canned Italian plum tomatoes, juice included
3 bay leaves
1 Tablespoon minced fresh sage or 1 teaspoon crumbled dried sage
1 teaspoon salt

½ teaspoon freshly milled black pepper
3 large carrots (8 ounces), trimmed, peeled and sliced into 1-inch lengths
1 pound green beans, washed, trimmed, and sliced into 1-inch lengths
5 medium-size long or round white potatoes (2 pounds), peeled and cut into 1½-inch cubes
2 Tablespoons minced Italian parsley leaves (optional garnish)

1. In a 6-quart Dutch oven, heat olive oil over medium heat until haze forms. Add meat in two batches and sauté, stirring constantly, until very lightly golden. Remove with a slotted spoon. Discard most of the pan drippings, leaving about 2 Tablespoons. Add onion and sauté, stirring constantly to loosen any fragments that might be stuck to bottom of pan, until barely tender, about 1 minute. Add garlic and sauté, stirring constantly, for an additional 30 seconds. Add tomatoes, bay leaves, sage, salt and pepper. Return meat to pan and bring to a boil over high heat, stirring constantly. Turn heat down to low and cook covered, stirring frequently, until meat is very tender when pierced with the tip of a knife, about 1½ hours. (Watch cooking liquid; if it starts to evaporate, add about ½ cup hot water.)

2. Add carrots and mix well. Cook covered over low heat until carrots are barely tender when tested with a fork, about 5 minutes. Add green beans and cook, covered, stirring frequently, until barely tender, about 15 minutes. Add potatoes and continue cooking, covered, stirring once or twice, until potatoes are done, about 10 minutes.

3. When ready to serve, remove bay leaves and transfer stew to a large platter. Garnish with minced parsley and serve immediately.

CHICKEN

Summer vacation was always a great joy for me because it meant I would be spending a few days at my Uncle Tony's poultry farm. The day started early in the morning with the gathering of eggs for market, went on to include the selection of chickens to be sold— from young broilers to plump roasters—and always ended at Uncle Tony's and Aunt Angie's table savoring the special taste of such favorites as Chicken Cacciatora or roast chicken. Those summers taught me a lesson that I value to this day: there is nothing like the taste of a fresh-killed chicken. I consider myself fortunate to have a poultry farm in my area, but realize this luxury is not available to everyone. With this in mind, I offer the following suggestions:

- □ *Chicken is extremely perishable and should be used within two days of its purchase.*
- □ *Wash chicken as soon as you get it home, or soak it in cold water with a little salt. Rinse thoroughly and blot dry with paper towel.*
- □ *If you are not going to use it the same day, rub a cut lemon all over chicken (the acid in the lemon will keep it fresh smelling). Place chicken in a nonaluminum bowl, cover and refrigerate overnight.*

BONING AND FILLETING CHICKEN BREASTS: CHICKEN SUPRÊMES

Each whole breast should weigh at least 1 pound before boning, so that you will have 4 large fillets plus 2 smaller fillets when finished.

YIELDS 6 FILLETS

1. Wash chicken breasts and blot dry with paper towel. Wrap each breast in plastic and place in freezer for 45 minutes (this makes boning process a lot easier).

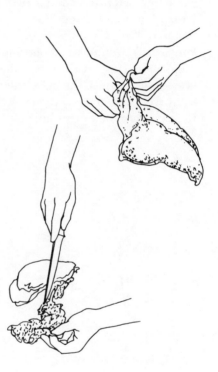

2. Place breast on work surface skin side up. Starting at the top of the breast (thickest part), slip your fingers under the skin and loosen it with your fingertips. Peel off skin, using knife only if necessary to avoid tearing meat. Trim off any membrane or bits of fat that may still be attached to the breast.

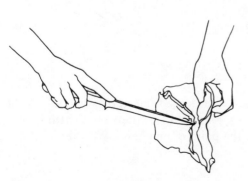

3. Look or feel for a pocket along the broad upper side of breast. Run your index finger in pocket along the upper part of breast to ribcage and loosen meat. Insert the tip of a boning knife into pocket between ribcage and meat, keeping the knife as close to the ribcage as

possible. Use a sawing motion to cut meat away from ribcage. Using knife, scrape meat towards center breastbone up and over the small fillet which should still be attached to one side of the breastbone. (The smaller strip extending lengthwise under the large fillet is called the filet mignon). With the point of the knife, work around wishbone and remove. Starting at the top of the breast, slice half of the large fillet away from center breastbone. Repeat process on other side of breast.

4. With the tip of the boning knife, cut away the small fillet from the side of the breastbone (ribcage can be saved for making chicken broth). To remove tough white tendons running along underside of small fillets, hold knife against end of tendon. With the other hand, pull tendon out against blade. Lightly pound the two small fillets between sheets of waxed paper to flatten.

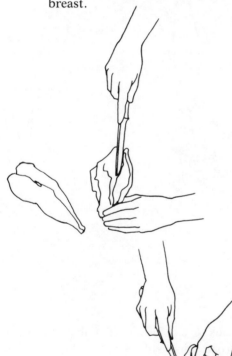

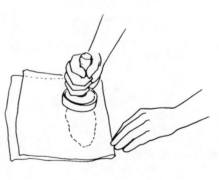

5. Slicing will be a lot easier if you wrap each large fillet in plastic and place in freezer for at least 20 minutes. Place chilled fillets on a cutting board. Hold single fillet firmly with the palm of one hand. With the

other hand, starting at the top of the fillet (thickest part), slice horizontally using a slight sawing motion; watch carefully as you slice to keep the pieces even. Place the fillets between sheets of waxed paper and very lightly pound to flatten, being careful not to tear the meat. Repeat process with other large fillets.

6. Chicken suprêmes (fillets) are now ready to use or they may be individually wrapped in plastic and aluminum foil. Freeze until needed.

A wise host or hostess will keep a supply in the freezer, ready for unexpected guests or a quick meal. Taken directly from the freezer, these versatile fillets will defrost in one hour.

Chicken suprêmes can be substituted for any recipe in this book calling for veal scallops or cutlets. This is not only economical, but a way of expanding your culinary repertoire.

□■□

CHICKEN SUPRÊMES WITH PIQUANT CAPER SAUCE
Petti di Pollo con Salsa Piccante

A very light entree, especially after pasta. You may also want to try the sauce on broiled or fried fillet of sole.

SERVES 8

3 large whole chicken breasts (3½ pounds), boned, skinned and filleted (see directions for preparing suprêmes, page 183)
½ cup Wondra flour
3 large eggs
1 teaspoon salt
½ teaspoon freshly milled black pepper

1½ cups fine dry breadcrumbs
2 Tablespoons minced Italian parsley leaves
½ cup freshly grated Parmigiano cheese
1½ cups vegetable oil, preferably corn

1. Place flour in a shallow bowl. In another shallow bowl, beat eggs with salt and pepper. In third shallow bowl, combine breadcrumbs, parsley and Parmigiano cheese. Dredge chicken fillets in flour mixture, dip in beaten egg and then coat with breadcrumb mixture. Arrange fillets in a single layer on a platter lined with waxed paper and refrigerate for at least 1 hour (chilling prevents breadcrumb coating from falling off during frying).

2. Adjust rack to center of oven and preheat to 200°F. In a 12-inch skillet, heat vegetable oil over medium-high heat until haze forms. Fry fillets in three batches until lightly golden on both sides. Drain on paper towels. Arrange fillets on ovenproof platter and keep warm in oven while preparing sauce.

CAPER SAUCE

1 Tablespoon olive oil
2 Tablespoons unsalted butter
2 Tablespoons minced shallot
1 cup chicken broth
3 Tablespoons capers, rinsed and well drained
½ cup dry vermouth

¼ cup fresh lemon juice
1 teaspoon salt
½ teaspoon freshly milled white pepper
1 teaspoon arrowroot
2 Tablespoons dry vermouth
2 Tablespoons minced Italian parsley leaves

1. In a 1½-quart saucepan, heat olive oil and butter over low heat. Add shallot and sauté, stirring constantly, until tender-crisp, about 2 minutes.
2. Add chicken broth, raise heat to medium-high and cook until broth is slightly reduced, about 5 minutes. Add capers, ½ cup vermouth, lemon juice, salt and pepper. Cook uncovered over low heat for another 3 minutes. Remove pan from heat.
3. Dissolve arrowroot in 2 Tablespoons vermouth and add to sauce. Return to low heat and continue to cook, stirring constantly, until slightly thickened, about 2 minutes. Add parsley and remove from heat.
4. To serve, arrange chicken fillets on a large platter in a slightly overlapping pattern. Spoon a little sauce on top of each fillet. Serve the remaining sauce separately.

CHICKEN WITH ARTICHOKE HEARTS AND MUSHROOMS
Pollo con Carciofi e Funghi

Plan on serving this spectacular entree for one of your dinner parties. This recipe can be completely assembled up to 3 hours before baking; cover with foil until ready to bake.

SERVES 8 TO 10

4 whole chicken breasts (4 pounds), boned and skinned
¼ cup Wondra flour
½ cup fine dry breadcrumbs
1 teaspoon salt
½ teaspoon freshly milled black pepper
¼ cup olive oil
2 Tablespoons unsalted butter

1 large yellow onion (10 ounces), halved and thinly sliced
2 packages (9 ounces each) frozen artichoke hearts, defrosted and well drained
1 pound medium mushrooms, trimmed, wiped and thinly sliced
1 cup chicken broth
½ cup dry vermouth

1. Cut each boned chicken breast in half and each half into thirds.
2. In a shallow bowl, combine flour, breadcrumbs, salt and pepper. Dredge chicken in flour mixture and shake off excess.
3. In a 12-inch skillet, heat olive oil over medium-high heat until haze forms, then add butter. Quickly sauté chicken in two batches until very lightly golden on both sides. Drain on paper towels.
4. Arrange chicken in a single layer in a 9 × 13-inch baking dish.
5. Pour off some of the pan drippings, leaving about 3 tablespoons. Add onion and sauté over medium heat until barely tender, about 2 minutes, stirring constantly to loosen any fragments that might be stuck to bottom of pan. Add artichoke hearts and continue to sauté, stirring frequently, until barely tender when tested with a fork at base of choke, about 2 minutes. Add mushrooms and sauté just until well incorporated, about 30 seconds. Stir in chicken broth and vermouth, then remove from heat. Spoon artichoke mixture between and over chicken pieces. Pour remaining pan juices over chicken.
6. When ready to bake, adjust rack to center of oven and preheat to 350°F. Bake uncovered, basting frequently with pan juices, until chicken and artichoke hearts are very tender when tested with the tip of a knife, about 35 to 40 minutes. Remove from oven and serve immediately.

STUFFED CHICKEN BREASTS
Petti di Pollo Imbottiti

Leaving the skin on the halved chicken breast insures added moisture and flavor. The stuffing, made with zucchini, Asiago and tarragon, is surprisingly different.

SERVES 6

3 whole chicken breasts (3½ pounds)
2 medium zucchini (12 ounces), washed, trimmed and coarsely grated (can be grated in food processor fitted with shredding disc; cut into 1-inch pieces before placing horizontally in feed tube)
2 Tablespoons olive oil
1 Tablespoon unsalted butter
1 cup thinly sliced scallions
½ cup freshly grated Asiago, Provolone or imported Swiss cheese, well packed

1½ cups fresh breadcrumbs
1 Tablespoon finely minced fresh tarragon or 1 teaspoon crumbled dried tarragon
½ teaspoon salt
½ teaspoon freshly milled black pepper
1 large egg yolk, lightly beaten
2 Tablespoons olive oil
1 large clove garlic, split in half
1 bunch curly parsley sprigs (garnish)

1. Wash chicken breasts and blot dry with paper towel. Place one chicken breast on work surface skin side down. With a boning knife, slice breast in half lengthwise right through middle of breastbone (do not remove breastbone, as this will help hold stuffing in place). Turn chicken skin side up. Insert the tip of the boning knife into thickest part of breast under skin. Make a pocket, using a sawing motion with boning knife, from center breastbone towards the ribcage and about ⅔ the length of breast. Repeat process with remaining breasts. Set aside.
2. Place grated zucchini in a strainer and squeeze out excess moisture with your hands.
3. In a medium skillet, heat 2 Tablespoons olive oil and butter over medium heat. Sauté scallions until barely tender, stirring constantly, about 1 minute. Add zucchini and sauté until tender-crisp, about 1 minute. Remove from heat and add cheese, breadcrumbs, tarragon, salt and pepper; mix well. Let mixture cool slightly. With a fork, thoroughly blend beaten egg yolk into stuffing. Divide stuffing into 6 portions and cool to room temperature.

4. Adjust rack to center of oven and preheat to 350°F. Brush a large baking pan with 1 Tablespoon olive oil.

5. Spoon stuffing into pockets of chicken breasts. With your fingers, press pockets to seal. Thoroughly rub split garlic over skin of each halved breast. Drizzle remaining 1 Tablespoon olive oil over chicken.

6. Bake for 30 minutes or just until skin starts to turn a very light golden color. Remove from oven and baste with pan juices. Continue to bake, basting frequently with pan juices, until breasts are deep golden, about 30 minutes.

7. Arrange a bed of curly parsley on a platter, arrange breasts on top and serve immediately.

CHICKEN ROLLS WITH TOMATO–MINT SAUCE
Pollo Involto con Salsa di Pomodoro e Menta

A wonderful dish to make when entertaining a crowd. Leaving the skin on the breasts after they are boned will add moisture and make them easier to roll. Chicken breasts can be cooked 1 day ahead; instead of discarding drippings, pour over breasts to keep moist. Cover with foil and refrigerate overnight. Reheat in 250°F oven for 30 minutes.

SERVES 12

4 large chicken breasts (5 pounds)
¼ cup unsalted butter
1 cup finely chopped yellow onion
1 cup grated parsnips (about 2 medium)
8 ounces lean ground pork
4 ounces mortadella or imported ham, finely diced
1 cup fresh breadcrumbs, well packed

2 Tablespoons finely minced fresh sage or 2 teaspoons crumbled dried sage
½ teaspoon salt
½ teaspoon freshly milled black pepper
¼ cup finely minced Italian parsley leaves
2 extra large egg yolks, lightly beaten

1. Wash chicken breasts and blot dry with paper towel. Wrap in plastic and place in freezer for 30 minutes (this makes boning easier). Place 1 breast

on work surface skin side up. Look or feel for a pocket along the broad upper side of breast. Run your index finger in pocket along the upper part of the breast to ribcage and loosen meat.

Insert the tip of a boning knife into pocket between ribcage and meat, keeping the knife as close to the ribcage as possible.

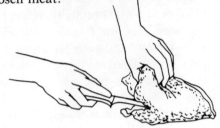

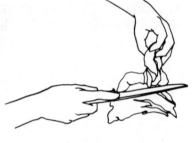

Use a sawing motion to cut meat away from ribcage.

Using knife, scrape meat towards center breastbone up and over the small fillet which should still be attached to one side of the breastbone.

Repeat process on other side of breast.
With the point of the knife, work around the wishbone to loosen and pull the wishbone out.

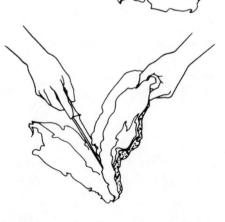

Scrape meat from center bone, being
careful not to tear meat. Remove
breastbone. With the tip of the
boning knife, cut away small fillets
from the side of the breastbone.
Remove tough white tendon by
holding knife against it and pulling
with your fingers. Save bones for
broth or discard.

2. Place the whole chicken breast skin side up between sheets of waxed paper
   and very lightly pound with a mallet to flatten. Place the small fillets between waxed paper and very lightly pound to flatten slightly.

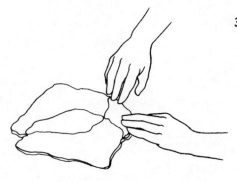

3. Place chicken breast skin side
   down on work surface. Place one
   small fillet vertically down center
   breast and place the other
   horizontally across top edge of
   breast on loose skin. Repeat
   boning procedure with the other 3
   breasts; line up boned breasts on
   work surface.

4. Melt butter in a medium skillet over low heat. Add onion and parsnips
   and cook, stirring frequently, until soft, about 6 minutes. Stir in pork
   and cook, stirring constantly, just until meat loses its pinkness, about 2
   minutes. Add remaining ingredients except egg yolks and mix well. Remove from heat and let mixture cool slightly. Stir egg yolks into mixture
   and blend thoroughly with a fork. Divide filling into 4 portions in pan.

5. Using a metal spatula, spread
   filling evenly over breasts.

Loosely roll into jelly roll shape; do not roll too tightly or breast will split in baking.

Sew closed with kitchen thread. Make sure you sew both ends so that filling will not come out during baking.

TO COOK

¼ cup olive oil

3 Tablespoons unsalted butter

1 large yellow onion (10 ounces), halved and sliced into ½-inch pieces

4 large carrots (8 ounces), trimmed, peeled, halved and quartered

½ teaspoon salt

½ teaspoon freshly milled black pepper

1 cup dry vermouth

2 cups coarsely chopped canned Italian plum tomatoes, juice included

2 Tablespoons finely minced fresh mint or 2 teaspoons crumbled dried mint

1 bunch curly parsley sprigs (garnish)

1. Adjust rack to center of oven and preheat to 350°F.
2. In a large ovenproof sauté pan, heat olive oil over medium heat until haze forms, then add butter. Very quickly sauté chicken rolls on all sides until very lightly golden. Remove and set aside.
3. Remove pan from heat and arrange onion and carrots in a single layer in bottom of pan. Place rolls in prepared pan with seam side down. Sprinkle with salt and pepper. Pour vermouth over chicken. Cover pan and bake for 1 hour, basting with pan juices every 15 minutes.
4. Remove from oven, transfer chicken rolls to platter and cover with foil.
5. Remove most of the pan drippings from pan, leaving about 3 Tablespoons. Leave onion and carrots in pan.
6. Place pan over medium heat and add tomatoes. Cook sauce, stirring frequently and scraping bottom of pan to loosen any fragments that might be stuck, for 15 minutes. Add mint and cook for an additional 5 minutes. Taste sauce and season with additional salt and pepper if needed.
7. Transfer sauce to food processor fitted with metal blade. Run machine nonstop until sauce is finely pureed. (If you do not have a processor, strain sauce through a food mill.) Transfer sauce to pan and keep warm over low heat.
8. Place chicken rolls on a cutting board and remove thread. Cut into ½-inch slices and arrange on a platter in a slightly overlapping pattern. Garnish with a border of curly parsley sprigs. Serve sauce separately.

BRAISED CHICKEN WITH TOMATO AND OLIVES
Pollo alla Cacciatora

This dish just bursts with robust Neapolitan flavor. A savory and delicious accompaniment would be Rice with Eggs and Cheese, page 127.

SERVES 4

1 frying chicken (3 pounds), cut into 8 pieces
½ cup Wondra flour
1 teaspoon salt
½ teaspoon freshly milled black pepper
5 Tablespoons olive oil
½ cup finely chopped yellow onion
1 teaspoon finely minced garlic
1 large red or green bell pepper (8 ounces), halved, cored and thinly sliced

½ cup dry vermouth
1 cup canned Italian plum tomatoes, coarsely chopped, including a little juice
1 Tablespoon minced fresh basil or 1 teaspoon crumbled dried basil
1 large bay leaf
½ cup oil-cured black olives (about 12), pitted and quartered

1. Wash chicken parts in cold water and blot dry with paper towel.
2. In a shallow bowl, combine flour, salt and pepper. Dredge chicken pieces in flour mixture and shake off excess (dredge just before sautéing or coating will become gummy).
3. In a large sauté pan, heat olive oil over medium-high heat until haze forms. Place all of the chicken pieces in pan skin side down and sauté until lightly golden on both sides. Remove and set aside. Pour off most of the pan drippings, leaving about 2 Tablespoons. Add onion, turn heat down to medium and cook, stirring constantly, until lightly golden, about 5 minutes. Add garlic and continue to cook, stirring constantly, until soft but not brown, about 1 minute. Add pepper and cook, stirring frequently, until barely tender when tested with fork. Add vermouth, turn heat to high and cook until liquid is slightly reduced, about 5 minutes.
4. Return chicken to pan and spoon most of the pepper-onion mixture on top. Add tomatoes, basil and bay leaf. Cover pan, turn heat to low and cook, basting frequently, until the juice runs clear when thigh is pierced with the tip of a small knife, about 30 minutes.
5. Preheat oven to 200°F. Transfer chicken to an ovenproof platter and place in oven to keep warm, leaving sauce in pan.

6. Discard bay leaf and turn heat to high. Cook sauce, stirring constantly, until slightly thickened, about 10 minutes. Stir in the olives and cook for an additional 2 minutes. Pour sauce over chicken and serve immediately.

BUTTERFLIED HERBED CHICKEN
Pollo alla Genovese

Basting with the herbed mixture during baking gives this dish its distinctive flavor. If you are a garlic lover, substitute 2 Tablespoons finely minced garlic for shallots. For an elegant presentation, serve on a bed of Zucchini with Roasted Peppers, page 256.

SERVES 6 TO 8

2 whole frying chickens, 2½ pounds each	1 heaping Tablespoon Dijon mustard
3 Tablespoons unsalted butter, room temperature	¼ cup fresh lemon juice
3 Tablespoons finely chopped shallots	½ teaspoon salt
2 Tablespoons minced fresh rosemary or 1 teaspoon powdered rosemary	½ teaspoon freshly milled black pepper
	1 small bunch curly parsley sprigs (optional garnish)

1. Adjust rack to center of oven and preheat to 350°F.

2. Wash chickens and blot dry with paper towel. To butterfly, place one chicken on work surface with breast side down. Using poultry shears, snip through one side of neck and down backbone. Snip along other side of backbone down to the tail. Discard backbone or save for making broth. Turn chicken over and clip wing tips off at the first joint. Flatten center breastbone by pounding with the palm of your hand. Turn chicken over again (skin side down) and slip out breastbone with a small sharp knife, being careful to keep skin intact.

3. Turn chicken (skin side up). Using index finger, loosen skin from flesh of chicken breasts, thighs and drumsticks; be careful not to puncture skin. Repeat entire procedure with the other chicken.

4. Combine remaining ingredients except parsley in a small bowl and mix well with a spoon. Reserve ¼ cup of the herbed mixture for basting.

5. With a small metal spatula or butter knife, spread mixture smoothly between meat and skin.
6. Place chicken skin side up on a rack in a shallow roasting pan. Using a small pastry brush, spread ⅓ of the reserved herb mixture over chicken. Bake for 20 minutes. Turn chicken over and spread another third of the herbed mixture on inside surface of chicken. Roast another 20 minutes. Turn chicken again (skin side up) and spread remaining herb mixture on top. Continue roasting until tender and golden brown, about 30 minutes (total cooking time is about 70 minutes). Using poultry shears, cut into quarters.
7. To serve, arrange on a platter and garnish with curly parsley sprigs, or arrange on a bed of sautéed red peppers and zucchini.

STUFFED CHICKEN LEGS
Coscie di Pollo Ripieni

Each chicken leg with thigh must weigh at least 7 to 8 ounces, so that it will be simple to bone and there will be enough meat left for stuffing. This dish is easy to eat with a knife and fork, because there are virtually no bones, and is an inexpensive and elegant way of serving the dark meat which many people prefer. Chicken can be cooked up to 2 hours before serving, covered and reheated over low heat.

SERVES 8

9 whole chicken legs with thighs, 7 to 8 ounces each (4½ pounds)
8 ounces Italian sweet sausage
2 Tablespoons unsalted butter
½ cup finely chopped scallions
1 cup finely chopped mushrooms (6 ounces)
3 Tablespoons minced Italian parsley leaves

1 Tablespoon minced fresh sage or 1 teaspoon crumbled dried sage
½ teaspoon salt
½ teaspoon freshly milled black pepper
½ cup fresh breadcrumbs, well packed
1 extra large egg, lightly beaten

1. Lay 1 chicken leg skin side down on a cutting board. Pull the leg as straight as possible. With a small paring knife, slit the meat from the thigh bone to the hip joint. Cut the thigh bone from the drumstick and discard. Scrape meat from drumstick bone. Cut off most of bone, leaving 1 inch of drumstick bone intact. Push back into place. Straighten the boned leg. Repeat with remaining legs; set aside.

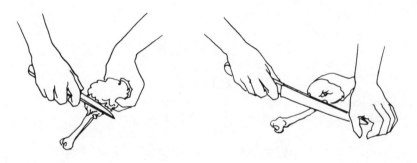

2. Skin one of the boned chicken legs. Coarsely chop meat and set aside for stuffing (can be chopped in food processor fitted with metal blade).
3. Place sausage and ½ cup water in a small saucepan. Cook covered over medium heat for 10 minutes. Let cool in liquid to almost room temperature. Remove casing from sausage; coarsely chop meat (can be chopped in food processor fitted with metal blade).
4. In a 10-inch skillet, melt butter over medium heat. Sauté scallions, stirring constantly, until barely tender, about 1 minute. Add mushrooms and cook, stirring constantly, until all the liquid is evaporated, about 3 minutes. Add sausage and reserved chopped chicken to skillet; cook just until chicken turns opaque, about 1 minute. Remove from heat and stir in parsley and sage. Season with salt and pepper; add breadcrumbs and mix well. Add lightly beaten egg and thoroughly blend into stuffing with a fork. Divide filling into 8 portions in pan; cool to room temperature.
5. Line up all the boned chicken legs on work surface with skin side down. Spoon 1 Tablespoon of stuffing into the cavity of one drumstick; spread

another Tablespoon down the center of the thigh, leaving a ¾-inch margin of meat all around. Pull the skin of the thigh up and around the stuffing to enclose completely. With kitchen twine, tie thigh and upper portion of leg at 1-inch intervals; do not tie too tightly or filling will come out during cooking. Repeat with remaining legs.

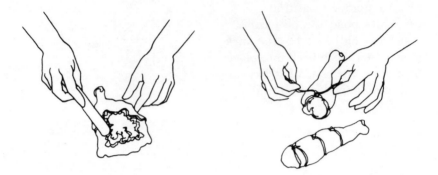

TO COOK

3 Tablespoons olive oil
2 Tablespoons unsalted
    butter
1½ cups thinly sliced scallions
1 teaspoon salt

½ teaspoon freshly milled
    black pepper
½ cup dry white wine
½ to 1 cup chicken broth

1. In a large sauté pan, heat olive oil over medium heat until haze forms, then add butter. Add the chicken legs and sauté on all sides until very lightly golden. Remove chicken and pour off most of the pan drippings, leaving about 2 Tablespoons. Add scallions and sauté until barely tender, scraping the bottom of pan with a wooden spoon to loosen any fragments that might be stuck. Return chicken to pan and season with salt and pepper. Add wine and ½ cup of the chicken broth. Turn heat to low and cook covered, basting frequently with pan juices, for an additional 25 minutes; if liquid evaporates during cooking, add a little more broth.
2. Transfer chicken to a platter and remove twine. Skim off any surface fat from pan with a large spoon. Pour remaining juices over chicken and serve at once.

TO CARVE A SMALL ROAST CHICKEN

Roast chicken (up to 3½ pounds) is easy to carve, provided you have the proper tools. Use a long pointed knife and a pair of poultry or kitchen shears for the following carving method.

1. Place chicken on a cutting board with breast side up. Bend the leg outwards and, with the tip of a knife, slice through the skin between the hip joint and breast to remove the whole leg (leaving thigh and drumstick in one piece). Repeat with the other leg.

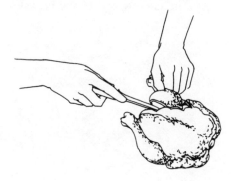

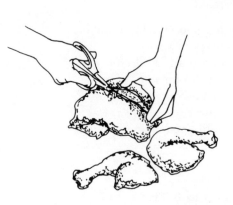

2. Turn chicken over on cutting board (breast side down). To remove backbone, use a pair of poultry or kitchen shears and snip through one side of neck and down backbone. Snip along other side of backbone down to tail; discard bone.

3. Split the bird in two by cutting straight down along the center of the breastbone with knife. Remove

the breastbone (which is now in two pieces) and trim away the flat piece of cartilage that is attached to the narrow end of the breast.

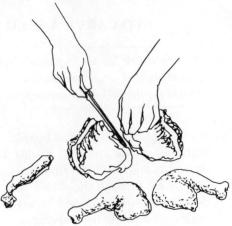

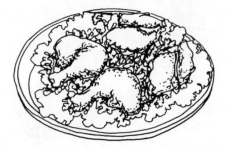

4. To serve, arrange quartered chicken on platter with skin side up.

ROAST CHICKEN WITH DRIED WILD MUSHROOMS
Pollo al Forno con Funghi Secchi

I prefer using a small fryer rather than a roasting chicken for this recipe, because it is moister, it cooks faster and it is less expensive. If entertaining 4 to 6 people, roast 2 chickens.

SERVES 2 TO 4

1 whole frying chicken (2½ to 3 pounds)
1 large clove garlic, split
1 large lemon, washed, dried and cut in half crosswise
1 Tablespoon minced fresh sage or 1 teaspoon crumbled dried sage
1 teaspoon salt

½ teaspoon freshly milled black pepper
½ ounce dried porcini mushrooms
2 Tablespoons unsalted butter
2 Tablespoons finely minced shallots

1. Adjust rack to center of oven and preheat to 400°F.
2. Remove fat from the rear cavity of the chicken. Cut off wing tips at the first joint. Rinse chicken under cold water and blot dry inside and out with paper towels. Rub bird inside and out with split garlic, then place

garlic in cavity. Rub outside of bird with ½ lemon. Squeeze the other half inside chicken and leave in cavity. Sprinkle with sage, salt and pepper. Truss chicken with kitchen twine (if you do not know how to truss, just tie legs and wings in place with twine).

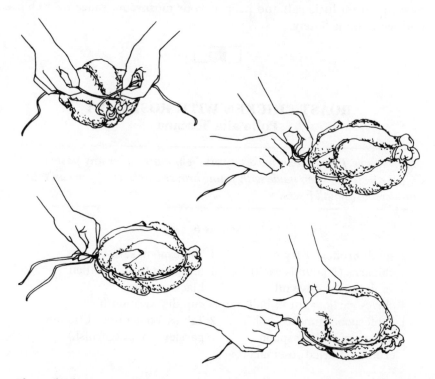

3. Place chicken on its side on a rack in a shallow roasting pan. Roast for 15 minutes. Turn chicken on its other side and roast another 15 minutes. Remove chicken from oven and lower temperature to 350°F. Place chicken on its back and return to oven. Baste every 15 minutes with pan juices and roast until the skin is nicely browned and crisp, about 1 hour. Transfer chicken to a platter, cool slightly and remove twine. Remove garlic and lemon from rear cavity and discard.

4. While chicken is roasting, soak dried mushrooms in ⅔ cup warm water for 30 minutes. Drain mushrooms in a strainer and reserve liquid. Pour liquid through strainer lined with paper towel to remove sand; set aside. Rinse mushrooms in cold water, blot dry with paper towel and chop finely.

5. Quarter chicken and place on a serving platter (see procedure for carving, page 199). Return chicken to oven and set at 200°F while making sauce.

6. Skim fat from roasting pan. Place pan over medium heat, add 2 Tablespoons mushroom liquid and scrape up any browned fragments in bottom of pan with wooden spoon; set aside.

7. In a 1½-quart saucepan, melt butter over medium heat; sauté shallots, stirring constantly, until tender-crisp, about 2 minutes. Add mushrooms and cook, stirring constantly, for another minute. Stir in mushroom liquid and pan juices; cook sauce, stirring frequently, for an additional 5 minutes. Season with a little salt and pepper. Pour mushroom sauce over chicken and serve immediately.

ROAST CHICKEN WITH ROSEMARY
Pollo alla Toscana

This simple Tuscan dish makes a very light entree after any pasta. It is most succulent when made with young broiler chickens; if you can't find broilers, use small fryers.

SERVES 6

2 small broiler or frying
   chickens (2 pounds each)
3 Tablespoons olive oil
4 cloves garlic, split in half
1 Tablespoon minced fresh
   rosemary or 1 teaspoon
   crumbled dried rosemary

1 Tablespoon salt
1 teaspoon freshly milled
   black pepper
¼ cup dry vermouth
2 Tablespoons minced Italian
   parsley leaves (garnish)

1. Wash chickens and blot dry with paper towels. Cut chickens in half lengthwise with poultry shears. Trim off wing tips at the first joint.
2. Adjust rack to center of oven and preheat to 350°F. Brush the bottom of a large jelly roll pan with 1 Tablespoon of the olive oil.
3. Rub each chicken half on both sides with 2 of the split pieces of garlic, rosemary, salt and pepper. Arrange chickens breast side up in baking pan. Place remaining garlic around chicken. Drizzle remaining olive oil over chicken.
4. Bake for 20 minutes. Turn chicken over (breast side down) and baste with pan juices. Brush half of the vermouth over inside surface of chicken. Return to oven and continue baking for another 20 minutes. Turn chicken again (breast side up) and brush with remaining vermouth. Continue baking, basting twice with pan juices, until golden brown, about 20 minutes (total cooking time is about 1 hour).
5. To serve, cut each piece in half between breast and thigh with poultry shears. Arrange on a platter and garnish with minced parsley.

FISH AND SEAFOOD

FILLETS OF SOLE FLORENTINE
POACHED FISH ROLLS IN TOMATO SAUCE
BAKED HALIBUT STEAKS
SWORDFISH WITH SWEET AND SOUR SAUCE
BAKED SWORDFISH STEAKS
COD STEW

CLEANING MUSSELS

MUSSELS WITH HOT TOMATO SAUCE

CLEANING SQUID

FISH SOUP
SEAFOOD SALAD

Whether it was on the channel of the Manasquan River or deep-sea fishing in the Atlantic Ocean, some things never seemed to change. Standing between Uncle Bill and Uncle Henry, two perfectly outfitted fishermen who always seemed to have the latest, most intricate equipment, would be my father, holding an antiquated rod and reel. As the day progressed, Uncle Bill and Uncle Henry would good-naturedly tease my father about his outdated equipment and spend a great deal of time untangling their lines. My father, on the other hand, would take a different approach—he would tilt his hat over his eyes, assume a comfortable position and fall asleep until he felt a tug on the line. At the end of the day, my father would always take the prize for catching the biggest fish.

The fish were packed in ice, brought home, scaled and cooked that night or, at the latest, the next day. As he scaled the fish, my father would say to me, "Smell the fish, Anna, it smells of the sea. Look at these clear, bright eyes. That is what you look for when you buy fish."

Friends and neighbors anxiously awaited my father's return from a fishing trip. I was the daughter chosen to deliver the catch, always with specific directions: "Cook it today!"

The crisp, clear scent of the sea is the same smell one should look for in selecting a seafood store. When shopping, don't be afraid to let your nose interview the fish. Freshness is the key to quality. For this, a reliable fish dealer is your best guarantee.

FILLETS OF SOLE FLORENTINE
Pesce alla Fiorentina

This tasty Florentine specialty can be completely assembled up to 5 hours before baking. Cover dish with plastic wrap and refrigerate until ready to bake.

SERVES 6

3½ pounds spinach
6 thin slices fillet of sole, preferably lemon sole (about 1½ pounds)
1 Tablespoon grated lemon rind
1½ cups fresh breadcrumbs, well packed
2 Tablespoons olive oil
2 Tablespoons unsalted butter
1 cup thinly sliced scallions

1 teaspoon minced garlic
¼ cup minced Italian parsley leaves
1 teaspoon salt
½ teaspoon freshly milled black pepper
1 Tablespoon unsalted butter, softened
2 Tablespoons (approx.) olive oil
1 large lemon, sliced into wedges (optional garnish)

1. Stem spinach and wash several times in lukewarm water to remove sand. Place spinach in a 5-quart pot and cover (do not add water; the final rinse water clinging to the leaves will be sufficient to steam them). Cook covered over medium heat until spinach is limp, about 3 minutes. Transfer to a colander, refresh under cold water and drain well. Squeeze out excess moisture with your hands. Finely chop spinach (can be chopped in food processor fitted with metal blade). Set aside.

2. Wash fillets in cold water and blot dry with paper towel. If fillets are more than ½ inch thick, pound lightly between sheets of waxed paper to flatten. Line up fillets on work surface with broad ends facing you.

3. In a small bowl, combine lemon rind with breadcrumbs. Remove 6 Tablespoons of the mixture and reserve.

4. In a large skillet, heat 2 Tablespoons olive oil over medium heat until haze forms, then add 2 Tablespoons butter. Add scallions and sauté, stirring constantly, until barely tender, about 2 minutes. Add garlic and sauté, stirring constantly, until soft but not brown, about 1 minute. Add spinach and sauté, stirring constantly, until well combined, about 1 minute. Add breadcrumb mixture, parsley, salt and pepper. Cook, stirring constantly, until no moisture is left in bottom of pan, about 1 minute. Remove from heat and let cool slightly.

5. Grease bottom and sides of a 9 × 11-inch baking dish with softened butter.

Sprinkle 3 Tablespoons of the reserved breadcrumb mixture evenly in bottom of baking dish. Spoon ⅔ of the spinach mixture evenly over breadcrumb mixture and spread with metal spatula. Set aside.

6. With a metal spatula, spread remaining spinach mixture (about 2 heaping Tablespoons) over each fillet. Starting with the broad ends, roll fillets up tightly and secure with toothpicks. Arrange fillets seam side down on bed of spinach. Sprinkle top of fillets with remaining 3 Tablespoons of breadcrumb mixture.

7 When ready to bake, adjust rack to center of oven and preheat to 350°F.

8. Just before placing baking dish in oven, drizzle about ½ teaspoon olive oil over each rolled fillet. Bake uncovered until fish barely flakes when tested with a fork, about 25 to 30 minutes.

9. Very carefully remove toothpicks and rearrange rolls seam side down on bed of spinach.

10. To serve, slice spinach in between fillets and lift out with a metal spatula, so that each portion will have a rolled fillet on top of a bed of spinach. Garnish each plate with a lemon wedge and serve immediately.

POACHED FISH ROLLS IN TOMATO SAUCE
Rollatini di Pesce al Pomodoro

The fillets are stuffed, rolled and poached in tomato sauce. Most succulent!

SERVES 6

TOMATO SAUCE

¼ cup olive oil
1 cup thinly sliced scallions
2 teaspoons finely minced garlic
1 can (35 ounces) Italian plum tomatoes, coarsely chopped, including juice (can be chopped in food processor fitted with metal blade)

1 teaspoon salt
½ teaspoon freshly milled black pepper
½ teaspoon sugar
1½ Tablespoons minced fresh basil or 1½ teaspoons crumbled dried basil

In a large sauté pan, heat olive oil over medium-high heat until haze forms. Add scallions and sauté, stirring constantly, until barely tender, about 2 minutes. Add garlic and sauté, stirring constantly, until soft but not brown, about 1 minute. Stir in remaining ingredients and cook sauce uncovered, stirring frequently, until slightly thickened, about 20 minutes. Set aside.

TO ASSEMBLE AND COOK

6 slices fillet of sole, each fillet about 6 inches long (about 1½ pounds)
1 cup fine dry breadcrumbs
1 cup small pimiento-stuffed green olives (about 24), well drained and finely chopped

3 Tablespoons minced Italian parsley leaves
½ teaspoon salt
¼ teaspoon freshly milled black pepper
1 extra large egg, lightly beaten

1. Rinse fillets in cold water and blot dry with paper towel. If fillets are more than 8 inches long, slice in half horizontally; if more than ½ inch thick, pound lightly between sheets of waxed paper to flatten.
2. In a shallow bowl, combine breadcrumbs, olives, parsley, salt and pepper. Stir in beaten egg and mix well. Divide filling into 6 portions in bowl.
3. Line up fillets on work surface with broad ends facing you. Using a metal spatula, spread breadcrumb mixture over each fillet. Starting with broad end, roll fillets up tightly and secure with toothpicks.
4. Bring sauce to a boil over high heat, then turn down to low. Arrange rolled fillets seam side down in a single layer in pan. Simmer rolls over very low heat, partially covered, basting frequently, until easily flaked when tested with a fork, about 10 to 12 minutes.
5. Transfer to a platter and remove toothpicks. Spoon remaining sauce over rolls and serve immediately.

BAKED HALIBUT STEAKS
Pesce Infornata

The thin slices of lemon and sautéed scallion not only add subtle flavor, but also keep the steaks moist while baking. Swordfish, salmon or cod steaks can be substituted for the halibut.

SERVES 6

6 halibut steaks, 1½ inches thick (about 4½ pounds)
2 Tablespoons unsalted butter
2 cups thinly sliced scallions
¼ cup Wondra flour
1 cup fine dry breadcrumbs
6 Tablespoons sesame seed (natural, not hulled)
2 Tablespoons minced fresh tarragon or 2 teaspoons crumbled dried tarragon
¼ cup minced Italian parsley leaves
1 teaspoon salt
1 teaspoon freshly milled black pepper
½ cup (approximately) olive oil
2 large lemons, very thinly sliced
½ cup dry vermouth
1 bunch parsley sprigs (garnish)

1. Rinse steaks in cold water and blot dry with paper towel.
2. In a small skillet, melt butter over low heat and sauté scallions, stirring constantly, until barely tender, about 1 minute; set aside.
3. On a large flat plate, combine flour, breadcrumbs, sesame seed, tarragon, parsley, salt and pepper.
4. Adjust rack to center of oven and preheat to 400°F. Brush the bottom of a large jelly roll pan with 3 Tablespoons olive oil.
5. Brush a very light coating of olive oil on both sides of steaks. Firmly press steaks into flour mixture on both sides. Arrange steaks in a single layer in baking pan and sprinkle each with sautéed scallions. Cover each steak with thin slices of lemon in a slightly overlapping pattern. Drizzle tops of steaks with about 2 Tablespoons olive oil. Bake, basting twice with vermouth, until steaks barely flake when tested with a fork, about 15 to 20 minutes.
6. With 2 metal spatulas, very carefully transfer steaks to a serving platter. Pour pan juices over steaks and garnish platter with parsley sprigs. Serve immediately.

SWORDFISH WITH SWEET AND SOUR SAUCE
Pesce Spada Agrodolce

This piquant tomato sauce keeps the swordfish moist in cooking. If you wish, the sauce can be made earlier in the day, and halibut or cod steaks can be substituted for swordfish.

SERVES 6

SWEET AND SOUR SAUCE

2 Tablespoons olive oil
1 cup thinly sliced yellow onion
2½ cups canned Italian plum tomatoes, well drained and coarsely chopped (can be chopped in food processor fitted with metal blade)
½ teaspoon salt
½ teaspoon freshly milled black pepper
2 Tablespoons imported red wine vinegar
2 Tablespoons sugar
2 Tablespoons minced fresh mint or 2 teaspoons crumbled dried mint

In a medium skillet, heat olive oil over medium heat until haze forms. Add onion, turn heat to low and cook, stirring frequently, until soft but not brown, about 5 minutes. Stir in tomatoes, salt and pepper. Raise heat to medium and cook sauce uncovered, stirring frequently, until slightly thickened, about 15 minutes. Add vinegar, sugar and mint; mix well. Remove from heat and set aside.

TO ASSEMBLE AND COOK

2½ pounds swordfish steaks, about 1 inch thick
½ cup Wondra flour
1 teaspoon salt
½ teaspoon freshly milled black pepper
½ cup vegetable oil, preferably corn
Several fresh mint sprigs (optional garnish)

1. Rinse steaks and blot dry with paper towel. Cut steaks into 6 servings.
2. In a shallow bowl, combine flour with salt and pepper. Dredge steaks on both sides and shake off excess (dredge just before sautéing so coating will not get gummy).
3. In a large sauté pan, heat vegetable oil over medium-high heat until haze forms. Add steaks and quickly sauté on both sides to seal in juices, about 30 seconds on each side. Drain steaks on paper towels. Discard oil from pan. In same pan, evenly spread half of the sweet and sour sauce. Arrange steaks

in a single layer on top of sauce and cover with remaining sauce. Cook steaks, covered, just until fish flakes when tested with a fork, about 10 minutes.

4. To serve, arrange steaks on a large platter and spoon sauce over each. Garnish with mint sprigs and serve immediately.

BAKED SWORDFISH STEAKS
Pesce Spada al Forno

Succulent swordfish steaks are baked in a bed of aromatic vegetables accented with thyme and dry white wine. Halibut, salmon or cod steaks can be substituted.

SERVES 6

6 Tablespoons unsalted butter
1 cup finely chopped yellow onion
2 cups carrot cut into ¼-inch cubes
2 cups celery, strings removed, cut into ¼-inch cubes
1 Tablespoon grated lemon rind
3 Tablespoons fresh lemon juice
2 Tablespoons minced fresh thyme or 2 teaspoons crumbled dried thyme

1 teaspoon salt
½ teaspoon freshly milled black pepper
2½ pounds swordfish steaks, about 1 inch thick
½ cup Wondra flour
½ teaspoon salt
½ teaspoon freshly milled black pepper
½ cup vegetable oil, preferably corn
½ cup dry white wine

1. Adjust rack to center of oven and preheat to 350°F.
2. Melt butter in a large skillet over low heat. Add onion and sauté, stirring constantly, until soft but not brown, about 5 minutes. Add carrot, celery, lemon rind and juice. Increase heat to medium-high and sauté, stirring constantly, until mixture is soft and slightly glazed, about 10 minutes. Stir in thyme, 1 teaspoon salt, ½ teaspoon pepper and remove from heat. Spread half of the vegetable mixture evenly in the bottom of a 10 × 14-inch baking dish.

3. Rinse steaks and blot dry with paper towel. Cut steaks into 6 servings.
4. In a shallow bowl, combine flour with remaining salt and pepper. Dredge steaks on both sides and shake off excess (dredge just before sautéing or flour coating will get gummy).
5. In a large skillet, heat vegetable oil over medium-high heat until haze forms. Add steaks and quickly sauté on both sides to seal in juices, about 30 seconds on each side. Drain steaks on paper towels.
6. Arrange steaks in a single layer on top of the vegetable mixture. Spread remaining vegetable mixture evenly over each steak. Pour wine over vegetable mixture.
7. Cover dish tightly with foil and bake for 15 minutes. Remove foil and spoon some of the pan juices over vegetable mixture. Bake uncovered until fish barely flakes when tested with a fork, about 5 to 10 minutes. Serve immediately.

COD STEW
Merluzzo in Umido

A fabulous one-dish meal, prepared with a minimum of fuss and savored by fish lovers.

SERVES 6

3 pounds cod fillets, 1½ inches thick
6 Tablespoons olive oil
1 large yellow onion (8 ounces), cut into ½-inch slices
5 large celery ribs (10 ounces), strings removed, cut into 2-inch lengths
3 large Idaho potatoes (1½ pounds), peeled and sliced into ½-inch rounds
1 teaspoon salt

1 teaspoon freshly milled white pepper
4 large leeks (8 ounces), trimmed, halved lengthwise and thoroughly washed
½ cup jumbo Greek-style green olives (about 10), pitted and quartered (see note)
2 Tablespoons dark raisins
2 Tablespoons pine nuts (pignoli)
¼ cup water

1. Rinse fillets with cold water and blot dry with paper towel. Cut fillets into 3-inch strips. Set aside.
2. Drizzle 4 Tablespoons olive oil in bottom of 6-quart Dutch oven. Place onion in a single layer in pan. Arrange celery in a single layer on top of onion.

Place sliced potatoes on top and sprinkle with half of the salt and pepper. Arrange leeks in a single layer over potatoes. Place cod fillets in a single layer on top of leeks. Sprinkle olives between pieces of fish. Scatter raisins and pine nuts on top of fish and season with remaining salt and pepper. Drizzle remaining 2 Tablespoons olive oil over fish and add water.

3. Cover pan and cook over medium-low heat, basting frequently with cooking liquid, until potatoes are cooked when tested with the tip of a fork, about 30 to 40 minutes. Check cooking liquid frequently; if the Dutch oven is not a heavy one, you may have to add a few more tablespoons of water to keep mixture moist.

4. To serve, use two large serving spoons to carefully lift each portion into individual bowls. Spoon a little of the pan juices on top and serve immediately.

Note: Greek olives can be purchased in gourmet or Italian specialty shops. If unavailable, substitute bottled jumbo Spanish olives; drain well before pitting and slicing.

CLEANING MUSSELS

Buy mussels only when you can find small to medium ones; large mussels tend to be rather tough. Always buy a few more than the recipe calls for, to allow for discarding any that are open or that do not open after steaming.

Using a stiff wire brush, scrub mussels under running water to remove any dirt or foreign matter clinging to shell. With a small paring knife, cut or pull off the "beards" (looks like a twisted fibre connected to inside of shell). Discard any mussels that are open. Rinse again in cold water. Place mussels in a large pail, cover with cold water and add 2 Tablespoons salt. Sprinkle with 2 Tablespoons cornmeal or oatmeal. The mussels will open in the cold water and feed on the cornmeal or oatmeal; this will remove a considerable amount of the sandy residue that shellfish of this kind usually have. Soak mussels for at least 2 hours. Rinse again in cold water and drain well in a colander. Place mussels in a single layer in a large skillet with 1 cup water. Cover and bring to a boil over high heat just until they open, about 2 minutes. As soon as they are open, transfer with tongs to colander. Discard any mussels that do not open. If you are preparing a large number of mussels, steam in two batches. Let mussels cool slightly before removing them from their shells. Place in a strainer and drain well.

MUSSELS WITH HOT TOMATO SAUCE
Cozze con Pomodoro Piccante

Make this dish for guests who have a passion for mussels, and watch them devour every mouthful. Serve with crusty Italian bread for dunking in the sauce. You can also substitute squid for the mussels; see note at end of recipe.

SERVES 6

HOT TOMATO SAUCE

¼ cup olive oil
¼ cup unsalted butter
1 cup finely chopped yellow onion
1½ teaspoons finely minced garlic
2 cans (35 ounces each) Italian plum tomatoes, coarsely chopped, juice included (can be chopped in two batches in food processor fitted with metal blade)

2 large bay leaves
2 Tablespoons minced fresh basil or 2 teaspoons crumbled dried basil
1 teaspoon sugar
1 teaspoon salt
1 teaspoon crushed red pepper flakes
⅓ cup fresh lemon juice
½ cup dry vermouth

In a large sauté pan, heat olive oil over medium heat until haze forms, then add butter. Add onion, turn heat to low and sauté until soft but not brown, stirring frequently, about 5 minutes. Add garlic and cook, stirring constantly, until soft but not brown, about 2 minutes. Stir in tomatoes, bay leaves, basil, sugar, salt and red pepper. Bring sauce to a boil over high heat. Lower heat to medium and cook sauce uncovered, stirring frequently, until slightly thickened, about 45 minutes. Add lemon juice and vermouth. Turn heat to high and cook, stirring constantly, until slightly reduced, about 5 minutes.

TO ASSEMBLE AND COOK

6½ pounds medium mussels (see directions for cleaning and shelling, page 212)

2 Tablespoons minced Italian parsley leaves

1. Add shelled mussels to heated sauce. Turn heat to medium-high and cook, stirring constantly, for 5 minutes (do not cook any longer or mussels will toughen). Remove from heat and discard bay leaves. Add parsley and mix well.

2. To serve, ladle into individual bowls and accompany with crusty Italian
bread.

Note: You can substitute 3 pounds of squid for mussels. Follow directions for
cleaning and slicing squid. Add to sauce and cook over low heat partially covered, stirring frequently, until squid is tender when tested by tasting, about 50
minutes.

CLEANING SQUID

Grasp the tentacles with one hand.
Hold the body sac in the other hand.
Pull firmly but gently to remove the
tentacles together with the innards
and ink sac (the ink sac will still be
attached to the tentacles).

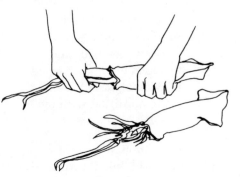

Cut the tentacles just above the eyes
and discard innards from the eyes
down.

Push the beak out from the center of
the tentacles and slice off. Under cold
running water, peel off as much of
the skin on the tentacles as will come
off. Cut the tentacles into 1-inch
pieces and set aside.

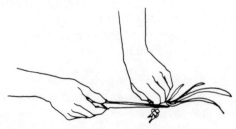

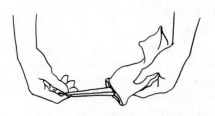

Pull out the transparent quill from the body sac and discard. Thoroughly wash out the inside of the sac.

Gently pull off and reserve the flaps attached to the body sac to avoid tearing the sac. Peel the speckled membrane from the flaps; peel the membrane from the body sac under cold running water.

Slice the sac into ½-inch-wide rings. Wash the tentacles, flaps and sliced rings under cold running water. Transfer to strainer and blot thoroughly dry with paper towel.

FISH SOUP
Zuppa di Pesce

Every Italian family has its own recipe for Zuppa di Pesce. Even my husband, who is not a fish lover, adores it. A good fish stock is the most important ingredient in this dish. Any type of white fish, such as sea bass, snapper, halibut steaks or fresh cod steaks, can be substituted for the haddock or tilefish.

SERVES 6

FISH STOCK

7 Tablespoons olive oil
1 large leek (5 ounces), trimmed, halved lengthwise, washed thoroughly and finely chopped
½ cup finely chopped carrots
½ cup finely chopped celery
½ cup dry vermouth
2½ pounds fish heads, eyes removed

3½ cups water
1 large bay leaf
1 Tablespoon minced fresh thyme or 1 teaspoon crumbled dried thyme
2 teaspoons salt
1 teaspoon freshly milled black pepper

1. In a 6-quart stockpot, heat olive oil over medium heat until haze forms. Sauté leek, carrot and celery, stirring constantly, until soft but not brown, about 5 minutes. Add vermouth, turn heat to high and bring to a boil. Boil briskly for 30 seconds. Add fish heads, water, bay leaf, thyme, salt and pepper. Turn heat down to low and cook stock uncovered, stirring frequently, for 50 minutes. Remove from heat, cover pan, and let stock rest for at least 1 hour so that all the flavors meld together.
2. With a pair of tongs, remove large pieces of bone from stock and discard. Strain stock through the coarse disc of a food mill set over a large bowl. Make sure you extract all the juices from the fish trimmings as well as the vegetables before discarding them. Scrape the bottom of the food mill periodically with a rubber spatula.

Note: Stock can be made up to 2 days ahead, covered and refrigerated until needed. It can also be placed in containers and frozen up to 1 month.

TO COOK

1½ cups Italian plum tomatoes, coarsely chopped, juice included (can be chopped in food processor fitted with metal blade)

1 pound squid, cleaned and sliced (see directions, page 214)

2 dozen littleneck clams

2 pounds tilefish steaks, 2 inches thick, cut into 3-inch serving pieces

2 pounds fillet of haddock, cut into 3-inch serving pieces

8 ounces medium shrimp, shelled and deveined

1 large loaf Italian bread, sliced and toasted

2 Tablespoons minced Italian parsley leaves (garnish)

1 Tablespoon grated lemon rind (garnish)

1. Transfer fish stock to a 5-quart sauté pan. Add tomatoes and squid. Cook partially covered over low heat, stirring frequently, until squid is tender when tasted, about 50 minutes.

2. While squid is cooking, scrub clams with a stiff brush under cold running water. Place clams in a large skillet with just enough water to cover the bottom. Cover pan and place over high heat until clams open, about 1 to 2 minutes; discard any clams that do not open. Remove clams from their shells and set aside.

3. Add tilefish (or the thickest fish used) to sauté pan. Spoon stock over fish and cook uncovered over low heat, basting frequently, for 2 minutes. Add haddock; continue basting and cooking for another 3 minutes. Add shrimp and cook just until they turn pink, about 3 minutes. Total cooking time for tilefish and haddock is about 6 to 8 minutes, or until fish barely flakes when tested with a fork.

4. Add clams, spoon stock over and remove from heat. Taste stock and season with additional salt and pepper, if needed.

5. To serve, place 2 slices of toasted bread in each large individual soup bowl. Place fish and shellfish over bread and spoon stock on top of each portion. Combine parsley and lemon; sprinkle on top of each portion and serve immediately.

SEAFOOD SALAD
Insalata di Gamberi e Pettine

Beat the heat in style with this lovely seafood salad, which can be the highlight of any summertime meal. It can also be served as a first course. Shrimp and scallops can be cooked a day ahead and packed separately in jars with ice water and lemon wedges. Drain thoroughly and blot dry with paper towel before tossing with dressing. You can substitute 1 pound of cooked jumbo lump crabmeat for either of the seafoods.

SERVES 6

1 teaspoon salt
1 pound medium shrimp, shelled and deveined
1 teaspoon salt
1 pound bay scallops, thoroughly washed to remove sand
1½ cups thinly sliced celery, strings removed

½ cup medium-size pimiento-stuffed green olives (about 18), well drained and halved
1 large head romaine lettuce (1½ pounds) (garnish)

1. In a 4-quart pot, bring 2 quarts of water to a boil and add 1 teaspoon salt. Place shrimp in pot and cover. As soon as water returns to a boil, uncover and cook shrimp until they turn pink, about 2 minutes; do not overcook or shrimp will be tough. Drain in a strainer, rinse under cold water and blot dry with paper towel.
2. In a 10-inch skillet, bring 2 cups of water to a boil and add 1 teaspoon salt. Place scallops in pan in a single layer and cover. As soon as water returns to a boil, uncover and cook scallops for 1 minute. Transfer to strainer, rinse under cold water and drain well; blot dry with paper towel.
3. Two hours before serving, combine shrimp, scallops, celery and olives in a large bowl.
4. Discard any bruised outer leaves from romaine. Trim tough bottom ends and wash several times in cold water to remove sand. Spin dry in a salad spinner or blot dry with paper towel. Set aside.

DRESSING

½ cup olive oil
1 Tablespoon grated lemon
  rind
¼ cup fresh lemon juice
½ teaspoon sugar
1 teaspoon salt

½ teaspoon freshly milled
  white pepper
3 Tablespoons minced Italian
  parsley leaves
3 Tablespoons snipped chives

1. In a small bowl, combine all ingredients and mix well with a wire whisk (can be done in food processor fitted with metal blade).
2. Pour dressing over seafood, cover with plastic wrap and refrigerate for 2 hours (do not marinate any longer or the seafood will get soggy).
3. To serve, arrange lettuce leaves around edge of a large platter. Toss seafood salad again and transfer to center of platter; serve immediately.

VEGETABLES

ARTICHOKE HEARTS WITH PEAS

FRIED ARTICHOKE HEARTS

ASPARAGUS AND CARROTS WITH SESAME SEED

ASPARAGUS AND TOMATOES

SAUTÉED BEET GREENS

BROCCOLI WITH CHESTNUTS

SAUTÉED BROCCOLI AND MUSHROOMS

BROCCOLI WITH OLIVES

BRUSSELS SPROUTS WITH FENNEL

BAKED CELERY AND MUSHROOMS

BRAISED CELERY, CARROTS AND ROMAINE

FRIED CELERY

SAUTÉED CUCUMBERS

SAUTÉED EGGPLANT

EGGPLANT MANICOTTI

CURLY ENDIVE WITH PROSCIUTTO

BRAISED ESCAROLE

STUFFED ESCAROLE

FENNEL AND MUSHROOMS

SAUTÉED GREEN BEANS AND CHERRY TOMATOES

GREEN BEANS WITH TOMATO SAUCE

SAUTÉED MUSHROOMS

PARSNIPS AND CARROTS

FLUFFY POTATO PIE

POTATOES WITH PANCETTA AND ROSEMARY

PARSLEYED POTATOES

SAUTÉED PUMPKIN

SWISS CHARD WITH TOMATOES

BAKED ZUCCHINI

ZUCCHINI WITH GARLIC AND TOMATO

ZUCCHINI WITH ROASTED PEPPERS

My father lovingly tended his garden, from the early lettuces, green beans, eggplant and tomatoes of summer to fall's finale of broccoli, celery and cauliflower. We practically ate right from the garden, and when Mamma called me to pick the vegetables for dinner, that was exactly what she meant!

Vegetables play as important a role in my menus today as they did in the meals of my childhood. I can't recall a dinner Mamma served that didn't have at least two different vegetables. The wide range of vegetables available to us year round provides unending and exciting combinations of color, texture and taste.

Fresh vegetables are used exclusively in these recipes, with the exception of artichoke hearts and tiny green peas, which are available in the frozen food section of most supermarkets.

I offer you the same advice I give my students: In planning a menu, always select two alternative vegetable recipes. List the ingredients needed for each and bring this list along when you do your shopping. If the vegetable of your first choice does not meet your standards of freshness and quality, go with the second choice. Remember, a vegetable which is unavailable today may very well appear in abundance at your greengrocer tomorrow.

ARTICHOKE HEARTS WITH PEAS
Carciofi e Piselli

The distinctive flavoring of prosciutto and fennel truly enhances this dish.

SERVES 8 TO 10

3 Tablespoons olive oil
3 Tablespoons unsalted butter
1 cup finely chopped yellow onion
4 ounces thinly sliced prosciutto or boiled ham, cut into ¼-inch cubes
2 packages (9 ounces each) frozen artichoke hearts, defrosted and well drained

2 packages (9 ounces each) frozen tiny peas, defrosted and well drained
2 Tablespoons minced fresh fennel fronds or ½ teaspoon fennel seed
1 teaspoon salt
½ teaspoon freshly milled black pepper

In a large sauté pan, heat olive oil over medium heat until haze forms, then add butter. Sauté onion, stirring constantly, until barely tender when tested with a fork, about 2 minutes. Add prosciutto or ham and cook, stirring constantly, until soft but not brown, about 1 minute. Add artichoke hearts and mix well with a wooden spoon. Turn heat to low, cover pan and cook, stirring once or twice, until artichokes are barely tender when tested with fork, about 5 minutes. Stir in peas and fennel, cover pan and continue to cook until peas are tender (test by tasting), about 5 minutes. Season with salt and pepper. Transfer vegetables to a serving bowl and serve immediately.

FRIED ARTICHOKE HEARTS
Carciofi Fritti

Not only a savory accompaniment to any chicken, meat or fish dish, but an excellent appetizer as well.

SERVES 8

2 packages (9 ounces each) frozen artichoke hearts
1 teaspoon salt
½ cup Wondra flour
3 large eggs
1 teaspoon salt
½ teaspoon freshly milled black pepper
2 Tablespoons grated lemon rind
2 cups (approximately) fine dry breadcrumbs
2 cups vegetable oil, preferably corn
1 medium lemon, cut into thin wedges (garnish)

1. Rinse frozen artichoke hearts in a strainer under warm running water to defrost. In a medium skillet, bring 2 cups water to a boil and add 1 teaspoon salt. Place artichokes in a single layer in pan and cook, covered, over medium heat until barely tender when tested with a fork, about 3 minutes (watch carefully so that they do not fall apart in pan). Using a pair of tongs, transfer artichoke hearts to a colander. Let cool slightly; blot thoroughly dry with paper towel.
2. Place flour in a shallow bowl. In another shallow bowl, beat eggs with 1 teaspoon salt and pepper. In third bowl, combine lemon rind with breadcrumbs. Dredge artichoke hearts in flour and shake off excess. Lightly coat with egg, letting the excess drip off; thoroughly coat in breadcrumb mixture. Arrange in a single layer on a platter lined with waxed paper. Refrigerate for at least 1 hour to set coating.
3. In a deep 12-inch skillet, heat vegetable oil over medium-high heat until haze forms. Fry artichokes on both sides until lightly golden (you will have to fry in two or three batches; do not crowd pan). Transfer with tongs to paper towels to drain.
4. To serve, arrange on a large platter and garnish with lemon wedges.

ASPARAGUS AND CARROTS WITH SESAME SEED
Asparagi e Carota con Sesamo

In our home, delicious sesame-seeded Italian bread is served every night with dinner. What does one do with the sesame seeds that accumulate at the bottom of the bag?

SERVES 8

1 pound carrots	1½ cups thinly sliced scallions
2 teaspoons salt	1 teaspoon salt
3 pounds asparagus	½ teaspoon freshly milled
3 Tablespoons olive oil	black pepper
2 Tablespoons unsalted	2 Tablespoons sesame seed,
butter	lightly toasted

1. Scrub carrots well. Trim ends and peel with a vegetable peeler. Slice into thin 3 × ½-inch strips. Boil carrots in 2 quarts boiling water with 1 teaspoon salt until barely tender, about 4 minutes. Transfer to a colander, refresh under cold water, drain well and blot dry with paper towel. Set aside.
2. Wash asparagus several times in cold water to get rid of sand. Using a sharp knife, cut off tough part at base of spear. With a vegetable peeler, peel stalks, starting at base of spear and leaving tips intact. Slice stalks diagonally into 3-inch lengths; reserve tips. Half fill a large skillet with water. Bring to a boil, covered, over high heat, then add 1 teaspoon salt. Place asparagus bottoms in pan and cook uncovered until barely tender when tested with the tip of a knife, about 2 minutes. Add tips and cook for another minute. Drain in a colander, refresh under cold water and blot dry with paper towel. (Vegetables can be prepared up to this point several hours ahead and finished off when ready to serve.)
3. In a 12-inch skillet, heat olive oil over medium heat until haze forms, then add butter. Sauté scallions, stirring constantly, until tender-crisp, about 2 minutes. Add asparagus and carrots; sauté very briefly, just until vegetables are coated, about 1 minute. Season with 1 teaspoon salt and pepper. Remove from heat, add sesame seed and toss with vegetables. Transfer to a platter and serve immediately.

ASPARAGUS AND TOMATOES
Asparagi e Pomodoro

To insure even cooking, buy asparagus spears that are all the same size. Asparagus can be cooked earlier in the day and finished off with tomato just before serving.

SERVES 6

2 pounds asparagus (medium size, not jumbo)
1 teaspoon salt
4 plum tomatoes or 2 medium-size ripe tomatoes (10 ounces)

3 Tablespoons olive oil
1¼ cups thinly sliced scallions
1 teaspoon salt
½ teaspoon freshly milled black pepper

1. Wash asparagus several times in cold water to get rid of sand. Using a sharp knife, cut off tough part at base of spear. Peel stalks with a vegetable peeler, starting at base of spear and leaving tips intact. Half fill a large skillet with water. Bring to a boil, covered, over high heat and add 1 teaspoon salt. Add asparagus in one or two layers (they should be covered with water). Boil uncovered until barely tender-crisp when tested with the tip of a knife, about 3 minutes. Drain in a colander, rinse under cold water and blot dry with paper towel. Set aside.
2. Blanch tomatoes in a small pan of boiling water for 1 minute. Transfer to colander and refresh under cold water. Peel tomatoes, squeeze some of the seeds out and chop coarsely.
3. In a large skillet, heat olive oil over medium-high heat until haze forms. Add scallions and sauté, stirring constantly, until tender-crisp, about 1 minute. Add tomatoes, salt, pepper and sauté, stirring constantly, for an additional minute. Add asparagus and sauté, carefully turning in the tomato-scallion mixture with a wooden spoon (you must turn asparagus gently so that tips don't break off). Cook until well coated with tomato-scallion mixture, about 2 minutes; when finished, the asparagus should still be crisp.
4. Transfer to a platter and serve immediately.

SAUTÉED BEET GREENS

Most people throw away the beet greens and stems, but I enjoy them more than the beets themselves.

SERVES 6

Tops and stems from 3 pounds of beets
1 Tablespoon salt
¼ cup olive oil

2 cloves garlic, split in half
1 teaspoon salt
½ teaspoon freshly milled black pepper

1. Wash beet tops several times in cold water to remove sand. Cut stems into 2-inch lengths. Leave green tops whole if about 2 inches in length; if larger, slice in half horizontally.
2. In a 6-quart pot, bring 4 quarts of water to a boil and add 1 Tablespoon salt. Cook stems until barely tender when pierced with a fork, about 25 minutes. Add greens and cook until greens are tender, about 10 minutes. Drain well in a colander and refresh under cold water. Squeeze out excess moisture with your hands.
3. In a 12-inch skillet, heat olive oil over medium heat until haze forms. Add garlic, sauté until lightly golden and discard. Add greens and stems; sauté, stirring constantly, until well coated with olive oil, about 2 minutes. Season with salt and pepper. Transfer to a platter and serve immediately.

BROCCOLI WITH CHESTNUTS
Broccoli con Castagne

Chestnuts add a festive note to broccoli in this fine dish for fall or winter.

SERVES 8

8 ounces dried chestnuts (see note)
1 large or 2 small bunches broccoli (about 2½ to 3 pounds)
1 Tablespoon salt
3 Tablespoons finely chopped shallots

¼ cup olive oil
¼ cup unsalted butter
1 teaspoon salt
½ teaspoon freshly milled black pepper

1. Boil chestnuts in 3 cups boiling water until tender, about 45 minutes. Drain chestnuts in a colander, let cool to room temperature and blot dry with paper towel. Slice thinly and set aside.
2. Remove florets, leaving about 1 inch of stem. Cut or break florets into 1-inch pieces. Wash in cold water, drain and set aside. Remove and discard the coarse leaves from stems and cut off about ½ inch of tough lower part of stalk. Wash stalks thoroughly and peel with a vegetable peeler. Cut stalks in half lengthwise (if stalks are extremely large, cut into quarters), then into 1-inch pieces. Boil stalks in 4 quarts boiling water with 1 Tablespoon salt until barely tender when tested with a fork, about 5 minutes. Add florets and continue cooking until barely tender when tested with fork, about 2 minutes. With a skimmer, transfer broccoli to colander, rinse under cold water and blot dry with paper towel.
3. In a large sauté pan, heat olive oil over medium heat until haze forms, then add butter. Turn heat to low, add shallots, and stir constantly until soft but not brown, about 2 minutes. Add sliced chestnuts and sauté, stirring constantly, until lightly glazed, about 5 minutes. Add broccoli and toss over low heat with a wooden spoon until mixture is well combined and broccoli is warmed through. Season with salt and pepper.
4. Transfer to a platter, spoon most of the chestnuts over broccoli and serve immediately.

Note: Dried chestnuts are available in gourmet and Italian specialty shops. If unavailable, use fresh chestnuts and cook as follows: Using 12 ounces fresh chestnuts, cut an X on the round side of each. Boil in 3 quarts boiling water until shells open, about 15 minutes. Drain chestnuts in a colander; shell and peel them while they are still hot. Place chestnuts in a skillet and add enough water to cover. Cover pan and simmer over low heat until chestnuts are tender when tested with the tip of a knife, about 30 to 35 minutes. Transfer to colander, drain well and cool to room temperature.

SAUTÉED BROCCOLI AND MUSHROOMS
Broccoli e Funghi Saltati

You can almost call this dish an Italian stir-fry!

SERVES 8

1 large bunch broccoli (2 pounds)
¼ cup olive oil
2 large cloves garlic, split in half
12 ounces medium mushrooms, wiped, trimmed and thinly sliced
½ teaspoon salt

½ teaspoon freshly milled black pepper
¼ cup freshly grated Parmigiano cheese

1. Separate broccoli florets from stems. Wash florets and stems separately in cold water. Drain separately in strainers. Cut florets into bite-size pieces. Trim bottoms of stems. Peel stems with a vegetable peeler. Cut in half horizontally, then slice each stem into 2 × ½-inch strips.
2. In a large sauté pan, heat olive oil over medium heat until haze forms. Add garlic and sauté, stirring constantly, until lightly golden; discard. Add broccoli stems and cook, stirring constantly, until barely tender, about 2 minutes. Add florets and continue to sauté, stirring constantly, until tender-crisp, about 3 minutes. Add mushrooms and cook, stirring constantly, until tender-crisp, about 1 minute. Season with salt and pepper and remove from heat.
3. Transfer to a platter, sprinkle with Parmigiano cheese and serve immediately.

BROCCOLI WITH OLIVES
Broccoli ed Oliva

The pungent flavor of black oil-cured olives gives this broccoli dish its excitement.

SERVES 6

1 large bunch broccoli (2 pounds)
1 Tablespoon salt
¼ cup olive oil
1 teaspoon finely minced garlic

¼ cup medium-size oil-cured black olives (about 8), pitted and thinly sliced
1 teaspoon salt
½ teaspoon freshly milled black pepper
3 Tablespoons freshly grated Parmigiano cheese

1. Wash broccoli and drain well. Remove and discard the large coarse leaves; cut off the tough lower part of the stalk (about ½ inch). Peel stalks with a vegetable peeler. If stalks are large, cut lengthwise into halves or quarters. Cook broccoli in 4 quarts of boiling water with 1 Tablespoon salt until stalks are tender when tested with a fork, about 7 minutes. Drain in a colander, refresh under cold water and blot thoroughly dry with paper towel.
2. In a 12-inch skillet, heat olive oil over medium heat until haze forms. Sauté garlic, stirring constantly, until very lightly golden, about 1 minute. Stir in olives and sauté, stirring constantly, just until they puff a little, about 1 minute. Add broccoli, turn heat to low and cook just until broccoli is warmed through. Season with 1 teaspoon salt and pepper.
3. Transfer to a platter and sprinkle with freshly grated Parmigiano cheese. Serve immediately.

BRUSSELS SPROUTS WITH FENNEL
Cavoli di Brusselle e Finocchio

Try to select small Brussels sprouts of uniform size. This dish can be prepared 2 hours ahead of serving, but omit lemon juice and breadcrumbs. Reheat, uncovered, over medium heat, adding juice and crumbs.

SERVES 8

1 small fennel bulb
(1½ pounds) or 2 teaspoons
fennel seed
1½ pounds Brussels sprouts
(1 quart)
1 Tablespoon salt
¼ cup olive oil
½ cup thinly sliced onion

½ teaspoon sugar
1 teaspoon salt
½ teaspoon freshly milled
black pepper
2 Tablespoons fresh lemon
juice
3 Tablespoons fine dry
breadcrumbs

1. Cut off the upper stalks of fennel. With a vegetable peeler, lightly peel outside bulb to remove strings. Slice bulb in half vertically and remove center core using a V cut. Slice thinly lengthwise. (If fresh fennel is unavailable, add fennel seed to skillet with Brussels sprouts.)
2. Wash the Brussels sprouts, trim off tough outer leaves and cut a shallow cross in the bottom of each. In a 5-quart saucepan, bring 4 quarts of water to a boil. Add 1 Tablespoon salt and Brussels sprouts. Cook sprouts, covered, until tender when tested with the tip of a knife inserted in bottom of sprout, about 10 to 15 minutes. Transfer to a colander, refresh under cold water and blot dry with paper towel.
3. In a large sauté pan, heat olive oil over medium heat until haze forms. Add onion and fennel; sauté, stirring frequently, until both are tender-crisp, about 4 minutes. Add Brussels sprouts, sugar, 1 teaspoon salt and pepper; sauté, stirring constantly, for an additional 2 minutes. Stir in lemon juice and breadcrumbs. Cook, stirring constantly, until well combined, about 30 seconds. Transfer to platter and serve immediately.

BAKED CELERY AND MUSHROOMS
Sedano con Funghi al Forno

Most Americans use celery raw, but in Italy it is widely eaten as a cooked vegetable. This combination makes a perfect accompaniment for chicken, veal or fish. The casserole can be completely assembled several hours ahead, covered with plastic wrap and refrigerated until ready to bake.

SERVES 8

1 large or 2 small bunches celery (about 2 pounds)
1 teaspoon salt
1 pound medium mushrooms
½ cup medium-size pitted black olives (about 12), well drained and finely chopped
¾ cup fine dry breadcrumbs
¼ cup freshly grated Romano cheese
¼ cup minced Italian parsley leaves
1 teaspoon salt
½ teaspoon freshly milled black pepper
9 Tablespoons olive oil

1. Separate celery stalks, cut off leaves and trim bottoms of stalks. Using a vegetable peeler, remove coarse strings. Wash celery and cut into 2 × ½-inch strips. Cook in 5 quarts boiling water with 1 teaspoon salt until barely tender when tested with fork, about 8 minutes. Transfer to a colander, refresh under cold water and blot dry with paper towel.
2. Wipe mushrooms with a damp cloth, trim ends and slice thinly.
3. In a shallow bowl, combine remaining ingredients except olive oil. Divide breadcrumb mixture into 4 portions in bowl.
4. Brush a 9 × 11-inch ovenproof baking dish with 1 Tablespoon olive oil. Arrange half of the celery strips in a single layer in dish. Sprinkle one portion of the breadcrumb mixture over celery and drizzle with 2 Tablespoons olive oil. Place half of the sliced mushrooms in a single layer over celery. Sprinkle with another portion of breadcrumb mixture and drizzle with 2 Tablespoons olive oil. Make two more layers, using ingredients in this order: celery, breadcrumb mixture, olive oil, mushrooms, breadcrumb mixture, olive oil.
5. When ready to bake, adjust rack to center of oven and preheat to 350°F. Bake uncovered until lightly golden on top, about 35 minutes. Serve immediately.

BRAISED CELERY, CARROTS AND ROMAINE
Sedano con Carote e Lattuga

Feel free to substitute lettuce, escarole or curly endive for the romaine in this braised mixture, or to use a little of each (see note).

SERVES 6

1 large head romaine lettuce (1½ pounds)
¼ cup olive oil
1 cup thinly sliced yellow onion
5 large celery ribs (4 ounces), strings removed, sliced into thin 2 × ½-inch strips

4 large carrots (6 ounces), peeled and sliced into thin strips same size as celery
1 teaspoon salt
½ teaspoon freshly milled black pepper
2 Tablespoons fine dry breadcrumbs (optional)

1. Separate romaine leaves and trim any bruised tips. Wash several times in lukewarm water to remove grit. Drain well and blot dry with paper towel. Cut leaves crosswise into 1-inch lengths. (If leaves are exceptionally large, slice down the middle before cutting crosswise.)
2. In a 5-quart Dutch oven, heat olive oil over medium heat until haze forms. Add onion, celery and carrots; sauté, stirring frequently, until all three are tender-crisp, about 3 minutes. Stir in romaine and cook, covered, stirring frequently, for 5 minutes. Remove cover and cook until romaine is tender when tested with a fork, about 5 minutes. Season with salt and pepper. There should be just a little liquid left in the pan after vegetables have cooked; if there is too much liquid, raise heat to high, add breadcrumbs and toss until most of the liquid is absorbed. Transfer to a bowl and serve immediately.

Note: This is a great vegetable dish to make when you have different types of salad greens on hand. Don't throw away those outer leaves; just follow the cleaning procedure for romaine. It's also a terrific dish to make at the end of the week when you haven't used up all your salad greens.

FRIED CELERY
Sedano Fritto

You can serve these fried celery sticks as an appetizer or side dish.

SERVES 6

1 large or 2 small bunches of celery (2 pounds)
1 teaspoon salt
1 cup Wondra flour
3 extra large eggs
1½ teaspoons salt

1 teaspoon freshly milled black pepper
2½ cups fine dry breadcrumbs
2 cups vegetable oil, preferably corn

1. Separate celery stalks, cut off leaves and trim bottoms of stalks (save the hearts of celery for salad). Remove coarse strings using a vegetable peeler. Wash celery and cut into 3 × ½-inch strips. Cook in 5 quarts boiling water with 1 teaspoon salt until barely tender when tested with fork, about 8 minutes. Transfer to a colander, refresh under cold water and blot thoroughly dry with paper towel.

2. Place flour in a shallow bowl. In another shallow bowl, beat eggs with 1½ teaspoons salt and pepper. Place breadcrumbs in third shallow bowl. Dredge celery sticks in flour, dip in beaten eggs and then thoroughly coat in breadcrumbs. Refrigerate on a platter lined with waxed paper for at least 1 hour (chilling prevents coating from coming off during frying).

3. In a large sauté pan or deep skillet, heat vegetable oil over medium-high heat until haze forms. Fry celery sticks in three batches until lightly golden on all sides. Drain on paper towels.

4. Arrange fried sticks in an overlapping pattern on a platter and serve immediately.

SAUTÉED CUCUMBERS
Cetrioli Saltati

For a perfect sauté, select dark green, extremely firm cucumbers no more than 6 to 7 inches long.

SERVES 6

4 medium cucumbers
2 Tablespoons olive oil
1 large clove garlic, split in half
2 Tablespoons fine dry breadcrumbs

1 teaspoon salt
½ teaspoon freshly milled black pepper
1 Tablespoon minced Italian parsley leaves (garnish)

1. Wash cucumbers in cold water and dry with paper towel. Peel cucumbers with a vegetable peeler. Cut in half lengthwise and remove seeds with a melon ball scoop or spoon. Trim ends and cut crosswise into ¼-inch slices. Place cucumber slices in a deep bowl, cover with about 5 ice cubes and fill bowl with cold water. Refrigerate at least 1 hour (soaking will insure crispness after sautéing). Drain well in a strainer and blot thoroughly dry with paper towel.
2. In a 12-inch skillet, heat olive oil over medium-high heat until haze forms. Add garlic and sauté, stirring constantly, until lightly golden; discard with a slotted spoon. Add cucumbers and sauté, stirring constantly, until tender-crisp (test by tasting), about 2 minutes. Turn heat to high and add breadcrumbs. Cook, stirring constantly, until no liquid is left in bottom of pan, about 30 seconds. Season with salt and pepper. Transfer to a platter and garnish with minced parsley. Serve immediately.

SAUTÉED EGGPLANT
(Melanzana Saltata)

Select glossy, firm eggplant for this very simple but tasty dish.

SERVES 6

¼ cup olive oil
½ cup finely chopped yellow
  onion
1 medium-size green pepper
  (5 ounces), halved, cored
  and finely chopped
1 large or 2 medium-size
  eggplants (1½ pounds),
  washed, dried, ends
  trimmed, peeled and cut
  into 1-inch cubes
4 canned Italian plum
  tomatoes, well drained,
  halved, seeded and coarsely
  chopped

2 Tablespoons minced fresh
  basil or 2 teaspoons
  crumbled dried basil
1 teaspoon salt
½ teaspoon freshly milled
  black pepper
2 Tablespoons minced Italian
  parsley leaves
½ cup freshly grated
  Parmigiano cheese

1. In a 12-inch skillet, heat olive oil over medium heat until haze forms. Add onion and pepper; sauté, stirring constantly, until soft but not brown, about 3 minutes. Add eggplant and sauté until barely tender when tested with a fork, about 2 to 3 minutes. Stir in tomatoes, basil, salt and pepper. Continue to cook, stirring constantly, until well incorporated, about 2 minutes. Remove from heat; stir in parsley and freshly grated Parmigiano cheese. Transfer to a platter and serve immediately.

EGGPLANT MANICOTTI
Manicotti di Melanzane

These little wrapped bundles are substantial enough for a delicious meat-less main course. Make this Sicilian dish when you can find firm, un-blemished eggplants. Be sure to pick 2 eggplants that are the same shape, so that they will be uniform when rolled. The dish can be prepared up to 6 hours in advance, covered with plastic wrap and refrigerated until ready to bake. If baking right from refrigerator, increase baking time by 10 min-utes.

SERVES 6—MAIN COURSE
SERVES 8—FIRST COURSE

TOMATO SAUCE

2 Tablespoons olive oil
¼ cup finely chopped yellow onion
2 cups canned concentrated crushed tomatoes
1 teaspoon minced fresh basil or ½ teaspoon crumbled dried basil

¼ teaspoon sugar
½ teaspoon salt
¼ teaspoon freshly milled black pepper
1 jar (7 ounces) roasted red peppers or pimientos, well drained and finely chopped

In a 2-quart saucepan, heat olive oil over medium heat until haze forms. Turn heat down to low and sauté onion until soft but not brown, about 3 minutes. Add remaining ingredients except peppers. Turn heat up to medium and cook sauce uncovered, stirring frequently, until slightly thickened, about 10 min-utes. Stir in peppers and cook for an additional 5 minutes. Set aside.

TO PREPARE EGGPLANT

3 Tablespoons olive oil
2 medium eggplants (2¼ pounds)

½ cup olive oil (approximately)

1. Position rack 6 inches from broiler and preheat oven to broil setting. Coat a large jelly roll pan with 3 Tablespoons olive oil.
2. Wash eggplants and dry with paper towel. Trim the tops and bottoms of eggplants, but do not peel. Cut lengthwise into ¼-inch slices, discarding the first and last slice of each eggplant. Lightly brush both sides of each slice with olive oil. Arrange slices in a single layer in pan; do not crowd (if pan is

not large enough, do eggplant in two batches). Broil for 3 minutes on each side or until very lightly golden. Layer slices on paper towel, with more paper towels between layers to absorb some of the moisture. Let eggplant cool slightly while making filling.

FILLING

1½ cups whole milk ricotta cheese

4 ounces whole milk Mozzarella cheese, coarsely grated

¼ cup freshly grated Romano cheese

2 Tablespoons finely minced Italian parsley leaves

2 large egg yolks, lightly beaten

½ teaspoon salt

¼ teaspoon freshly milled white pepper

In a medium bowl, mix ricotta, Mozzarella and Romano cheeses with a fork. Add parsley and mix well. Stir in egg yolks, salt and pepper; mix until well combined.

TO ASSEMBLE AND COOK

3 Tablespoons freshly grated Romano cheese (garnish)

1 Tablespoon minced Italian parsley leaves (garnish)

1. Adjust rack to center of oven and preheat to 350°F.
2. Evenly spread ¼ cup sauce in the bottom of a large jelly roll pan.
3. Line up eggplant slices on a large work surface with short ends facing you. Spoon 1½ Tablespoons filling in the center of each slice. With a metal spatula, spread filling, leaving a ½-inch margin on all sides. Starting with short end, roll up like a jelly roll. Arrange eggplant rolls seam side down in prepared pan. Spoon 1 Tablespoon sauce over each roll.
4. Bake for 25 minutes. Do not fret if the cheese starts to ooze out during the first 10 minutes; the filling will be firm by the time they are finished baking.
5. To serve, arrange in a single layer on a large platter. Sprinkle a little Romano cheese on top of each roll and garnish with minced parsley. Serve with remaining sauce.

CURLY ENDIVE WITH PROSCIUTTO
Scarola Riccia con Prosciutto

Curly endive, in the same family as escarole, is sometimes called curly chicory in the produce markets. It is available most of the year, but is especially good during the winter months. If curly endive is unavailable, substitute 3 pounds spinach with stems removed. Steam spinach until limp, about 3 minutes.

SERVES 6 TO 8

2 large heads curly endive (about 2½ pounds)
2 Tablespoons olive oil
2 Tablespoons unsalted butter
3 Tablespoons finely chopped shallots
4 ounces thinly sliced prosciutto, cut into 2 × ½-inch strips
½ teaspoon salt
½ teaspoon freshly milled black pepper

1. Discard any wilted or bruised leaves from curly endive. Separate leaves, cut off tough bottom ends of greens (about 2 inches) and discard. Slice greens into 3-inch lengths; wash several times in lukewarm water to get rid of grit. Place endive in a 5-quart pot and cover. Do not add water; the final rinse water clinging to the leaves will be sufficient to steam them. Cook, covered, over medium heat until leaves are limp, about 7 to 8 minutes. Transfer to a colander and drain well. Let cool slightly and squeeze out excess moisture with your hands.

2. In a large sauté pan, heat olive oil over medium heat until haze forms, then add butter. Turn heat to low and add shallots. Sauté, stirring constantly, until soft but not brown, about 2 minutes. Add prosciutto and continue to sauté, stirring constantly, until soft, about 1 minute. Add endive and cook partially covered, stirring frequently, until leaves are soft when tested with a fork (test by tasting), about 10 to 15 minutes. Uncover pan and turn heat to high. Cook, stirring constantly, until most of the liquid in the bottom of pan has evaporated, about 1 minute. Season with salt and pepper; remove from heat. Transfer to a bowl and serve immediately.

BRAISED ESCAROLE
Scarola alla Mamma

A good vegetable dish for winter, when escarole is abundant at the produce market. You can substitute curly endive for the escarole. This can be prepared up to 3 hours before serving. Reheat, covered, over low heat, and add breadcrumb mixture just before serving.

SERVES 6 TO 8

2 large heads escarole (about 2½ pounds)
1 teaspoon salt
½ cup fine dry breadcrumbs
2 Tablespoons freshly grated Romano cheese
2 Tablespoons minced Italian parsley leaves

¼ cup olive oil
2 cloves garlic, split in half
1 teaspoon salt
1 teaspoon freshly milled black pepper

1. Discard any wilted or bruised leaves from escarole. Separate leaves, cut off tough bottom ends of greens (about 1 inch) and discard. Slice greens into 3-inch lengths and wash several times in lukewarm water to get rid of grit. Place escarole in a 5-quart pot, add 1 teaspoon salt and cover. Do not add water; the final rinse water clinging to leaves will be sufficient to steam them. Cook, covered, over medium heat until leaves are limp, about 5 minutes. Transfer to a colander and drain well. Let cool slightly and squeeze out excess moisture with your hands.
2. In a small bowl, combine breadcrumbs, Romano cheese and parsley; set aside.
3. In a large sauté pan, heat olive oil over medium heat until haze forms. Turn heat to low and add garlic; sauté, stirring constantly, until lightly golden, then discard with a slotted spoon. Add escarole and cook partially covered, stirring frequently, until leaves are soft when tested with a fork (test by tasting), about 10 to 15 minutes. Season with 1 teaspoon salt and pepper. Turn heat to high and add breadcrumb mixture. Cook uncovered, stirring constantly, until well combined and no liquid is left in bottom of pan, about 1 minute. Transfer to a bowl and serve immediately.

STUFFED ESCAROLE
Scarola Imbottita

A lovely, hearty entree to serve during the cold winter months, this is perfect when preceded by a steaming bowl of soup. I can remember Nonna Louisa telling me, "Anna, the success of this dish depends on the size of the escarole—make sure you pick large, well-rounded heads with unblemished outer leaves."

SERVES 6 TO 8

STUFFING

8 ounces Italian sausage
3 Tablespoons unsalted butter
1 cup finely chopped yellow onion
3 cups coarse fresh breadcrumbs, well packed
¼ cup minced Italian parsley leaves
½ cup freshly grated Romano cheese
1 teaspoon salt
½ teaspoon freshly milled black pepper
3 large eggs, lightly beaten

1. In a 2½-quart saucepan, place sausage and add ¼ cup cold water. Cover pan, bring to a boil and turn heat down to low. Steam sausage for 15 minutes. Remove sausage and let cool slightly; remove casings and coarsely chop meat (can be chopped in food processor fitted with metal blade).
2. In a small saucepan, melt butter over low heat. Add onion, cover pan and steam until soft, about 5 minutes.
3. In a large bowl, combine sausage, steamed onion, and all the remaining ingredients except eggs. Add lightly beaten eggs and blend thoroughly with a fork. Divide stuffing into three portions and shape each into a ball; set aside.

TO ASSEMBLE AND COOK

3 large heads escarole (about 3 pounds)
1 Tablespoon salt
⅓ cup olive oil
¼ cup water
3 large cloves garlic, split in half

1. If tips of some of the outer leaves of escarole are blemished, trim with kitchen shears (do not trim too much, as these leaves are

needed for wrapping the stuffing).
Wash heads thoroughly in warm
running water, opening leaves very
carefully. Trim approximately ⅛
inch from bottom core of escarole.
Open escarole leaves. Using a
small paring knife, very carefully
remove the pale green short leaves
from center (save tender leaves for
salad).

2. In a large pot, bring 6 quarts of
   water to a boil with 1 Tablespoon
   salt. Blanch 1 head of escarole at a
   time for about 2 minutes, or just
   until leaves are limp. Drain each
   head well in a colander. Let cool
   slightly.

3. Place escarole on work surface and
   open leaves carefully. Place one
   ball of stuffing in center of each
   escarole. Enclose stuffing with
   leaves and tie with kitchen twine
   into round bundles.

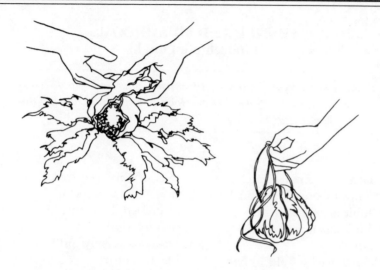

4. Arrange escarole bundles upright in a 5-quart Dutch oven. Add olive oil and water to Dutch oven. Place garlic in between bundles of escarole. Cook covered over medium heat, basting frequently with pan juices, until escarole is extremely tender when tested with the tip of a knife at base of bundle, about 30 minutes (watch cooking liquid carefully; if liquid starts to evaporate, add a little more water). Remove from heat and let rest for at least 15 minutes.

5. To serve, remove twine and slice each head into 4 wedges. Arrange on a platter and serve immediately.

Note: Stuffed escarole can be made up to 4 hours before serving. Reheat in Dutch oven over low heat, basting frequently with cooking liquid.

FENNEL AND MUSHROOMS
Finocchio e Funghi

This side dish of fennel teamed with mushrooms and tomatoes capitalizes on fennel's truly different flavor. Good to make from late fall through January, when it is available fresh.

SERVES 6

1 large or 2 small fennel bulbs (about 1¼ pounds)
2 Tablespoons olive oil
2 Tablespoons unsalted butter
2 cloves garlic, split in half
5 canned Italian plum tomatoes, well drained, halved, seeded and finely chopped
¼ cup chicken broth
1 teaspoon minced fresh thyme or ½ teaspoon crumbled dried thyme
1 teaspoon salt
½ teaspoon freshly milled black pepper
1 pound medium mushrooms, wiped and thinly sliced
2 Tablespoons fine dry breadcrumbs

1. Cut off the upper stalks of fennel. With a vegetable peeler, lightly peel outside of bulb to remove strings. Slice bulb in half vertically and remove center core using a V cut. Slice thinly lengthwise and cut slices into 1½-inch lengths.

2. In a large sauté pan, heat olive oil over medium heat until haze forms, then add butter. Add garlic, sauté until lightly golden and discard with a slotted spoon. Add fennel, tomatoes, broth, thyme, salt and pepper. Cover pan, turn heat to low and cook until fennel is tender when tested with a fork, about 10 minutes. Uncover pan, turn heat to high and add mushrooms. Cook uncovered, stirring constantly, just until mushrooms start to exude juices, about 1 minute. Add breadcrumbs and continue cooking, stirring constantly, until very little moisture is left in bottom of pan, about 1 minute. Transfer to a platter and serve immediately.

SAUTÉED GREEN BEANS AND CHERRY TOMATOES
Fagiolini Verdi e Pomodori Saltati

*Make this beautiful combination when you can find tender green beans
and ripe cherry tomatoes.*

SERVES 6

1 pound green beans
1 teaspoon salt
1 pint cherry tomatoes
3 Tablespoons olive oil
1 cup thinly sliced scallions
1 teaspoon salt
1 teaspoon freshly milled
    black pepper

2 Tablespoons olive oil
2 cloves garlic, split in half
1 Tablespoon minced fresh
    basil or 1 teaspoon
    crumbled dried basil

1. Wash green beans, trim both ends and boil in 4 quarts boiling water with 1 teaspoon salt until tender when tested with a fork, about 5 minutes. Drain in a colander, rinse under cold water and blot dry with paper towel.
2. While beans are cooking, wash cherry tomatoes, remove stems and blot dry with paper towel.
3. In a 10-inch skillet, heat 3 Tablespoons olive oil over medium heat until haze forms. Add scallions and sauté, stirring constantly, until barely tender, about 2 minutes. Add green beans and sauté, stirring constantly, about 3 minutes. Season with half of the salt and pepper; set aside.
4. In an 8-inch skillet, heat 2 Tablespoons olive oil over medium heat until haze forms. Sauté garlic until very lightly golden and discard. Stir in basil and sauté, stirring constantly, for 30 seconds. Add tomatoes and toss and swirl in pan until they are just heated through and coated with olive oil, about 1 minute (this must be done very quickly or the skins will split). Season with remaining salt and pepper.
5. Arrange beans in border around outside of platter. Place cherry tomatoes in center and serve immediately.

GREEN BEANS WITH TOMATO SAUCE
Fagiolini Verdi con Pomodoro

Adding oregano after the sauce has finished cooking will prevent the bitter aftertaste one gets from cooking this herb too long.

SERVES 6

1½ pounds green beans
1 teaspoon salt
3 Tablespoons olive oil
3 Tablespoons finely chopped yellow onion
1 can (35 ounces) Italian-style tomatoes, well drained and coarsely chopped (can be chopped in food processor fitted with metal blade)
1 teaspoon salt
½ teaspoon freshly milled black pepper
½ teaspoon sugar
⅛ teaspoon freshly grated nutmeg
1 Tablespoon minced fresh basil or 1 teaspoon crumbled dried basil
1 teaspoon minced fresh oregano or ½ teaspoon crumbled dried oregano

1. Wash green beans, trim both ends and slice into 2-inch lengths. Cook beans in 5 quarts boiling water with 1 teaspoon salt until tender-crisp, about 5 to 7 minutes. Test by tasting. Drain in a colander, rinse under cold water and set aside.
2. In a 12-inch skillet, heat olive oil over medium-high heat until haze forms. Add onion, turn heat to low and cook, stirring frequently, until soft but not brown, about 5 minutes. Stir in tomatoes, 1 teaspoon salt, pepper, sugar, nutmeg and basil. Increase heat to medium-high and bring to a boil, stirring constantly, then reduce heat to medium-low. Cook uncovered, stirring frequently, until sauce is slightly thickened, about 15 minutes. Add oregano and mix well.
3. Add green beans to sauce and mix well. Cook uncovered over low heat, stirring constantly, until heated through, about 3 minutes. Transfer to a bowl and serve immediately.

SAUTÉED MUSHROOMS
Funghi Saltati

Try to select button mushrooms with smooth, unblemished skins. The caps should be closed, so that no gills show around stems.

SERVES 6

1½ pounds medium mushrooms
¼ cup olive oil
3 cloves garlic, thinly sliced
2 Tablespoons fine dry breadcrumbs

1 teaspoon salt
½ teaspoon freshly milled black pepper
2 Tablespoons minced Italian parsley leaves

1. Wipe mushrooms with a damp cloth and trim bottoms of stems. Slice mushrooms about ¼ inch thick.
2. In a 12-inch skillet, heat olive oil over medium-high heat until haze forms. Add garlic, sauté until lightly golden and discard with a slotted spoon. Add mushrooms; quickly toss with a wooden spoon until mushrooms are well coated with olive oil. Cook, stirring constantly, just until mushrooms begin to exude their juices, about 1 minute. Add breadcrumbs and quickly toss with mushrooms until no liquid is left in pan. Season with salt and pepper; remove from heat. Add parsley and mix lightly just to incorporate. Transfer to a small platter and serve immediately.

PARSNIPS AND CARROTS
Pastinaca e Carota

Parsnips are young and tender when they are about 8 inches in length. Try to select carrots the same size for this surprisingly delicious combination.

SERVES 6

1 pound parsnips, washed, trimmed and lightly peeled with a vegetable peeler
1 pound carrots, washed, trimmed and lightly peeled with a vegetable peeler
2 teaspoons salt
2 Tablespoons olive oil

2 Tablespoons unsalted butter
1 cup thinly sliced scallions
½ teaspoon salt
½ teaspoon freshly milled black pepper
1 Tablespoon minced Italian parsley leaves (garnish)

1. Cook parsnips and carrots separately, each in 2 quarts boiling water with 1 teaspoon salt, until barely tender when tested with a fork (cooking time will vary depending on size; carrots will cook faster). Transfer to separate colanders and rinse with cold water. Blot vegetables dry with paper towel. Quarter vegetables and cut into 2-inch lengths.
2. In a large skillet, heat olive oil over medium heat until haze forms, then add butter. Sauté scallions, stirring constantly, until barely tender, about 2 minutes. Add parsnips and carrots; continue cooking, stirring constantly, until vegetables are easily pierced with the tip of a fork, about 3 to 4 minutes. Season with ½ teaspoon salt and pepper; remove from heat.
3. Transfer to a platter and garnish with parsley. Serve immediately.

FLUFFY POTATO PIE
Pure di Patate

Select round or long white boiling potatoes for this creamy potato pie; baking potatoes will fall apart in cooking and are too mealy for this dish. Potato pie can be completely assembled up to 4 hours before baking, covered with plastic wrap and refrigerated until ready to bake. Increase baking time by 10 minutes if baking straight from refrigerator.

SERVES 8

1 Tablespoon unsalted butter, softened

2 Tablespoons fine dry breadcrumbs

2 pounds boiling potatoes, peeled and quartered

1 Tablespoon salt

¼ cup unsalted butter

½ cup milk

2 large eggs

4 ounces Mozzarella cheese, coarsely grated

¼ cup freshly grated Parmigiano cheese

½ teaspoon salt

½ teaspoon freshly milled white pepper

3 Tablespoons minced Italian parsley leaves

1. Grease the bottom and sides of a deep 10-inch pie or quiche dish with 1 Tablespoon softened butter. Sprinkle bottom and sides of dish with 1 Tablespoon dry breadcrumbs.
2. Place potatoes in a 5-quart pot and add enough cold water to cover by 1 inch. Bring to a boil, covered, and add 1 Tablespoon salt. Cook potatoes, covered, until tender when tested with a fork, about 20 to 30 minutes.
3. In a small saucepan, heat ¼ cup butter and milk over low heat until butter is completely melted.
4. Drain potatoes well in a colander. Transfer to a large bowl and mash with a wire whisk or electric mixer. Add milk mixture and whip until fluffy.
5. In a shallow bowl, beat eggs with Mozzarella and Parmigiano cheese; beat into potato mixture until well incorporated. Add ½ teaspoon salt, pepper and parsley; mix well. Using a metal spatula, spread potato mixture evenly in prepared dish; sprinkle remaining 1 Tablespoon breadcrumbs on top.
6. When ready to bake, adjust rack to center of oven and preheat to 350°F. Bake pie until lightly golden and puffed on top, about 30 to 40 minutes. Remove from oven and let rest for 5 minutes before serving. Slice into wedges to serve.

POTATOES WITH PANCETTA AND ROSEMARY
Patate con Pancetta e Rosmarino

Russet-type baking potatoes give a creamier texture to this dish than Idahos do. It can be completely assembled up to 3 hours before baking.

SERVES 8

¼ cup unsalted butter
6 large Russet baking potatoes (3 pounds), peeled
1 Tablespoon salt
1 large yellow onion (12 ounces), halved and thinly sliced
4 ounces pancetta or very lean bacon, finely diced

1 Tablespoon minced fresh rosemary or ½ teaspoon powdered rosemary
1 teaspoon salt
1 teaspoon freshly milled black pepper

1. Dot the bottom of a 9 × 13-inch ovenproof baking dish with 2 Tablespoons butter. Set aside.
2. In a 5-quart pot, place potatoes and add enough cold water to cover by 2 inches. Bring to a boil, covered, and add 1 Tablespoon salt. Cook potatoes, covered, until they are still a bit firm when tested with the tip of a knife, about 20 minutes. Drain potatoes and let cool slightly. Slice into ½-inch rounds and set aside.
3. While potatoes are cooking, melt remaining 2 Tablespoons butter in a 1½-quart saucepan over low heat. Add onion, cover, and cook until soft, about 6 minutes.
4. Spread ⅓ of the cooked onion evenly in bottom of baking dish. Place half of the potatoes in a single layer over onions. Sprinkle half the rosemary over potatoes. Season with half of the salt and pepper. Spread half of the remaining onion over potatoes. Sprinkle half of the diced pancetta or bacon on top. Repeat second layer with remaining potatoes, rosemary, salt, pepper, onion and pancetta. Cover baking dish with foil.
5. When ready to bake, adjust rack to center of oven and preheat to 350°F. Bake until potatoes are cooked when tested with a fork, about 1 hour. Remove from oven. Adjust rack to 6 inches from broiler and turn oven to broil setting. Remove foil from baking dish and broil until potatoes are lightly golden, about 5 minutes. Serve immediately.

PARSLEYED POTATOES
Patate Lesse con Prezzemolo

Red-skinned waxy potatoes are the type best suited for boiling. Just a slight hint of garlic rounds out this dish.

SERVES 6

2 pounds small red-skinned potatoes
1 Tablespoon salt
1 large clove garlic, split in half
¼ cup olive oil

1 teaspoon salt
½ teaspoon freshly milled black pepper
3 Tablespoons minced Italian parsley leaves

1. Scrub potatoes well with a vegetable brush. In a 5-quart pot, place potatoes and add enough cold water to cover by 1 inch. Bring to a boil, covered, and add 1 Tablespoon salt. Uncover, reduce heat to medium-high and cook until tender when tested with the tip of a knife, about 15 to 20 minutes; if potatoes vary in size, remove smaller ones first to prevent overcooking. Drain potatoes in a colander and quarter (do not peel).
2. Rub serving bowl with split garlic; discard garlic. Toss hot potatoes in serving bowl with olive oil, 1 teaspoon salt and pepper. Add parsley and toss again. Serve immediately or at room temperature.

SAUTÉED PUMPKIN
Zucca Saltata

My students thought I was off the wall when I made this as a vegetable, but they ate their words after tasting it!

SERVES 6

1 wedge (2 pounds) fresh
  pumpkin
½ cup olive oil
2 cloves garlic, split in half
2 Tablespoons imported red
  wine vinegar

1 teaspoon salt
½ teaspoon freshly milled
  black pepper

1. Peel and seed pumpkin. Using a metal spoon, scrape out fibers and discard. Cut pumpkin into ¼-inch-thick slices, then cut slices into 1 × 2-inch rectangular pieces.
2. In a 12-inch skillet, heat olive oil over medium-high heat until haze forms. Sauté garlic until lightly golden, then discard with a slotted spoon. Add half of the pumpkin (do not crowd) and sauté, turning once, until lightly golden and tender when tested with a fork. Using a slotted spoon, remove and drain on paper towel. Repeat with remaining pumpkin. Discard all the oil from skillet. Return pumpkin to skillet and add vinegar, salt and pepper. Cover pan, turn heat to low and cook for an additional 3 minutes. Remove from heat and let pumpkin rest in pan for 10 minutes so that the flavors meld together. Transfer to a platter and serve warm, but not hot.

SWISS CHARD WITH TOMATOES
Bietole Saltate

Swiss chard, with its delicate, spinach-like flavor, is usually available from mid-June through October.

SERVES 6

3 pounds Swiss chard
1 teaspoon salt
¼ cup olive oil
1 teaspoon minced garlic

½ cup coarsely chopped
   peeled and seeded tomatoes
1 teaspoon salt
½ teaspoon freshly milled
   black pepper

1. Trim off any wilted or discolored edges from leaves. Cut the leaves away from the stalks. Trim bottoms of stalks. With a small knife, peel away the transparent membrane attached to the stalk on both sides. Wash leaves and stalks separately in cold water several times to get rid of grit; drain well. Cut leaves and stalks crosswise into 2-inch lengths.

2. Boil the stalks, uncovered, in 4 quarts boiling water with 1 teaspoon salt, until barely tender when tested with a fork, about 15 to 20 minutes. Add leaves and cook for an additional minute. Transfer to a colander, refresh under cold water and drain well. Squeeze out any excess moisture with your hands.

3. In a 12-inch skillet, heat olive oil over medium-high heat until haze forms. Turn heat to low and add garlic. Sauté, stirring constantly, until very lightly golden, about 1 minute. Add chopped tomatoes, salt and pepper; cook, stirring constantly, for an additional minute. Add chard leaves and stems. Cook, covered, stirring once or twice, until stalks are very tender when tested with a fork, about 10 minutes. Transfer to a bowl and serve immediately.

BAKED ZUCCHINI
Zucchini al Forno

Baking zucchini slices on the top rack of the oven will insure crispness. When finished, they will taste like they are pan-fried.

SERVES 6

2 Tablespoons olive oil
2 pounds medium zucchini
2 extra large eggs
1½ cups fine dry breadcrumbs
¼ cup freshly grated Romano cheese
1 teaspoon minced garlic
2 teaspoons minced Italian parsley leaves

1 Tablespoon minced fresh basil or 1 teaspoon crumbled dried basil
½ teaspoon salt
½ teaspoon freshly milled black pepper
2 Tablespoons (approximately) olive oil

1. Adjust rack to upper portion of oven and preheat to 375°F. Brush a large jelly roll pan with 2 Tablespoons olive oil. Set aside.
2. Scrub zucchini and blot dry with paper towel. Trim ends. If zucchini are about 6 inches in length, leave whole; if larger, slice in half crosswise. Cut lengthwise into ¼-inch slices, discarding the first and last slice of each zucchini.
3. In a shallow bowl, beat eggs with a fork. In another shallow bowl, combine all of the remaining ingredients except olive oil. Dip zucchini slices in egg, then dredge on both sides in breadcrumb mixture. Arrange slices in a single layer in pan. Drizzle about ½ teaspoon olive oil over each slice. Bake until slices are lightly golden on top, about 5 minutes. Remove from oven and turn slices. Continue to bake until slightly crusty and lightly golden, about 5 to 7 minutes.
4. Using a metal spatula, transfer to a platter. Arrange in a slightly overlapping pattern and serve immediately.

ZUCCHINI WITH GARLIC AND TOMATO
Zucchini con Aglio e Pomodoro

Fragrant with basil and pungent with garlic.

SERVES 6

4 large ripe plum tomatoes
  or 2 ripe tomatoes (12
  ounces)
2 pounds medium zucchini
¼ cup olive oil
2 teaspoons minced garlic
2 Tablespoons minced fresh
  basil or 2 teaspoons
  crumbled dried basil

1 teaspoon salt
½ teaspoon freshly milled
  black pepper
1 Tablespoon minced Italian
  parsley leaves (garnish)

1. Blanch tomatoes in boiling water for 1 minute. Refresh under cold water and remove skins. Slice in half lengthwise and squeeze gently to remove seeds. Cut into ½-inch cubes. Set aside.
2. Scrub zucchini, blot dry with paper towel and trim ends. Cut zucchini at a 20° angle into ½-inch slices.
3. In a 12-inch skillet, heat olive oil over medium heat until haze forms. Add garlic, turn heat to low and sauté, stirring constantly, until very lightly golden. Add tomatoes, zucchini and basil. Turn heat to medium and cook, stirring constantly, until zucchini is tender-crisp when tested with a fork, about 5 minutes. Season with salt and pepper; remove from heat. Transfer to a bowl, garnish with parsley and serve immediately.

ZUCCHINI WITH ROASTED PEPPERS
Zucchini con Peperoni

Zucchini should be cooked tender-crisp so that its texture contrasts with the roasted peppers. If red peppers are unavailable, substitute 2 jars (7 ounces each) pimientos, well drained and thinly sliced.

SERVES 6 TO 8

¼ cup olive oil
¾ cup thinly sliced yellow onion
2 pounds small zucchini, washed, trimmed and sliced into 2 × ½-inch strips

2 large red bell peppers (1 pound), roasted, peeled and thinly sliced (see directions for roasting peppers, page 8)
1 teaspoon salt
½ teaspoon freshly milled black pepper

In a 12-inch skillet, heat olive oil over medium heat until haze forms. Add onion, turn heat to low and cook, stirring constantly, until soft but not brown, about 4 minutes. Add zucchini and cook, stirring frequently, until barely tender when tested with a fork, about 3 minutes. Stir in roasted peppers and continue to cook for an additional minute. Season with salt and pepper; remove from heat. Transfer to a bowl and serve immediately.

SALADS

ASPARAGUS VINAIGRETTE

BEET SALAD

CAULIFLOWER—TOMATO SALAD

CURLY ENDIVE—SPINACH—MANDARIN SALAD

GREEN SALAD WITH MUSTARD VINAIGRETTE

GREEN BEAN AND NEW POTATO SALAD

ORANGE—AVOCADO SALAD

ROMAINE, WATERCRESS AND TOMATO SALAD WITH GORGONZOLA DRESSING

TOMATO SALAD WITH RICOTTA SALATA

ZUCCHINI SALAD

FOOD PROCESSOR MAYONNAISE

In the summer months I have a vegetable garden where I can pick fresh greens daily. During the winter, however, practicality deems it necessary to gather salad fixings from local greengrocers and markets.

My weekly shopping ritual is not without a system. As soon as I've put away my groceries, I go to work on the salad greens. Each is washed and thoroughly dried with the aid of a salad spinner. Next, each is wrapped in paper toweling. The greens are then placed in separate plastic bags, closed with twist ties and refrigerated until needed throughout the week. Please refer to the ingredients section of this book for specific procedures for cleaning parsley and scallions.

Before you discard any outer leaves from salad greens, or if you find yourself with soon-to-be-wilting vegetables, please read my recipe for Braised Celery, Carrots and Romaine, page 233.

ASPARAGUS VINAIGRETTE
Insalata di Asparagi

Try to select asparagus of uniform size. Adding the dressing to the chilled asparagus will insure beautiful green color.

SERVES 6

1½ pounds large asparagus
1 Tablespoon salt
8 unblemished romaine lettuce leaves (garnish), washed and blotted dry with paper towel
¼ cup imported white wine vinegar
1 teaspoon salt
½ teaspoon sugar
½ teaspoon freshly milled black pepper
½ cup olive oil
2 Tablespoons minced Italian parsley leaves
1 Tablespoon minced fresh basil or 1 teaspoon crumbled dried basil

1. Using a sharp knife, cut off tough part at base of each asparagus spear. With a vegetable peeler, peel stalks starting at base of spear and leaving tips intact. Wash several times in cold water to remove sand; drain well in a colander.
2. In a deep 12-inch skillet, bring 1½ quarts of water to a boil over high heat and add 1 Tablespoon salt. Place asparagus in one to two layers in pan (they should be covered with water). Boil uncovered until tender when stalk is tested with the tip of a knife, about 10 minutes; the exact time will depend on thickness and tenderness of asparagus. Using a pair of tongs, carefully transfer to colander and refresh under cold water. Drain thoroughly and blot dry with paper towel.
3. Arrange border of romaine leaves on a large platter. Place asparagus in center of platter and refrigerate until needed.
4. In a shallow bowl, combine vinegar, 1 teaspoon salt and sugar; mix with a wire whisk until sugar and salt are dissolved. Add pepper, olive oil, parsley and basil; whisk again until thoroughly blended.
5. Pour dressing over asparagus just before serving.

BEET SALAD
Insalata di Barbabietola

In selecting fresh beets, try to choose those that are no more than 2 inches in diameter (the larger ones tend to be fibrous). Also, select beets that do not have a break in the skin, as splits allow color to escape in boiling. Don't throw away the stems and tops; see directions for cooking beet greens, page 227.

SERVES 6 TO 8

1 small red onion (2 ounces), peeled and thinly sliced
3 pounds whole beets
1 Tablespoon salt
½ cup olive oil
¼ cup imported red wine vinegar

12 fresh mint leaves or 2 teaspoons dried mint
1 teaspoon salt
½ teaspoon freshly milled black pepper
4 short fresh mint sprigs (garnish)

1. Place sliced onion in a small bowl with 3 ice cubes and cover with cold water. Refrigerate for at least 1 hour. (Soaking the onion will insure crispness.)
2. Clean and trim beets, leaving 2 inches of the stems and the root ends intact (this will prevent color from oozing out during boiling). Wash beets thoroughly in cold water. Place in a large pot and cover with cold water. Bring to a boil, covered, and add 1 Tablespoon salt. Cook beets, partially covered, over high heat until tender when pierced with the tip of a small knife, about 30 minutes to 1 hour depending on size.
3. Drain in a colander and refresh under cold water. While beets are still warm, slip off skins. Quarter beets and cut into ½-inch wedges.
4. Place beets in a serving bowl. Drain onions, blot dry with paper towel and add to beets.
5. Place olive oil, vinegar, mint, salt and pepper in food processor fitted with metal blade. Run machine nonstop until mint leaves are finely minced. Pour dressing over beets and toss well. Cover with plastic wrap and refrigerate until well chilled.
6. When ready to serve, toss again and garnish with a few sprigs of fresh mint.

CAULIFLOWER–TOMATO SALAD
Insalata di Cavolfiore e Pomodoro

Adding the cauliflower to the dressing while still warm will bring out the full flavor of this salad.

SERVES 8

1 pint cherry tomatoes
1 large head cauliflower
(about 2 pounds)
1 Tablespoon salt
1 large clove garlic, split in
half
1 teaspoon salt
½ teaspoon sugar
¼ cup imported white wine
vinegar
½ teaspoon freshly milled
white pepper
½ cup olive oil
1 small bunch curly endive
(garnish)
¼ cup minced Italian parsley
leaves

1. Wash cherry tomatoes and remove stems. Halve tomatoes and place in a strainer set over a bowl. (If cherry tomatoes are very small, leave whole).
2. Cut cauliflower into medium-size florets, leaving about 1 inch of stem. Using a small paring knife, trim heavy skin from stems. Cook cauliflower in 4 quarts boiling water with 1 Tablespoon salt until tender (test by tasting), about 10 minutes. Drain well in a colander and refresh briefly under cold water. Blot dry with paper towel.
3. While cauliflower is cooking, make dressing. Rub garlic in the bottom and around the sides of a large bowl; discard garlic. Add salt and sugar to bowl and pour in vinegar. Stir until salt and sugar are dissolved (this is best done with your index finger so that you can feel when the salt and sugar have dissolved). Add pepper and olive oil; mix thoroughly with a fork. Add cauliflower to dressing and mix well. Cover with plastic wrap and marinate at room temperature for at least 1 hour.
4. Discard any bruised leaves from curly endive and trim tough lower stems. Wash several times in cold water and drain well. Blot dry with paper towel or spin dry in a salad spinner. Arrange a border of curly endive on a large platter. Refrigerate until needed.
5. Just before serving, toss cauliflower with tomatoes and parsley. Transfer to garnished platter and serve immediately.

CURLY ENDIVE–SPINACH–MANDARIN SALAD
Insalata con Mandarino

A refreshing salad any time of year, and especially good with the fish recipes in this book.

SERVES 6 TO 8

1 large head curly endive or chicory (1¼ pounds)
1 pound spinach
1 cup thinly sliced celery, strings removed
½ cup thinly sliced scallions
1 can (11 ounces) mandarin oranges, well drained
½ cup slivered almonds, toasted (garnish)

1. Discard tough outer leaves from curly endive. Break off tough bottom ends of greens and discard. Wash greens several times in cold water. Drain well and blot dry with paper towel or spin dry in a salad spinner. Tear greens into bite-size pieces and set aside.
2. Wash spinach clusters several times in cold water until there is not a grain of sand left. Remove stems and discard. Blot leaves dry with paper towel or spin dry in salad spinner. If spinach leaves are very large, tear into bite-size pieces. Set aside.

DRESSING

1½ teaspoons honey, preferably orange blossom
⅓ cup fresh lemon juice
1 teaspoon salt
1 teaspoon freshly milled black pepper
⅔ cup olive oil

1. Place honey, lemon juice and salt in a large salad bowl and stir until salt is dissolved (this is best done with your index finger so that you can feel when the salt is dissolved). Add pepper and olive oil; beat with fork or wire whisk to incorporate.
2. Add the salad ingredients except almonds and toss well. Sprinkle top of salad with toasted almonds and serve immediately.

GREEN SALAD WITH MUSTARD VINAIGRETTE
Insalata Verde

A good salad to serve from late fall through the winter months, when all of these vegetables are readily available.

SERVES 6

1 large head romaine lettuce (1¼ pounds)
1 medium head escarole (12 ounces)
1 large head Belgian endive (3 ounces)
½ cup thinly sliced celery, strings removed

1 medium cucumber, peeled, halved lengthwise, seeded and thinly sliced
½ cup thinly sliced scallions
2 Tablespoons minced Italian parsley leaves

1. Discard tough outer leaves from romaine and escarole. Break off and discard tough bottom ends of greens; wash greens several times in cold water. Drain well and blot dry with paper towel or spin dry in a salad spinner. Tear into bite-size pieces; set aside.
2. Halve Belgian endive lengthwise. Cut out bitter center core; wipe leaves with a damp cloth to remove sand. (Slice thinly and set aside.)

MUSTARD VINAIGRETTE DRESSING

¼ cup imported white wine vinegar
½ teaspoon sugar
1 teaspoon salt

1 teaspoon freshly milled black pepper
1 teaspoon Dijon mustard
½ cup olive oil

1. Place vinegar, sugar and salt in a large salad bowl and stir until sugar and salt are dissolved (this is best done with your index finger so that you can feel when the sugar and salt have dissolved). Add pepper and mustard; stir with a fork or wire whisk until well combined. Add olive oil and beat with fork or whisk to incorporate.
2. Add all the salad fixings and toss well. Serve immediately.

GREEN BEAN AND NEW POTATO SALAD
Insalata di Fagiolini Verdi e Patate

Small new potatoes make an attractive salad, especially when embellished with tender green beans.

SERVES 6 TO 8

1½ pounds green beans
1 Tablespoon salt
2 pounds small red-skinned
  potatoes
1 Tablespoon salt
½ cup olive oil
¼ cup imported red wine
  vinegar

¼ cup snipped fresh chives or
½ cup thinly sliced
  scallions
3 Tablespoons minced Italian
  parsley leaves
1 teaspoon salt
½ teaspoon freshly milled
  black pepper

1. Trim both ends of beans. Wash several times in cold water and drain in a colander. Cut beans into 2-inch lengths. Cook uncovered in 4 quarts boiling water with 1 Tablespoon salt until tender-crisp when tested with a fork, about 10 to 12 minutes. Transfer to colander and rinse under cold water. Drain well and blot dry with paper towel. Set aside.
2. Scrub potatoes well with a vegetable brush. Place in a large pot with enough water to cover by 2 inches. Cover pot, bring to a boil and then add 1 Tablespoon salt. Uncover pot, reduce heat to medium-high and cook until potatoes are tender when tested with the tip of a knife, about 15 to 20 minutes; if potatoes vary in size, remove small ones first to prevent overcooking. Transfer to colander and let stand just until cool enough to handle.
3. In the same bowl in which you are serving salad, combine all the remaining ingredients and blend thoroughly with a wire whisk.
4. Peel potatoes and cut into 1-inch cubes. Transfer to bowl and toss gently with dressing (this must be done while the potatoes are still warm so they will absorb the full flavor of the dressing).
5. Add the green beans after the potatoes have cooled down to room temperature; gently toss again. This salad is best served at room temperature.

ORANGE–AVOCADO SALAD
Insalata d'Arancia con Avocado

To select the perfect avocados for this artfully arranged salad, look for ones that yield slightly when pressed gently with fingertips; if very soft, they are overripe. If they are as hard as a rock, buy them ahead of time and leave at room temperature for 2 to 3 days.

SERVES 8

5 large navel oranges
2 large avocados

3 medium heads Belgian
endive

1. Cut a slice from the top and bottom of oranges to expose the fruit. Peel the oranges and remove all the white membrane. Slice crosswise into ¼-inch-thick rounds and place in a strainer set over a bowl for at least 30 minutes to drain off excess juice.
2. Peel and pit avocados and cut into ½-inch cubes. Place in bowl and set aside.
3. Separate leaves from Belgian endive; wipe each leaf with a damp cloth to remove sand. On a large oval or round platter, arrange an outer border of endive leaves.

DRESSING

⅓ cup fresh lemon juice
⅔ cup olive oil
1½ teaspoons salt
½ teaspoon freshly milled
white pepper
½ teaspoon sugar

1 teaspoon Dijon mustard
3 Tablespoons snipped fresh
chives or 3 scallions, cut
into ½-inch lengths
¼ cup Italian parsley leaves

1. Combine all of the above ingredients in food processor fitted with metal blade. Run machine nonstop until chives or scallions and parsley are finely minced and dressing is creamy.
2. Pour half of the dressing over avocados and toss gently.
3. Arrange a border of oranges in a slightly overlapping pattern on endive and mound avocados in center of platter. Spoon remaining dressing over oranges and endive; serve immediately.

ROMAINE, WATERCRESS AND TOMATO SALAD WITH GORGONZOLA DRESSING
Insalata Mista con Gorgonzola

Gorgonzola and lemon bring out the full flavor of this salad. If you like a lighter dressing, substitute yogurt or sour cream for the ricotta. If Gorgonzola cheese is unavailable, substitute another blue-veined cheese. Dressing can be stored in refrigerator up to 5 days. It will definitely thicken, and can be thinned down by whisking in a little milk.

SERVES 6

1 small red onion (2 ounces), thinly sliced

1 medium head romaine lettuce (1 pound)

1 large bunch of watercress (6 ounces)

3 large, ripe tomatoes (1 pound), washed, cored and thinly sliced

1. Place sliced onion in a small bowl with 3 ice cubes and cover with cold water. Refrigerate for at least 1 hour. (Soaking the onion will insure crispness.)
2. Discard tough outer leaves from romaine. Break off tough bottom ends and wash leaves several times in cold water. Drain well and blot dry with paper towel or spin dry in a salad spinner. Tear greens into 3-inch pieces; set aside.
3. Wash watercress several times in cold water, drain well and blot dry with paper towel or spin dry in salad spinner. Remove tough lower stems. Set aside.
4. Arrange an outer border of romaine leaves on individual salad plates. Arrange watercress in a circular pattern on top of romaine. Place sliced tomatoes in an overlapping pattern in center of plate. Refrigerate until ready to serve, but not more than 1 hour.
5. Just before serving salad, drain onions in a strainer and blot dry with paper towel. Arrange a few slices of onion on top of tomatoes.

GORGONZOLA DRESSING

½ cup mayonnaise, preferably homemade (page 269)

½ cup whole milk ricotta cheese

4 ounces Gorgonzola cheese, crumbled

3 Tablespoons fresh lemon juice

¼ cup Italian parsley leaves

½ teaspoon salt

½ teaspoon freshly milled black pepper

1. Combine all ingredients in food processor fitted with metal blade. Run machine nonstop until you have a smooth, creamy mixture. Transfer to a bowl, cover and refrigerate until ready to serve. (Dressing can be made up to 4 hours ahead. If it becomes too thick, just whisk with a fork before serving.)
2. When ready to serve, spoon 2 heaping Tablespoons of dressing on top of each salad and serve immediately.

TOMATO SALAD WITH RICOTTA SALATA
Insalata di Pomodoro con Ricotta Salata

In late summer, when basil and New Jersey tomatoes are at the peak of their season, I serve this salad at least once a week. If semi-soft ricotta salata is unavailable, substitute whole milk Mozzarella cheese.

SERVES 6

5 large ripe tomatoes (about 2½ pounds), washed, cored and cut into ¼-inch slices

¼ cup (approximately) extra virgin olive oil

1 teaspoon salt

1 teaspoon freshly milled black pepper

2 ounces ricotta salata cheese (semi-soft variety), grated on coarse holes of grater

2 Tablespoons minced fresh basil or 2 teaspoons crumbled dried basil

1. Arrange tomato slices in a slightly overlapping pattern on a large platter.
2. Drizzle olive oil over tomatoes and season with salt and pepper. Sprinkle ricotta salata over tomatoes. Sprinkle basil over cheese and serve immediately.

ZUCCHINI SALAD
Insalata di Zucchini

Alive with the flavor of summer, this is best made when you can find small, firm zucchini.

SERVES 6

2 pounds small zucchini
(about 6)
1 teaspoon salt
1 clove garlic, split in half
½ cup olive oil
2 Tablespoons minced Italian
parsley leaves
1 Tablespoon minced fresh
mint or 1 teaspoon
crumbled dried mint

1 teaspoon salt
½ teaspoon freshly milled
black pepper
¼ cup imported white wine
vinegar

1. Scrub zucchini under cold running water until the skins feel clean and smooth. Trim both ends. Bring 3 quarts of water to a rolling boil and add 1 teaspoon salt. Add zucchini. When water returns to boil, cook until barely tender when tested with the tip of a knife, about 3 minutes. Transfer to a colander and refresh under cold water. Blot dry with paper towel. Halve zucchini lengthwise and slice again into 2 × ½-inch strips.
2. Rub a serving bowl with garlic and leave in bowl. In a shallow bowl, combine all the remaining ingredients except vinegar (see note); mix with a wire whisk until well combined. Place zucchini in bowl and combine with dressing. Marinate, covered, in refrigerator for at least 2 hours.
3. When ready to serve, remove garlic and add vinegar; toss well and serve immediately.

Note: If vinegar is added to dressing and tossed with warm zucchini it will produce bleached spots on the skin. Adding the vinegar to the chilled zucchini will insure bright green color. This is also a good tip to remember if you are cooking asparagus, green beans or broccoli for a cold vinaigrette dressing.

FOOD PROCESSOR MAYONNAISE

One of the joys of owning a food processor is making homemade mayon-naise. It is prepared in a matter of seconds, and once you taste it you may never buy mayonnaise again. This is a very thick, tart mayonnaise; if you like it thinner, use 1 whole extra large egg rather than yolks. You can also substitute fresh lemon juice or imported white wine vinegar for the apple cider vinegar for a less tart result. Remember: To form a perfect emulsion, the egg yolks and oil must be at room temperature.

YIELDS 1½ CUPS

2 extra large egg yolks, room temperature
3 Tablespoons apple cider vinegar
1 teaspoon sugar
1 teaspoon Dijon mustard
1 teaspoon salt
½ teaspoon freshly milled white pepper
1¼ cups corn oil, preferably Mazola, room temperature

Insert metal blade in food processor. Combine all ingredients except oil in work bowl. Add ¼ cup oil and run machine nonstop for 10 seconds. Uncover and scrape down the sides of the work bowl with a rubber spatula. Replace cover and turn machine on. With the motor running, pour remaining oil through the feed tube in a very fine, steady stream; the mixture will emulsify and become thick. Using a rubber spatula, transfer to jar; cover with a tight-fitting lid. Keep refrigerated until needed. Mayonnaise will keep up to 2 weeks in refrigerator.

DESSERTS

FRUIT AND MOLDED DESSERTS

TARTS AND TORTES

CAKES AND CREAM PUFF PASTRY

While desserts are not traditionally the highlight of an Italian meal, they have always had a special place at our table.

There were two major influences in my education as a dessert maker. From each I acquired the techniques, methods and procedures I use in my kitchen today. From my mother I learned the organizational skills needed to interpret the less structured approach of my father-in-law, a well-respected pastry chef.

Assisting my mother always seemed like assisting a chemist in a lab. Everything was accurately premeasured and placed into separate bowls before any dessert was started. If eggs were to be separated, she would tell me, "Anna, make sure you wipe out that shell with your thumb, you can always tell a good cook if she wipes out her eggs." She would also tell me, "Anna, in cooking you can add a little more seasoning or whatever to suit your own taste, but in preparing any dessert, you must be accurate in your measurements so everything will come out perfectly."

The scene changed a little during the 14 years we lived with my father-in-law. Assisting him always meant working on a grand scale, using the methods and techniques he was accustomed to from his days at the pastry shop. While I never saw him use a measuring spoon or cup, he precisely weighed all the flour, sugar, shortening and eggs before adding them to any recipe. I can remember wall-to-wall flour as I assisted him. He always worked at high speed, as though he were on a production schedule. His unbelievable wealth of knowledge was at my disposal whenever I asked for his criticism. If it were a dessert, he would taste it for the necessary adjustment. If it were a cake or pastry dough I was working on, he would take a small piece in his hand, roll it between his fingers and immediately tell me it should have more flour, less egg or whatever other change was needed. Any of his recipes that I have revised for this book have been broken down to standard measurements.

If you are in doubt about any ingredient being used, check the glossary on ingredients.

When preparing any of the baked desserts, make sure you check the position of the oven rack for perfect results.

I have tried to take today's taste into consideration in creating the recipes in this chapter, and have cut back on sugar whenever possible. There are many desserts here for the diet-conscious. While whipped cream is frequently suggested for a topping or garnish, it is not essential.

For the grand finale of a simple supper or a special dinner party, I offer the following collection of desserts ranging from a light, yet satisfying, apple cream whip to a glorious Cassata laced with Grand Marnier (as you read through the dessert chapter you will notice how much I like this splendid liqueur).

Fruit and Molded Desserts

GLAZED ORANGE PEEL

GLAZED POACHED APPLES WITH MARINATED FRUIT

BLUEBERRIES FLAMBÉ

LINDA'S GRAPES WITH COGNAC

FRESH ORANGE COMPOTE

STUFFED PEACHES

STUFFED POACHED PEARS

STRAWBERRIES ALL'ANNA

STRAWBERRIES WITH PASTRY CREAM AND SAUCE

APPLE CREAM WHIP

APRICOT MOUSSE

GRAND MARNIER MOUSSE

COLD MANDARIN SOUFFLÉ

ORANGE CREAM

RICOTTA MOUSSE WITH RASPBERRY SAUCE

CARAMEL CUSTARD

PAPA'S RICE PUDDING

RICOTTA PUDDING

FROZEN MOCHA SURPRISE

PINEAPPLE—COCONUT PARFAITS

BISCUIT TORTONI

GLAZED ORANGE PEEL

Make glazed peel when you can find large, unblemished California navel oranges, usually available late December through March. The peel is great to have on hand for several desserts in this chapter, or to slice thinly and use for garnishing. Once made, the glazed orange peel will keep in the refrigerator up to 1 year. Remember to turn the jar periodically so that the peel remains well coated with syrup.

YIELDS ABOUT 1 QUART

4 large, thick-skinned navel 2½ cups sugar
oranges (about 2 pounds) 1½ cups water

1. With a sharp knife, cut a small slice from the top and bottom of each orange. With tip of knife, divide orange skin into 6 sections. Very carefully peel off each section right to the orange itself.
2. Place the peels in a 3-quart saucepan and cover with cold water. Bring to a boil and cook for 30 seconds. Drain, rinse under cold water, cover again with cold water, bring to a boil and cook for 3 minutes. Drain, rinse, cover with water and bring to a boil again for another 3 minutes. Drain and rinse under cold water. Blot dry with paper towel and place in a single layer on work surface with skin side down. While peels are still warm, scrape away most of the pith (white membrane) with a teaspoon, leaving about ⅛ inch of pith. Set peel aside.
3. In a 2-quart saucepan, combine sugar and water and bring to a boil over medium heat. Stir and wash down any crystals clinging to the sides of the pan, using a brush dipped in cold water, until sugar is completely dissolved. Boil syrup undisturbed for 5 minutes.
4. Pack the orange peels in a 1-quart sterilized jar and fill jar with hot syrup. Secure with a tight-fitting lid and let cool to room temperature. Refrigerate overnight.
5. Once a day for the next 4 days, pour the syrup from jar into saucepan and bring to a boil; boil syrup for 1 minute. Pour hot syrup back into jar and cover. Let cool to room temperature and refrigerate. Let stand in refrigerator for 2 days after final boiling before using.

GLAZED POACHED APPLES WITH MARINATED FRUIT

Pick Golden Delicious apples, all the same size and without any bruise marks, for this surprisingly delicious combination.

SERVES 6

MARINATED FRUIT

½ cup dried peaches (about 6   ½ cup dark raisins
   large halves)   ¼ cup Cognac
½ cup water

1. Place peaches and water in a small saucepan. Cook uncovered over medium-high heat until peaches are tender when pierced with a fork, about 3 minutes. Drain in a strainer and let cool slightly. Blot dry with paper towel and cut into ¼-inch cubes.
2. In a small bowl, combine peaches, raisins and Cognac. Let fruit macerate, turning once or twice, until raisins are soft and Cognac is completely absorbed into fruit, at least 2 hours (can be covered and placed in refrigerator overnight).

POACHED APPLES

6 medium Golden Delicious   ¾ cup sugar
   apples (2¼ pounds)   ¼ cup fresh lemon juice
2 cups water

1. Peel apples and halve lengthwise. With a teaspoon or melon scoop, hollow out center core.
2. In a 12-inch skillet, combine water, sugar and lemon juice. Bring to a boil over high heat, reduce heat to low and simmer syrup for 5 minutes. Add apples to skillet, cut side down. Poach over low heat, spooning syrup over apples constantly, until they are barely tender when tested with a fork, about 6 minutes. Using a slotted spoon, transfer apples to a large platter, cut side up. Discard syrup or save for additional poaching.

GLAZE AND TOPPING

¾ cup peach preserves   1 cup heavy cream
3 Tablespoons Cognac   1 Tablespoon confectioners'
1 Tablespoon grated lemon   sugar
   rind
½ cup finely chopped pecans
   (optional garnish)

1. Strain preserves into a 1-quart saucepan. Add Cognac and lemon rind. Heat the glaze over low heat, stirring constantly.
2. Spoon the marinated fruit mixture into the center cavity of each halved apple. Transfer apples to individual serving plates and pour glaze over each serving. Sprinkle the edge of each halved apple with pecans.
3. Whip cream with confectioners' sugar until stiff. Place a dollop of whipped cream on each apple half and serve immediately. Apples are best served at room temperature.

BLUEBERRIES FLAMBÉ

The perfect dessert for a warm summer evening or whenever fresh blueberries are in season.

SERVES 8

2 pints blueberries
1½ quarts vanilla ice cream
1 cup blueberry preserves
1 Tablespoon grated lemon rind

¼ cup fresh lemon juice
½ cup Cognac

1. Wash each pint of blueberries separately. Drain well in a strainer and blot thoroughly dry with paper towel. Set aside.
2. Scoop out vanilla ice cream into individual serving bowls and place in freezer until needed.
3. In a 12-inch skillet, combine preserves, lemon rind and juice. Cook over medium heat, stirring constantly, until preserves are melted, about 2 minutes. Add half of the blueberries and cook, stirring constantly, until blueberries are soft, about 5 minutes. Add remaining blueberries and mix well. Pour Cognac over blueberry mixture and ignite; shake pan until flame goes out. Remove from heat and spoon mixture over ice cream. Serve immediately.

LINDA'S GRAPES WITH COGNAC

Choose the largest, sweetest black grapes you can find (taste one or two before purchasing), because there is very little sugar in this distinctive dessert.

SERVES 8

2 pounds large black grapes	½ cup sour cream
¼ cup Cognac	1 teaspoon pure vanilla
1 cup heavy cream	extract
2 Tablespoons confectioners'	2 Tablespoons firmly packed
sugar	dark brown sugar

1. Wash grapes in cold water, drain in a strainer and blot dry with paper towel. Cut each grape in half and remove seeds. Place in strainer again to drain.
2. In a medium bowl, combine grapes with Cognac. Divide among broiler-proof 3-ounce ramekins and refrigerate until needed.
3. Whip cream with confectioners' sugar until stiff. Using a rubber spatula, fold in sour cream and vanilla. Cover with plastic wrap and refrigerate.
4. When ready to serve, adjust rack to 6 inches from broiler and preheat oven to broil setting.
5. With a metal spatula, spread cream mixture over grapes. Sprinkle a little brown sugar on top of each ramekin.
6. Set ramekins on a large cookie sheet and place under broiler. Broil until brown sugar is melted, about 1 to 2 minutes; watch carefully, as sugar burns easily. Remove from oven and serve immediately.

FRESH ORANGE COMPOTE

A delectable, refreshing dessert. This is a good opportunity to save some of the skins and make Glazed Orange Peel, page 275.

SERVES 8

10 large navel oranges (5½ pounds)	6 Tablespoons Mandarine Napoléon liqueur
½ cup sugar	

1. With a sharp knife, cut a small slice from the top and bottom of each orange. With tip of knife, divide orange skin into 6 sections. Peel each section, removing most of the white membrane as you peel. Reserve some of the skins for making glazed orange peel or discard. With a vegetable peeler, remove all the white membrane from oranges. Cut out each orange segment, removing its protective membrane as you cut. Cut each segment in half and transfer to a large strainer set over a bowl. With a wooden spoon, lightly press oranges in strainer. Measure out ¼ cup juice.

2. In a 1-quart saucepan, combine juice with sugar. Bring to a boil, turn heat to low and cook, stirring constantly, until slightly thickened, about 4 minutes. Remove from heat and let syrup cool slightly.

3. Transfer orange segments to a serving bowl, add liqueur and toss lightly. Blend in syrup and stir to coat evenly. Cover with plastic wrap and refrigerate for at least 2 hours. (This can be done the night before, but toss oranges in syrup once or twice to make sure they are completely coated.)

TOPPING

1 cup heavy cream
1 Tablespoon confectioners' sugar
1 Tablespoon Mandarine Napoléon liqueur
½ cup slivered toasted almonds (optional garnish)
¼ cup finely chopped glazed orange peel (optional garnish)

1. Whip cream with confectioners' sugar until stiff. Fold in liqueur and refrigerate, covered, until ready to use.
2. Just before serving, place orange segments in individual serving bowls (preferably glass) and pour a little syrup over each. Top dessert with a dollop of whipped cream; garnish with almonds and orange peel.

STUFFED PEACHES

Sample the bounty of late summer, when beautiful ripe peaches are at the peak of the season.

SERVES 6

4 ounces amaretti (Italian macaroons)
¼ cup toasted slivered almonds
1 Tablespoon unsalted butter, softened
6 medium-size ripe peaches (about 2 pounds)

½ cup (approximately) apricot preserves
3 Tablespoons unsalted butter, cut into ¼-inch cubes
½ cup amaretto liqueur

1. Break up amaretti and place in food processor fitted with metal blade or in blender. Add almonds and run machine nonstop until both are coarsely ground, about 30 seconds. Set aside.
2. Adjust rack to center of oven and preheat to 350°F. Grease the bottom and sides of a 13 × 9-inch ovenproof baking pan with 1 Tablespoon softened butter.
3. Blanch peaches in boiling water for 2 minutes. Rinse under cold water, drain and remove skins. Cut each peach in half; remove and discard stone.
4. Place peaches in prepared pan and spoon ½ teaspoon apricot preserves into each peach cavity. Spoon crumb mixture into each cavity and gently press down with fingertips. Dot the top of each peach half with butter. Sprinkle liqueur on top of each and bake until barely tender when tested with a fork, about 15 minutes.

TOPPING

1 cup heavy cream
1 Tablespoon confectioners' sugar

2 Tablespoons amaretto liqueur

1. Whip cream with confectioners' sugar until stiff. Fold in liqueur.
2. To serve, place two peach halves on each individual serving dish and garnish with a dollop of whipped cream. Peaches are best served warm.

STUFFED POACHED PEARS

Especially good for the winter months when Anjou pears are abundant.

SERVES 6

3 cups sugar
3 cups water
2 Tablespoons grated lemon
  rind

½ cup fresh lemon juice
6 firm pears, preferably
  Anjou (about 2½ pounds)

1. In a deep 12-inch skillet, combine sugar, water, lemon rind and juice. Bring to a boil over high heat, stirring frequently until sugar is completely dissolved. Turn heat down to low, cover pan and cook syrup for about 8 minutes while preparing pears.
2. Remove core and stem from each of the pears. Peel fruit with a vegetable peeler. Cut the pears in half lengthwise. Using a melon ball scoop, remove the center core. Cut away the fibrous line leading from the core to the stem end.
3. Place pear halves in syrup, cut side down; simmer uncovered for 5 minutes. Using two wooden spoons, gently turn pears every 5 minutes and continue cooking, basting frequently, until pears are tender when tested with a fork, about 15 to 20 minutes. Remove from heat, cover pan, and let pears cool to room temperature in syrup.

RICOTTA FILLING

1½ cups whole milk ricotta
  cheese
¼ cup confectioners' sugar
2 Tablespoons Cognac

1 Tablespoon instant espresso
  coffee powder
2 Tablespoons finely chopped
  pecans (optional garnish)

1. In a medium bowl, combine all ingredients except pecans. Blend thoroughly with a wire whisk.
2. When ready to serve, carefully remove pears from syrup and place 2 halves on each serving dish. (Syrup can be reserved for additional poaching or discarded.) Stuff the center cavities with ricotta filling and garnish each with chopped pecans. Pears are best served at room temperature.

STRAWBERRIES ALL'ANNA

This is my version of the famous Strawberries Romanoff.

SERVES 6

1 quart strawberries	½ pint vanilla ice cream
1 Tablespoon sugar	½ pint raspberry sherbet
2 Tablespoons brandy	½ cup heavy cream, whipped
2 Tablespoons Grand Marnier	until stiff

1. Wash and hull strawberries. Blot dry with paper towel, slice thinly and transfer to a large serving bowl. Sprinkle sugar over berries. Add brandy and Grand Marnier; mix well. Cover with plastic wrap and refrigerate berries for at least 1 hour.
2. When ready to serve, place vanilla ice cream and sherbet in food processor fitted with metal blade or blender. Run machine nonstop until smooth. Add to chilled berries and mix well. Using a rubber spatula, fold in whipped cream. Spoon into individual dessert dishes and serve immediately.

STRAWBERRIES WITH PASTRY CREAM AND SAUCE

Seasonal fruit such as peaches, nectarines or pineapple can be substituted for strawberries. You may want to make the strawberry sauce alone and serve it on top of vanilla ice cream for another dessert.

SERVES 6

PASTRY CREAM

1½ Tablespoons all purpose flour	2 extra large egg yolks
	1 cup milk
1½ Tablespoons cornstarch	3 Tablespoons Grand Marnier
½ cup sugar	1 cup heavy cream

1. In a deep 2-quart mixing bowl, combine flour and cornstarch with a wire whisk. Add sugar and whisk again until well combined.
2. In a small bowl, beat the egg yolks lightly with a fork.

3. In a heavy 2-quart saucepan, bring the milk to a boil over medium-high heat. Quickly pour half of the boiling milk into the flour mixture and whisk until smooth, about 10 seconds; meanwhile, return remaining milk to burner and turn heat to low. Add beaten egg yolks to flour mixture and whisk until blended, about 5 seconds. The remaining milk should again be boiling; quickly add the flour-egg yolk mixture to the milk and whisk vigorously over medium heat until very thick, about 30 seconds. Transfer pastry cream to a large, shallow bowl to hasten cooling. Cover with plastic wrap, lightly placing the wrap against the surface of the cream to prevent a skin from forming. Cool to almost room temperature and whisk in Grand Marnier. Refrigerate until well chilled, about 1 hour.

4. In a medium bowl, whip the cream until stiff. Whisk the pastry cream briefly to loosen. Using a rubber spatula, fold the whipped cream gently but thoroughly into the pastry cream (can be covered with plastic wrap and refrigerated up to 24 hours before serving).

STRAWBERRY SAUCE

1 package (10 ounces) frozen
strawberries in sugar syrup
1 Tablespoon Grand Marnier

1. Thaw berries in a strainer and reserve juices. Place berries in food processor fitted with metal blade or in blender and run machine nonstop until you have a smooth puree. Transfer puree to a small bowl.

2. Place the reserved juice in a small saucepan and cook over medium heat, stirring constantly, until thickened, about 6 minutes. Pour the hot syrup into the puree and mix well. Cover with plastic wrap and cool to room temperature. Stir in liqueur. Refrigerate, covered, until needed (can be made up to 48 hours before serving).

TO SERVE

1 quart strawberries, washed,
hulled and halved, or 4
cups cut-up fruit

Divide pastry cream among 6 serving bowls (preferably glass). Arrange fruit on top of pastry cream. Spoon 2 Tablespoons strawberry sauce on top of fruit and serve immediately.

APPLE CREAM WHIP

A light, luscious dessert to make when Granny Smiths are in season.

SERVES 8

2 pounds Granny Smith
  apples, peeled, quartered
  and cored
1 Tablespoon grated lemon
  rind
¾ cup sugar
1 cinnamon stick
  (approximately 4 inches
  long)
4 extra large egg whites

¼ teaspoon salt
⅛ teaspoon cream of tartar
¼ cup sugar
1 Tablespoon pure vanilla
  extract
1 cup heavy cream
2 Tablespoons finely grated
  semisweet chocolate
  (garnish)

1. In a heavy 3-quart saucepan, combine apples, lemon rind, ¾ cup sugar and cinnamon stick. Cook mixture, covered, over low heat, stirring frequently with a wooden spoon, until apples are soft, about 15 to 20 minutes. Mash the apples with the back of a spoon to break apart. Turn heat to high and cook, stirring constantly and mashing with spoon, until all the liquid is evaporated, about 5 minutes. Discard cinnamon stick and transfer mixture to a bowl. Cover with plastic wrap and chill for at least 2 hours.
2. Transfer mixture to food processor fitted with metal blade and puree with quick on/off turns. Transfer to a large bowl. (If you do not have a food processor, puree mixture through a food mill set over a bowl.)
3. Beat egg whites with salt and cream of tartar until they hold soft peaks. Gradually add remaining ¼ cup of sugar; continue beating until stiff and glossy. Fold in vanilla. Using a rubber spatula, fold egg whites gently but thoroughly into the apple puree.
4. Whip cream until stiff; fold into apple mixture.
5. Spoon mixture into individual serving bowls (preferably glass) and chill for at least 2 hours or overnight.
6. Just before serving, garnish each bowl with grated chocolate.

APRICOT MOUSSE

Refreshingly smooth, and not too sweet.

SERVES 8

1 pound dried apricots	3 Tablespoons apricot liqueur
4 large strips of lemon rind	or 1 Tablespoon pure
¼ cup fresh lemon juice	vanilla extract
1 cup unsweetened	4 extra large egg whites
applesauce	¼ teaspoon salt
½ cup sugar	½ teaspoon cream of tartar

1. Place apricots in a 2-quart saucepan and cover with 3 cups water. Bring to a boil, covered, and drain immediately in a strainer. Return apricots to pan.
2. Add lemon rind, juice, applesauce and half of the sugar to apricots; mix well. Turn heat to low and cook uncovered, stirring frequently, until apricots are quite soft when tested with a fork, about 8 to 10 minutes. Remove from heat and discard lemon rind. Let mixture cool slightly and add liqueur or vanilla.
3. Place apricot mixture in food processor fitted with metal blade or in blender. Run machine nonstop until you have a smooth puree. Transfer to a bowl, cover with plastic wrap and refrigerate until well chilled, about 1½ hours (you can do this the night before if you wish).
4. Beat egg whites with salt and cream of tartar until soft peaks form. Gradually add remaining sugar; continue beating until stiff and glossy. Using a rubber spatula, fold apricot puree a little at a time into beaten egg whites. Ladle mousse into individual serving bowls (preferably glass) and chill for at least 2 hours.

TOPPING

1 cup heavy cream	¼ cup toasted slivered
1 Tablespoon confectioners'	almonds (optional garnish)
sugar	
2 Tablespoons apricot liqueur	
or 1 teaspoon pure vanilla	
extract	

1. Whip cream with confectioners' sugar until stiff. Fold in liqueur or vanilla. Cover with plastic wrap and refrigerate until needed.
2. To serve, place a dollop of whipped cream on each individual mousse and garnish with toasted almonds.

GRAND MARNIER MOUSSE

A stunning way to cap a perfect meal. This is richly satisfying, so make the portions small.

SERVES 8

1 envelope unflavored gelatin
(1 Tablespoon)
½ cup orange juice
2 cups heavy cream
¾ cup sugar

2 cups sour cream
2 Tablespoons grated orange rind
3 Tablespoons Grand Marnier

1. In a small bowl, sprinkle gelatin over orange juice and let stand until gelatin is softened, about 5 minutes.
2. Lightly grease a 5-cup mold; set aside. In a heavy 3-quart saucepan, combine heavy cream and sugar. Cook over low heat, stirring constantly with a wire whisk, until sugar is completely dissolved, about 4 minutes. Stir in gelatin and cook, stirring constantly, until dissolved, about 1 minute. Remove from heat; whisk in sour cream until completely incorporated. Stir in orange rind and Grand Marnier. Pour into prepared mold and refrigerate for at least 4 hours or overnight.

TOPPING

1 cup heavy cream
1 Tablespoon confectioners' sugar
2 Tablespoons Grand Marnier

1 section of Glazed Orange Peel (page 275), sliced into thin strips (optional garnish)

1. Whip cream with confectioners' sugar until stiff. Add Grand Marnier and blend well.
2. When ready to serve, dip mold in warm water for 30 seconds. Invert mousse onto a serving platter. Completely coat mousse with whipped cream and garnish with thin strips of glazed orange peel.

Note: Dessert can also be spooned into individual glass bowls (4-ounce size) and refrigerated for 4 hours before serving. Place a dollop of whipped cream on each and garnish with a few strips of glazed orange peel.

COLD MANDARIN SOUFFLÉ

This refreshing cold soufflé is delectably flavored with Mandarine Napoléon liqueur. If it's unavailable, substitute Grand Marnier.

SERVES 8 TO 10

1 cup cold water
2 envelopes unflavored
   gelatin (2 Tablespoons)
6 extra large eggs, separated
1 can (6 ounces) frozen
   orange juice concentrate,
   thawed

¼ cup Mandarine Napoléon
   liqueur
1 cup heavy cream
¼ teaspoon salt
⅛ teaspoon cream of tartar
¾ cup sugar

1. Fit a collar of folded waxed paper around a 1½-quart soufflé dish; the collar should come 2½ inches above the rim. Fasten ends with transparent tape. Set aside.
2. Place water in the top of a double boiler. Sprinkle in gelatin and let stand until softened, about 5 minutes.
3. In a medium bowl, beat egg yolks lightly with a whisk. Blend yolks into gelatin mixture. Cook over simmering water, whisking constantly, until gelatin is completely dissolved and mixture is slightly thickened, about 4 minutes. Remove from heat.
4. In a small bowl, combine thawed juice with liqueur. Pour into yolk mixture and blend well with whisk. Transfer to a bowl, cover with plastic wrap and refrigerate just until mixture begins to set, about 1 hour.
5. Whip cream until stiff.
6. Whisk the chilled yolk mixture briefly to loosen. Using a rubber spatula, fold in the whipped cream.
7. Beat egg whites with salt and cream of tartar until soft peaks form. Gradually add sugar; continue beating until stiff and glossy. Fold gently but thoroughly into the yolk mixture in three batches. Pour into prepared soufflé dish and refrigerate until firm, about 5 hours or overnight.

TOPPING

1 cup heavy cream
1 Tablespoon confectioners'
   sugar
2 Tablespoons Mandarine
   Napoléon liqueur

12 canned mandarin orange
   segments, well drained
   (optional garnish)

1. Whip cream with confectioners' sugar until stiff. Fold in liqueur.
2. Remove collar from soufflé dish. Spread whipped cream over top of soufflé and garnish with mandarin orange segments.

Note: For a lovely presentation, place whipped cream in a pastry bag fitted with a fluted tip and pipe a decorative border around soufflé, then garnish with orange segments.

ORANGE CREAM

Light in texture, yet intensely rich in flavor.

SERVES 6

2 large navel oranges	6 extra large egg yolks
½ cup water	6 Tablespoons Grand Marnier
1 cup sugar	2 cups heavy cream

1. Dip oranges in hot water for 1 minute. Rinse under cold water and wipe with a damp cloth to remove waxy coating. Using a vegetable peeler or sharp knife, remove thin outer peel from oranges; slice into thin julienne strips and then chop finely. In a 1½-quart saucepan, combine the chopped peel with about 1½ cups water. Bring to a boil, lower heat and cook until tender, about 10 minutes (test by tasting). Drain in a strainer and blot dry with paper towel.

2. Using a sharp knife, remove and discard white membrane from oranges. Cut out each orange segment, removing its protective membrane as you cut. Place orange sections in a strainer with bowl underneath; reserve sections for garnish.

3. In a 1-quart saucepan, combine water and sugar. Bring mixture to a boil over medium heat, stirring and washing down any crystals clinging to the sides of the pan with a brush dipped in cold water until all sugar is dissolved. Turn heat to low and boil syrup undisturbed for 5 minutes. Add chopped peel and cook for another minute.

4. Beat egg yolks until thick and lemon-colored, about 5 minutes. Pour the hot syrup in a very thin stream into beaten egg yolks, beating constantly. Continue to beat until cool (the mixture will be very thick). Add liqueur and blend thoroughly with a rubber spatula.

5. Beat heavy cream until it holds soft peaks. Using a rubber spatula, gradually fold half of the yolk mixture into the whipped cream. Fold the cream mixture back into remaining yolk mixture. Pour into individual bowls (preferably glass) and refrigerate overnight, or place in freezer for 2 hours.

TOPPING

TOPPING

1 cup heavy cream
1 Tablespoon confectioners'
  sugar
2 Tablespoons Grand Marnier

1. Whip cream with confectioners' sugar until stiff. Fold in liqueur. Refrigerate, covered, until needed.
2. When ready to serve, garnish each dessert with a dollop of whipped cream and well drained orange sections.

RICOTTA MOUSSE WITH RASPBERRY SAUCE

This showstopper will please any epicure. Try the raspberry sauce on top of vanilla ice cream for another dessert.

SERVES 8

2 envelopes unflavored
  gelatin (2 Tablespoons)
⅓ cup fresh lemon juice
1 Tablespoon grated lemon
  rind

1 cup heavy cream
15 ounces whole milk ricotta
  cheese
½ cup sugar
4 extra large egg yolks

1. In a small saucepan, sprinkle gelatin over lemon juice and let stand until softened, about 5 minutes. Place over low heat and stir constantly until gelatin dissolves, about 2 minutes. Remove from heat, add lemon rind and cool slightly.
2. Whip cream until stiff; set aside.
3. Beat ricotta with sugar until smooth. Add egg yolks and beat until well combined. Blend in gelatin mixture. Using a rubber spatula, fold in whipped cream.
4. Lightly grease a 6-cup mold. Pour in mousse mixture and chill for at least 6 hours or overnight.

RASPBERRY SAUCE

2 packages (10 ounces each)
  frozen red raspberries in
  sugar syrup, thawed

3 Tablespoons Chambord or
  Grand Marnier liqueur

1. In a 1-quart saucepan, place thawed raspberries, including syrup. Cook over medium heat, stirring constantly, until slightly thickened, about 6

minutes. Transfer to a fine strainer set over a bowl. Using the back of a wooden spoon, press berries through strainer; discard seeds. Stir liqueur into raspberry puree. Cover with plastic wrap and refrigerate until needed. (Raspberry sauce can be made well ahead of time and kept up to 1 month in covered container in refrigerator.)

TO SERVE

1 quart strawberries, washed and hulled   5 fresh mint sprigs (optional garnish)

1. Dip mold into warm water for 30 seconds. Invert mousse onto a serving platter and garnish with strawberries and mint sprigs.
2. To serve, slice mousse into wedges. Top with a few strawberries and ladle chilled raspberry sauce over each serving.

CARAMEL CUSTARD

This custard is exquisitely smooth. Topped off with a beautiful golden caramel, it is the perfect dessert for a special dinner. The custard can be made up to 2 days before serving.

SERVES 8

CARAMELIZED SUGAR

¾ cup sugar   ¼ cup water

In a heavy 1-quart saucepan, combine sugar and water. Cook over low heat, stirring constantly, until sugar is dissolved. Increase heat to high and cook without stirring until sugar turns a golden caramel color, about 6 minutes. Pour a little of the caramel into each of eight 4-ounce custard cups, swirling and tilting cups until the sides are evenly coated. Set aside to harden.

CUSTARD

8 extra large egg yolks
3 cups heavy cream
⅓ cup sugar

1 Tablespoon pure vanilla extract

1. Adjust rack to center of oven and preheat to 350°F.
2. Place yolks in a medium bowl and beat lightly with a wire whisk.
3. In a heavy 2-quart saucepan, combine cream and sugar. Cook uncovered

over medium heat, stirring once or twice, until cream is scalded (when tiny bubbles form around edge of pan). Remove pan from heat. Slowly pour yolks into scalded cream, whisking gently as you pour. Stir in vanilla. Pour mixture through a fine strainer set over a wide-mouth 1-quart pitcher to remove any coagulated egg particles. Divide strained mixture among prepared custard cups. Arrange custard cups in a large baking pan. Pour hot water into pan to reach ⅔ up the sides of cups. Bake until knife inserted in center of custard comes out clean, about 25 minutes. Immediately remove from water and arrange custards on a rack to cool. When cooled to room temperature, cover each cup with plastic wrap and refrigerate until well chilled, about 4 hours or overnight.

4. Just before serving, dip a knife into warm water and run around the inside of each custard cup. Turn custards out onto individual dessert plates. Drizzle any caramel remaining in cup over custard. Serve immediately.

PAPA'S RICE PUDDING
Budino alla Casale

Not for the diet-conscious, this is the ultimate in rich, smooth perfection.

SERVES 10

1 cup converted long-grain rice, picked over to remove any dark grains
2 cups milk
2 cups water
1 Tablespoon unsalted butter
1 teaspoon salt
1 cinnamon stick (approximately 4 inches long)
½ cup sugar
1 Tablespoon pure vanilla extract

1 Tablespoon Grand Marnier
2 Tablespoons finely chopped Glazed Orange Peel (page 275) or 2 Tablespoons finely grated orange rind
4 cups (1 quart) heavy cream
¼ cup confectioners' sugar
3 Tablespoons finely grated semisweet chocolate (garnish)

1. In a heavy 4-quart saucepan, combine rice, milk, water, butter, salt and cinnamon stick. Bring to a boil, covered, over high heat. Turn heat to low; cook covered, stirring frequently, until liquid is completely absorbed into

rice, about 25 minutes. Stir in sugar; continue to cook over low heat, stirring constantly, for an additional 2 minutes. Transfer mixture to a large bowl and cool to room temperature. Discard cinnamon stick. Using a rubber spatula, fold in vanilla, Grand Marnier and orange peel. Cover with plastic wrap and refrigerate until thoroughly chilled, about 2 hours.

2. Whip cream with confectioners' sugar until stiff. Remove 1½ cups whipped cream and reserve for garnish. Using a rubber spatula, thoroughly fold remaining cream into pudding. Spoon into individual dishes and refrigerate until ready to serve.

3. Top each dessert with a dollop of reserved whipped cream. Garnish with grated chocolate and serve immediately.

RICOTTA PUDDING
Budino di Ricotta

My students think this tastes more like cheesecake than pudding. This dessert can be served hot or at room temperature, though it will definitely sink a little in the middle on cooling. If serving at room temperature, whip 1 cup heavy cream with 1 Tablespoon confectioners' sugar and place a dollop on each portion (this way no one will know what you are trying to camouflage). The cream can be sprinkled with a little grated semisweet chocolate if you wish.

SERVES 8

1 Tablespoon unsalted butter, softened
15 ounces whole milk ricotta cheese
½ cup sugar
3 large eggs, separated
2 Tablespoons all purpose flour
1 teaspoon pure vanilla extract

½ cup golden raisins, plumped in hot water and well drained
1 Tablespoon finely chopped Glazed Orange Peel (page 275) or 1 Tablespoon grated orange rind
¼ teaspoon salt
⅛ teaspoon cream of tartar
2 Tablespoons confectioners' sugar, sifted (garnish)

1. Adjust rack to center of oven and preheat to 350°F. Grease eight 4-ounce ramekins with softened butter and set aside.

2. Beat the ricotta cheese until smooth. Add ¼ cup sugar and continue beating until well combined. Add egg yolks one at a time, beating well after each addition. Add flour and vanilla. Stir in raisins and orange peel.

3. Beat egg whites with salt and cream of tartar until they hold soft peaks. Gradually add remaining ¼ cup sugar; continue beating until stiff and glossy. Using a rubber spatula, fold beaten egg whites gently but thoroughly into ricotta mixture. Divide among prepared ramekins.

4. Arrange ramekins in a large baking pan. Pour hot water into pan to reach at least 2 inches up the sides of ramekins. Bake until pudding is lightly golden and puffed on top, about 30 minutes. Remove from oven and transfer ramekins to a rack to cool for 15 minutes before serving. Dust top of each pudding with confectioners' sugar and serve immediately.

FROZEN MOCHA SURPRISE

A smooth and creamy dessert for full-fledged chocolate addicts. The surprise is that the center is filled with amaretto liqueur. Just sit back and watch the expression on your guests' faces!

SERVES 8

1 bar (8 ounces) semisweet chocolate (preferably Ghirardelli), broken into 1-inch pieces
2 teaspoons instant espresso coffee powder
⅓ cup hot water
2 teaspoons pure vanilla extract
8 extra large egg yolks
1 cup confectioners' sugar, sifted after measuring
2 cups heavy cream

1. Cut 8 strips of waxed paper 3 inches wide; fold each strip in half lengthwise. Fit eight 2-ounce ramekins tightly with folded waxed-paper strips to form collars standing 1 inch above rims. Fasten ends with transparent tape. Set aside.

2. Place chocolate in the top of a double boiler and melt over simmering water.

3. While chocolate is melting, dissolve coffee in hot water. When chocolate has melted, remove top of double boiler and stir in coffee. Stir in vanilla and let mixture cool to almost room temperature, stirring once or twice.

4. Beat egg yolks with confectioners' sugar until very thick and lemon-colored. Pour in chocolate mixture and beat again until well combined.
5. Whip cream until stiff. Using a rubber spatula, fold whipped cream gently but thoroughly into chocolate mixture in 2 batches.
6. Spoon mixture into ramekins and freeze until firm, about 4 hours or overnight (dessert can be made ahead and kept in freezer up to 3 days before serving).

TOPPING

1 cup heavy cream
1 Tablespoon confectioners' sugar
2 Tablespoons (approximately) amaretto liqueur

2 Tablespoons finely chopped toasted almonds

1. Whip cream with confectioners' sugar until stiff.
2. With the end of a wooden spoon, make a hole in the center of each ramekin, right down to the bottom. Fill the hole with about ½ teaspoon liqueur. Remove collars and top each dessert with a small dollop of whipped cream. Garnish with chopped almonds and serve immediately.

PINEAPPLE–COCONUT PARFAITS

A delicious fantasy to sweeten any event!

SERVES 8

1 can (20 ounces)
unsweetened crushed
pineapple
½ cup cold water
1 cup sugar
¼ teaspoon cream of tartar
1 cup heavy cream

3 extra large egg whites
¼ teaspoon salt
1 Tablespoon pure vanilla
extract
1 cup sweetened flaked
coconut

1. Thoroughly drain crushed pineapple in a strainer. Remove ½ cup pineapple, place in a small bowl, cover with plastic wrap and refrigerate; reserve for garnish.
2. In a heavy 2-quart saucepan, combine water, sugar and cream of tartar. Bring to a boil over medium-high heat, washing down any sugar crystals that cling to the sides of the pan with a brush dipped in cold water. Turn heat to medium and cook syrup without stirring until it reaches 240°F on candy thermometer (thread stage), about 10 minutes.
3. Meanwhile, whip cream until stiff; set aside.
4. Beat the egg whites with salt until they hold soft peaks. Add the boiling syrup in a slow, thin stream, adding about 3 Tablespoons of syrup at a time and returning pan to low heat for approximately 30 seconds between additions (when finished, the mixture will be firm and satiny). With a rubber spatula, fold in the vanilla and whipped cream. Fold in coconut and drained pineapple gently but thoroughly. Transfer to individual parfait glasses and freeze until firm, about 3 hours or overnight.

TOPPING

1 cup heavy cream
1 Tablespoon confectioners'
sugar

1. Whip cream with confectioners' sugar until stiff.
2. When ready to serve, place a dollop of whipped cream on top of each parfait; garnish with reserved pineapple.

BISCUIT TORTONI

Papa Casale always had a supply of this exquisitely smooth dessert in the freezer for unexpected guests.

SERVES 12

½ cup blanched almonds
4 ounces amaretti (Italian macaroons)
2 cups heavy cream
1 cup confectioners' sugar, sifted after measuring

2 Tablespoons amaretto liqueur
2 extra large egg whites
¼ teaspoon salt
⅛ teaspoon cream of tartar

1. Adjust rack to center of oven and preheat to 350°F. Place almonds on a cookie sheet and toast until lightly golden, about 5 to 7 minutes. Let cool slightly. Place in food processor fitted with metal blade or in blender and run machine nonstop until finely ground. Transfer to a bowl. Break cookies into pieces and place in food processor or blender. Run machine nonstop until finely ground. Add to almonds and mix well. Transfer half of the crumb mixture to another bowl and reserve.
2. Whip cream with half of the confectioners' sugar until stiff; transfer to a large, deep bowl. Using a rubber spatula, fold half of the crumb mixture and the liqueur into whipped cream.
3. Beat egg whites with salt and cream of tartar until they hold soft peaks. Gradually add remaining confectioners' sugar; continue beating until stiff and glossy. Using a rubber spatula, fold beaten egg whites into whipped cream mixture in two batches.
4. Line up twelve 3-ounce ramekins and sprinkle 1 teaspoon of the reserved crumb mixture evenly into the bottom of each. Spoon tortoni mixture into each dish and garnish with remaining crumbs. Cover each ramekin with plastic wrap and freeze until firm, about 5 hours or overnight. Serve directly from freezer. (If you are going to freeze tortoni longer than a week, cover each ramekin with a layer of foil over plastic wrap to prevent freezer burns. Tortoni can be kept in freezer up to 3 months.)

Note: Some gourmet shops carry a 2-ounce paper cup which is excellent for tortoni. If using the paper ramekin, your yield will be 16 instead of 12.

Tarts and Tortes

APPLE CUSTARD TART
Torta di Mele

Great eye appeal as well as taste. This tart must be made the same day it is served, so the custard will not crack around apples.

SERVES 8 TO 10

CRUST

1¾ cups all purpose flour (not unbleached)
¼ cup confectioners' sugar
½ teaspoon salt
½ cup (1 stick) unsalted butter, well chilled and cut into ½-inch cubes

1 large egg yolk
3 Tablespoons fresh lemon juice, strained and well chilled
1 Tablespoon apricot preserves, strained

Lightly grease the bottom and sides of an 11-inch tart pan with removable bottom.

FOOD PROCESSOR METHOD

1. Place flour, confectioners' sugar and salt in food processor fitted with metal blade and turn machine on/off 3 times to combine. Add butter to work bowl, distributing it evenly over surface of dry ingredients. Turn machine on and process until mixture looks like coarse meal, about 30 seconds.

2. In a small bowl, beat egg yolk and lemon juice with a fork. Sprinkle half of the liquid over flour mixture. Turn machine on/off 3 times until mixture looks crumbly. Add remaining liquid; turn machine on/off 3 to 4 times, just until the dough starts to cling together (do not let dough form ball). Gather all the dough from the work bowl and flatten into an 8-inch circle. Wrap in plastic and refrigerate for 20 minutes.

HAND METHOD

1. Sift flour, confectioners' sugar and salt into a medium bowl. Using a pastry blender or two knives, cut in butter until evenly distributed and mixture resembles coarse meal.

2. In a small bowl, beat egg yolk and lemon juice with a fork. Sprinkle half of the liquid over the flour mixture; lightly mix with fork until crumbly. Sprinkle remaining liquid over dough; lightly mix again until dough comes away from sides of bowl and holds together in a cohesive ball. Flatten dough into an 8-inch circle. Wrap in plastic and refrigerate for 20 minutes.

TO ROLL CRUST

1. Place dough on a lightly floured pastry cloth. Using a lightly floured stockinette-covered rolling pin, roll dough into a circle 2 inches larger in diameter than the tart pan. Trim excess dough with a pastry cutter.

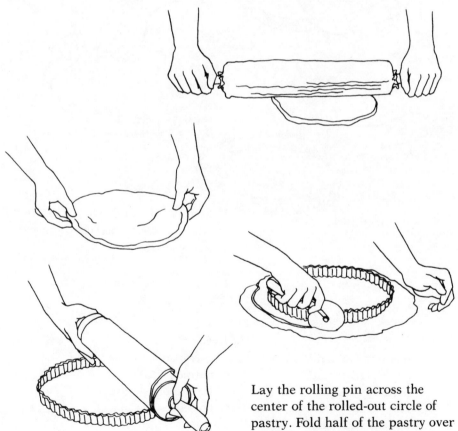

Lay the rolling pin across the center of the rolled-out circle of pastry. Fold half of the pastry over the rolling pin, then lift and lay across the center of the pan.

Gently unfold the pastry and ease
it into the pan so that the
overhang is even all around. Fold
in edge and press firmly against
sides of pan, letting dough extend
½ inch above rim.

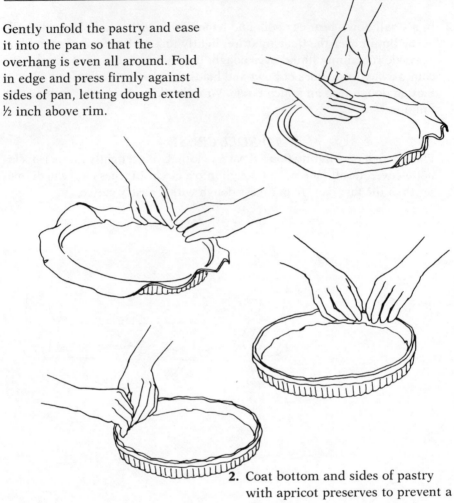

2. Coat bottom and sides of pastry
with apricot preserves to prevent a
soggy crust.

FILLING

5 medium Golden Delicious
  apples (1½ pounds)
3 extra large eggs
½ cup sugar
⅔ cup heavy cream
1 Tablespoon pure vanilla
  extract

¼ teaspoon freshly grated
  nutmeg
3 Tablespoons apricot
  preserves (for glaze)

1. Adjust rack to center of oven and preheat to 375°F.

2. Peel, quarter and core apples. Thinly slice each quarter crosswise several times without cutting all the way through. Starting from inside rim of pastry, arrange quartered apples in a circular pattern.

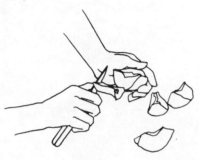

3. In a medium bowl, beat eggs and sugar with a wire whisk until pale and creamy. Add cream and vanilla; whisk again until well combined. Pour egg mixture over apples and sprinkle top of flan with nutmeg.

4. Place flan on a cookie sheet and bake for 20 minutes. Reduce oven temperature to 350°F and bake until custard filling is firm, about 25 minutes. Remove from oven and transfer to a rack to cool.

5. While flan is still warm, melt apricot preserves over low heat and strain. Brush preserves over cooked apples, taking care not to get glaze on custard.

6. When ready to serve, remove rim. Place flan on a large, flat plate with a folded piece of dampened paper towel in the center to prevent flan from sliding when slicing.

APPLE CHEESE TORTE

A luxurious blending of cream and a slight hint of lemon, topped off with apricot-glazed apples. This torte is best when made 1 day ahead of serving, covered with plastic wrap and refrigerated. Let stand at room temperature for about 30 minutes before serving.

SERVES 10 TO 12

CRUST

⅓ cup sugar
  Rind from 1 large lemon, cut into 1-inch pieces (food processor) or 1 Tablespoon grated lemon rind (hand method)
1¼ cups unbleached flour

¼ teaspoon salt
½ cup (1 stick) unsalted butter, well chilled and cut into ½-inch cubes
1 large egg yolk, lightly beaten

Adjust rack to center of oven and preheat to 350°F. Lightly grease the bottom and sides of a 10-inch springform pan or 10-inch fluted tart pan (2 inches deep) with removable bottom.

FOOD PROCESSOR METHOD

Place sugar and lemon rind in food processor fitted with metal blade. Run machine nonstop until rind is finely minced, about 1 minute. Using a rubber spatula, scrape inside of work bowl. Add flour and salt to work bowl; turn machine on/off to incorporate. Add butter to work bowl, distributing pieces evenly over the surface. Turn machine on and run until mixture is fine and crumbly, about 30 seconds. Add egg yolk and let machine run just until mixture begins to cling together, about 30 seconds (do not let dough form ball). Gather all the dough from work bowl and shape into a ball.

HAND METHOD

In a medium bowl, sift flour, salt and sugar together. Add 1 Tablespoon grated lemon rind; mix well. Using a pastry blender or two knives, cut in butter until evenly distributed and mixture resembles coarse meal. Sprinkle egg yolk over flour mixture and lightly mix with a fork until dough comes away from sides of bowl and holds together in a cohesive ball.

TO SHAPE CRUST

Dust fingertips lightly with flour. Press about half of the dough evenly into bottom of prepared pan. Break remaining dough into 4 equal chunks. Roll each piece between palms of your hands to form a rope about 1 inch in diameter and 6 inches long. Arrange evenly around base of pan (making ropes out of dough will make it easier to pat crust into place). Press dough about 2 inches up sides of pan, being careful to make top edge straight and even.

FILLING

2 packages (8 ounces each) cream cheese, room temperature, each package cut into 8 cubes	½ cup sugar 2 large eggs 1 teaspoon pure vanilla extract

FOOD PROCESSOR METHOD

Add half of all ingredients to work bowl fitted with metal blade (dividing the cream cheese mixture into two batches will give you a smoother texture). Run machine nonstop until you have a smooth mixture, stopping machine once or twice to scrape inside of work bowl with rubber spatula. Pour mixture into prepared pan and repeat with remaining ingredients.

HAND METHOD

Beat cream cheese with sugar until smooth. Add eggs one at a time, beating well to incorporate; add vanilla. Pour mixture into prepared pan.

TOPPING

⅓ cup sugar 1 teaspoon cinnamon 3 medium-size tart apples such as Granny Smith or Greening (1 pound), peeled, halved, cored and edges cut	flat (for food processor) or thinly sliced ½ cup apricot preserves ¼ cup sliced toasted almonds (garnish)

1. In a medium bowl, combine sugar and cinnamon.
2. If using food processor, fit with medium serrated slicer. Arrange apples in feed tube vertically; use firm pressure on pusher to slice.
3. Toss sliced apples in sugar mixture. Arrange over cream cheese layer in an overlapping pattern, starting from outside edge.
4. Bake until cheese mixture is set in center, about 1 hour and 15 minutes. Remove from oven and place on a rack.
5. While torte is still hot, melt apricot preserves over low heat and strain. Brush preserves on top of torte and garnish with toasted almonds.
6. When ready to serve, remove rim. Place torte on a flat plate with a folded piece of dampened paper towel in the center to prevent bottom of pan from sliding when slicing.

BLUEBERRY CREAM TORTE

Elegant and very easy to make. Sliced strawberries can be substituted for the blueberries.

SERVES 10 TO 12

CRUST

1 package (7½ ounces) Peek
Freans Sweet Meal biscuits
or 24 graham crackers (2⅜-
inch square size)
⅓ cup unsalted butter, melted

1. Adjust rack to center of oven and preheat to 350°F. Lightly grease the bottom of a 10-inch springform pan with vegetable shortening.
2. Break up biscuits or crackers and place in food processor fitted with metal blade or in blender. Run machine nonstop until reduced to fine crumbs, about 1 minute. Remove cover and pour melted butter over crumbs. Run machine until combined, about 1 minute, stopping to scrape inside of work bowl or container with a rubber spatula. Press crumbs into bottom of prepared pan and bake for 10 minutes. Remove from oven and set on a rack to cool to room temperature. Lightly grease sides of pan with vegetable shortening.

FILLING

2 pints blueberries
1 jar (10 ounces) currant or
strawberry jelly
1 envelope unflavored gelatin
(1 Tablespoon)
¼ cup fresh lemon juice

1 cup heavy cream
½ cup sugar
1 cup sour cream
1 Tablespoon grated lemon
rind

1. Wash each pint of blueberries separately. Drain well in strainer and blot dry with paper towel. Arrange half of the blueberries in a single layer over cooled crust.
2. In a small saucepan, melt jelly over low heat. Brush ⅓ of the melted jelly over blueberries. Set aside.
3. In a small bowl, sprinkle gelatin over lemon juice and let stand until gelatin is softened, about 5 minutes.
4. In a heavy 2-quart saucepan, combine heavy cream and sugar. Cook over low heat, stirring constantly with a wire whisk, until sugar is completely

dissolved, about 3 minutes. Stir in gelatin mixture and cook, stirring constantly, until dissolved, about 1 minute. Remove from heat; whisk in sour cream. Stir in lemon rind. Pour mixture over berries in crust and refrigerate until firm, about 2 hours.

5. Arrange remaining blueberries in a circular pattern over cream mixture. Reheat remaining jelly and brush over fruit. Refrigerate until set, about 4 hours or overnight.

6. When ready to serve, run knife around inside edge of pan and remove springform. Place on a platter with a folded piece of dampened paper towel in the center to prevent bottom of pan from sliding when slicing.

PUMPKIN CHIFFON TORTE

A spicy filling and a snappy crust; a light yet satisfying finale that captures the joy of Thanksgiving whenever it is served. Dessert can be made 2 days ahead of serving, covered with plastic wrap and refrigerated.

SERVES 12

CRUST

1 package (7 ounces) Peek Freans Ginger Crisp biscuits or 38 small gingersnaps
⅓ cup unsalted butter, melted

1. Adjust rack to center of oven and preheat to 350°F. Grease the bottom of a 10-inch springform pan with vegetable shortening.

2. Break up cookies and place in food processor fitted with metal blade or in blender. Run machine nonstop until reduced to fine crumbs, about 1 minute. Remove cover and pour melted butter over crumbs. Run machine until combined, about 1 minute, stopping to scrape inside of work bowl or container with rubber spatula. Press crumbs into bottom of pan and bake for 10 minutes. Remove from oven and set on a rack to cool to room temperature. Lightly grease sides of pan with vegetable shortening.

FILLING

2 envelopes unflavored
  gelatin (2 Tablespoons)
1 cup firmly packed dark
  brown sugar
1 teaspoon cinnamon
½ teaspoon freshly grated
  nutmeg

½ teaspoon ground ginger
2 cups milk
3 large eggs, separated
1 can (16 ounces) pumpkin
¼ teaspoon salt
⅛ teaspoon cream of tartar

1. In a heavy 2½-quart saucepan, mix together gelatin, ½ cup brown sugar, cinnamon, nutmeg and ginger. Using a wire whisk, stir in milk and egg yolks; blend well. Place over low heat and cook, whisking constantly, until gelatin dissolves and mixture thickens slightly, about 8 minutes. Remove from heat and stir in pumpkin. Transfer to a large bowl and cover with plastic wrap. Chill, stirring occasionally, just until mixture mounds when dropped from a spoon, about 35 minutes.
2. Beat egg whites until foamy. Add salt and cream of tartar and beat until soft peaks form. Gradually add remaining ½ cup brown sugar; continue beating until stiff and glossy. Using a rubber spatula, fold beaten egg whites gently but thoroughly into pumpkin mixture. Pour into crust and smooth top with a metal spatula. Chill overnight.

TOPPING

1 cup heavy cream
1 Tablespoon confectioners'
  sugar
1 teaspoon pure vanilla
  extract

1 Tablespoon coarsely grated
  semisweet chocolate
  (optional garnish)

1. Whip cream with confectioners' sugar until stiff. Fold in vanilla.
2. Up to 3 hours before serving, dip knife in cold water, run around inside of pan and remove ring. Place torte on a platter with a folded piece of dampened paper towel in the center to prevent bottom of pan from sliding when slicing. With a metal spatula, spread cream over entire surface of torte. Refrigerate until ready to serve. Just before serving, garnish top with grated chocolate.

TOASTED COCONUT CREAM TART
Torta di Crema

Another great do-ahead dessert. The crust can be made up to 3 days in advance, covered with plastic wrap and stored in a cool place. Prepare filling 1 day before serving, assemble tart and refrigerate until needed.

SERVES 8 TO 10

CRUST

1½ cups all purpose flour (not unbleached)
2 Tablespoons confectioners' sugar
½ teaspoon salt
¼ cup butter, well chilled and cut into ½-inch cubes

¼ cup vegetable shortening, well chilled and cut into small pieces
¼ cup orange juice, strained and well chilled

Using the bottom of an 11-inch tart pan with removable bottom as a pattern, cut a piece of parchment paper 2 inches larger than the rim. Set aside. Lightly grease bottom and sides of pan.

FOOD PROCESSOR METHOD

Place flour, confectioners' sugar and salt in food processor fitted with metal blade and turn machine on/off 3 times to combine. Add butter and shortening to work bowl, distributing them as evenly as possible over the surface of dry ingredients. Process until mixture looks like coarse meal, about 30 seconds. Sprinkle half of the orange juice over the flour mixture. Turn machine on/off 3 times until mixture looks crumbly. Add remaining juice; turn machine on/off 3 to 4 times, just until the dough starts to cling together (do not let dough form ball). Gather all the dough from work bowl and flatten into an 8-inch circle. Wrap in plastic and refrigerate for 20 minutes.

HAND METHOD

Sift flour, confectioners' sugar and salt into a medium bowl. Using a pastry blender or two knives, cut in butter and shortening until mixture resembles coarse meal. Sprinkle half of the orange juice over the flour mixture; lightly mix with a fork until crumbly. Sprinkle in remaining juice; lightly mix again until dough comes away from sides of bowl and holds together in a cohesive ball. Flatten dough into an 8-inch circle. Wrap in plastic and refrigerate for 20 minutes.

TO ROLL AND BAKE CRUST

1. Adjust rack to center of oven and preheat to 375°F.
2. Place dough on a lightly floured pastry cloth. Using a lightly floured stockinette-covered rolling pin, roll dough into a circle 2 inches larger in diameter than the tart pan. Lay the rolling pin across the center of the rolled-out circle of pastry. Fold half of the pastry over the rolling pin, then lift and lay across the center of the pan. Gently unfold the pastry and ease it into the pan so that the overhang is even all around. Fold in edge and press firmly against sides of pan, letting dough extend ¼ inch above rim. Prick all over bottom and sides of crust with a fork. Line the pastry with parchment paper. Weight with 2 cups rice or dried beans to prevent shrinking during baking. Bake for 10 minutes. Lower oven heat to 350°F and bake until edge of crust is very lightly golden, about 10 minutes. Remove from oven and very carefully remove weights and parchment paper. Return to oven and bake until bottom crust is lightly golden, about 5 to 10 minutes. Remove from oven and let cool to room temperature on a rack.

FILLING AND TOPPING

1¼ cups sweetened flaked coconut
1 envelope unflavored gelatin (1 Tablespoon)
½ cup milk, room temperature
4 extra large eggs, separated
⅔ cup sugar
3 Tablespoons Cognac
1 teaspoon pure vanilla extract
2 cups heavy cream
¼ teaspoon salt
⅛ teaspoon cream of tartar
1 Tablespoon apricot preserves, strained

1. Adjust rack to center of oven and preheat to 350°F. Spread coconut on a cookie sheet and bake until lightly toasted, about 5 minutes, stirring often to prevent burning (especially around edges). Set aside to cool.
2. Mix gelatin into milk with a fork and let stand until gelatin is softened, about 5 minutes.
3. Beat egg yolks with ⅓ cup sugar until thick and lemon-colored. Transfer mixture to the top of a double boiler set over simmering water (to avoid curdled yolks, water should not touch the upper section of the double boiler). Cook, stirring constantly with a wire whisk, until satiny, about 2 minutes. Add gelatin mixture and continue cooking, stirring constantly, until gelatin is completely dissolved, about 1 minute. Transfer mixture to a large bowl and let cool slightly. Add Cognac and vanilla. Cover with plastic wrap and cool to room temperature (can be placed in refrigerator for a few minutes to hasten cooling).
4. Whip cream until stiff. Using a rubber spatula, fold whipped cream into

yolk mixture; if yolk mixture has set, whisk briefly to soften before adding whipped cream.

5. Beat egg whites with salt and cream of tartar until they hold soft peaks. Gradually add remaining ⅓ cup sugar; continue beating until stiff and glossy. Using a rubber spatula, fold beaten egg whites gently but thoroughly into cream mixture.

6. Brush bottom of pastry shell with apricot preserves to prevent crust from getting soggy. Spoon in filling and smooth top with a metal spatula or knife. Sprinkle with toasted coconut. Refrigerate until set, about 5 hours or overnight.

7. Remove ring just before serving. Place tart on a large flat plate with a piece of dampened paper towel in the center to prevent bottom of pan from sliding when slicing.

ESPRESSO CREAM TART
Torta d'Espresso

Your guests will leave the table properly pampered after this dessert. Don't fret if you have a hairline crack in the bottom of the crust once the parchment paper is removed; this happens once in a while with a nut crust, but no one will know once the torte is filled.

SERVES 8 TO 10

CRUST

½ cup blanched almonds
1¾ cups unbleached flour
¼ cup confectioners' sugar
¼ teaspoon salt
6 Tablespoons unsalted butter, well chilled and cut into ½-inch cubes
¼ cup vegetable shortening, well chilled and cut into small pieces

1 large egg yolk
2 Tablespoons milk, well chilled
1 teaspoon pure vanilla extract

1. Using the bottom of an 11-inch tart pan with removable bottom as a pattern, cut a piece of parchment paper 2 inches larger than the rim. Set aside. Lightly grease bottom and sides of pan.

2. Adjust rack to center of oven and preheat to 350°F.

3. Place almonds on a cookie sheet and toast until lightly golden, about 5 to 7 minutes. Remove from oven and let cool to room temperature. Leave oven rack at same position for baking crust, but turn oven off.

4. Place almonds in food processor fitted with metal blade or in blender. Run machine nonstop until finely ground.

FOOD PROCESSOR METHOD

1. Leave ground almonds in food processor. Add flour, confectioners' sugar and salt and turn machine on/off 3 times to combine. Add butter and shortening to work bowl, distributing them as evenly as possible over the surface of the dry ingredients. Process until mixture looks like coarse meal, about 30 seconds.

2. In a small bowl, beat egg yolk, milk and vanilla with a fork. Sprinkle half of the liquid over the flour mixture. Turn machine on/off 3 times until mixture looks crumbly. Add remaining liquid and turn machine on/off 3 to 4 times, just until the dough starts to cling together (do not let dough form ball). Gather all the dough from work bowl and shape into a ball.

HAND METHOD

1. Grind almonds. Sift flour, confectioners' sugar and salt into a medium bowl. Add ground nuts and mix well with a fork. Using a pastry blender or two knives, cut in butter and shortening until evenly distributed and mixture resembles coarse meal.

2. In a small bowl, beat egg yolk, milk and vanilla with a fork. Sprinkle half of the liquid over the flour mixture and lightly mix with fork until mixture looks crumbly. Sprinkle remaining liquid over dough; lightly mix again until dough comes away from sides of bowl and holds together in a cohesive ball.

TO SHAPE AND BAKE CRUST

1. Preheat oven to 350°F.

2. Break dough into 10 chunks and place in bottom of prepared pan. Press evenly onto bottom and sides of pan, dusting hands with flour as necessary. Prick all over the bottom and sides of crust with a fork. Refrigerate for 30 minutes.

3. Line chilled pastry with parchment paper and press firmly onto dough. Weight with 2 cups rice or dried beans to prevent shrinking during baking. Bake until crust is lightly golden, about 30 minutes. Very carefully remove weights and paper and cool crust to room temperature on rack.

FILLING

1 Tablespoon instant espresso coffee powder	½ cup sugar
¾ cup water	3 Tablespoons coffee liqueur or brandy
1 envelope unflavored gelatin (1 Tablespoon)	2 cups heavy cream
2 extra large eggs, separated	¼ teaspoon salt
	⅛ teaspoon cream of tartar

1. In a small saucepan, combine coffee and water. Sprinkle gelatin over coffee and let stand until softened, about 5 minutes. Place over low heat and stir constantly until gelatin dissolves, about 2 minutes. Remove from heat and cool to room temperature, stirring occasionally, until slightly thickened.
2. Beat egg yolks with ¼ cup sugar until thick and lemon-colored. Stir in coffee mixture and liqueur or brandy. Transfer to a large bowl.
3. Whip cream until stiff. Remove ⅓ and reserve for topping. Using a rubber spatula, fold remaining cream into coffee mixture.
4. Beat egg whites with salt and cream of tartar until they hold soft peaks. Gradually add remaining ¼ cup sugar; continue beating until stiff and glossy. Using a rubber spatula, fold beaten egg whites gently but thoroughly into coffee mixture. Pour into pastry shell and smooth top with metal spatula. Refrigerate until firm, about 5 hours or overnight.

TOPPING

1 teaspoon confectioners' sugar	1 teaspoon grated semisweet chocolate
½ teaspoon instant espresso coffee powder	

1. Mix reserved whipped cream with confectioners' sugar and instant coffee. Cover and refrigerate until needed.
2. When ready to serve, place cream mixture in a pastry bag fitted with a fluted tip. Pipe border of cream onto tart and garnish with grated chocolate.
3. Remove rim and place tart on a flat plate with a piece of dampened paper towel in the center to prevent bottom of pan from sliding when slicing.

Cakes and Cream Puff Pastry

GOLDEN YELLOW CAKE

GLAZED ORANGE CAKE

RICOTTA CHEESECAKE

SICILIAN CAKE WITH CHOCOLATE FROSTING

SPECKLED CHOCOLATE SPONGE CAKE

ECLAIRS

ST. JOSEPH'S RICOTTA PUFFS

GOLDEN YELLOW CAKE

Almost like a poundcake in texture—very rich and buttery. Mamma made this cake at least once a week, and I find myself making it just as often. Cake can be made up to 2 days before serving, covered and kept in a cool place.

SERVES 12 TO 14

3 cups all purpose flour (not unbleached)
2½ teaspoons baking powder
1 teaspoon salt
1 cup (2 sticks) unsalted butter, room temperature
2 cups sugar

5 extra large eggs, room temperature
1 cup milk, room temperature
1 Tablespoon pure vanilla extract

1. Adjust oven rack ⅓ up from bottom of oven and preheat to 350°F. Grease a 10 × 4-inch tube pan with vegetable shortening. Dust pan lightly with flour; shake out excess and set aside.
2. In a shallow bowl, sift together flour, baking powder and salt; set aside.
3. With electric mixer on medium speed, cream butter and sugar until fluffy, about 5 minutes. Add eggs one at a time, beating well after each addition; scrape down inside of bowl with a rubber spatula. Turn speed down to low and add flour mixture alternately with milk in three batches, scraping down with rubber spatula after each addition. Stir in vanilla. Turn batter into prepared pan. Tap pan gently but firmly on work surface to dislodge any air bubbles. Bake until cake is lightly golden and tester inserted in center comes out clean, about 1 hour. Let cake cool in pan on a rack for about 5 minutes. Invert onto rack, remove pan, and invert again onto second rack. Let cake cool completely before transferring to cake plate and serving.

Variations: 1 cup of any of the following can be added to batter: chopped walnuts or pecans, sweetened flaked coconut, plumped raisins or chocolate chips.

GLAZED ORANGE CAKE

This cake has a nice, crunchy coating topped with orange glaze. When sliced, the cake is speckled with little bits of glazed orange. Can be made up to 3 days before serving, covered and kept in a cool place.

SERVES 12 TO 14

1 Tablespoon unsalted butter, softened

3 Tablespoons fine dry breadcrumbs, sifted through fine strainer

3 cups all purpose flour (not unbleached)

2½ teaspoons baking powder

1 teaspoon salt

1 cup (2 sticks) unsalted butter, room temperature

2 cups sugar

4 extra large eggs, room temperature

1 cup heavy cream, room temperature

2 teaspoons pure vanilla extract

2 Tablespoons finely chopped Glazed Orange Peel (page 275)

1. Adjust oven rack ⅓ up from bottom of oven and preheat to 350°F. Grease a 10 × 4-inch tube pan with 1 Tablespoon softened butter, making sure pan is completely coated. Dust with breadcrumbs and shake out excess. Set aside.
2. In a medium bowl, sift together flour, baking powder and salt; set aside.
3. With electric mixer on medium speed, cream butter and sugar until fluffy, about 5 minutes. Add eggs one at a time, beating well after each addition. Turn speed down to low and add flour mixture alternately with cream in three batches, scraping down inside bowl with a rubber spatula. Stir in vanilla and orange peel.
4. Turn batter into prepared pan and spread evenly with a metal spatula. Tap pan very gently on work surface to dislodge any air bubbles (if you tap too firmly, the breadcrumb coating will fall off). Bake until cake is lightly golden and tester inserted in center comes out clean, about 1 hour. Let cake cool in pan on a rack for about 5 minutes. Invert onto another rack. Remove pan, leaving the cake upside down. Place cake (on rack) over a large piece of aluminum foil and prepare glaze.

GLAZE

½ cup orange juice, strained
½ cup sugar

1. In a 1-quart saucepan, combine orange juice and sugar. Cook over low heat, stirring once or twice, until sugar is completely dissolved, about 3 minutes.

2. Brush warm glaze all over hot cake until completely absorbed. Let cake cool completely on rack. Transfer to a cake plate. Cover with cake cover and store in a cool place.

RICOTTA CHEESECAKE
Torta di Ricotta

The addition of cream cheese to the ricotta gives this cake its smooth texture. I have tested it with several brands of ricotta cheese, and with certain brands little cracks developed on top. Don't fret if this happens; the cracks will minimize in cooling.

SERVES 12

1 package (7 ounces) Peek Freans Shortcake Biscuits or 28 vanilla wafers	3 Tablespoons unsalted butter, melted and cooled

1. Adjust oven rack ⅓ up from bottom of oven and preheat to 375°F. Lightly grease the bottom of a 9-inch springform pan with vegetable shortening.

2. Break cookies into 1-inch pieces and place in food processor fitted with metal blade or in blender. Run machine nonstop until reduced to fine crumbs, about 1 minute. Remove cover and pour melted butter over crumbs. Run machine until combined, about 1 minute, stopping to scrape inside of work bowl or container with rubber spatula. Press crumbs into bottom of prepared pan and bake for 10 minutes. Remove from oven and set on a rack to cool to room temperature. Lightly grease sides of pan with vegetable shortening.

FILLING

1 package (8 ounces) cream cheese, cut into 1-inch cubes	1 Tablespoon pure vanilla extract
1 cup sugar	3½ Tablespoons finely chopped Glazed Orange Peel (page 275) or 2 Tablespoons grated orange rind
2 pounds whole milk ricotta cheese, well drained in strainer	
4 extra large eggs	12 thin strips Glazed Orange Peel (garnish)
2 Tablespoons all purpose flour	

1. With electric mixer on medium speed, beat cream cheese with sugar until smooth, about 3 minutes. Add ricotta and beat again until absolutely smooth, about 5 minutes. Add eggs one at a time, beating well after each addition; stop machine once or twice and scrape sides of bowl with rubber spatula to make sure everything is well combined. Blend in flour and vanilla. Stir in orange peel.

2. Pour cheese mixture into crust. Set pan on a cookie sheet to catch any drips. Bake until lightly golden around outside edge, about 50 minutes. Turn oven off and leave cake in oven for another hour. Remove and cool on a rack to room temperature. Cover with plastic wrap and refrigerate overnight or, preferably, 2 days.

3. When ready to serve, run knife around inside of pan and remove springform. Place cake on a platter with a folded piece of dampened paper towel in the center to prevent bottom of pan from sliding when slicing.

4. Garnish with strips of glazed orange peel.

SICILIAN CAKE WITH CHOCOLATE FROSTING
Cassata alla Siciliana

A true cassata is made with a hollowed-out spongecake that is completely filled with the ricotta mixture. I find that layering the ricotta filling between slices of spongecake makes a rich enough dessert. The entire cake must be assembled 1 day before serving. The spongecake can be made up to 3 days before that, or frozen up to a month ahead; allow 4 hours for cake to defrost before filling and frosting. This is an extravagant ending for any formal dinner or holiday, especially Christmas. It is my version of Papa Casale's recipe.

SERVES 12 TO 14

EGG YOLK SPONGECAKE

7 large egg yolks
1 large egg
1⅓ cups sugar
1¾ cups cake flour or all purpose flour (not unbleached)
1½ teaspoons baking powder

¼ teaspoon salt
1 Tablespoon grated orange rind
½ cup orange juice
1 teaspoon pure lemon extract

1. Adjust oven rack ⅓ up from bottom of oven and preheat to 325°F.
2. Using the bottom of a 10-inch springform pan as a pattern, cut a piece of parchment paper the same size. Grease bottom of pan with vegetable shortening. Place circle of parchment into prepared pan; smooth the paper down with your hands.
3. With electric mixer on medium speed, beat egg yolks and whole egg until thick, about 5 minutes. Gradually add sugar and beat until glossy, about 5 minutes.
4. In a shallow bowl, sift flour, baking powder and salt.
5. In a small glass measuring cup, mix orange rind, juice and lemon extract.
6. At medium speed, add flour and juice mixtures alternately in three batches, beating until well blended and scraping inside of bowl with rubber spatula after each addition.
7. Pour batter into prepared pan and tap gently on work surface to release any air bubbles. Bake until no imprint remains when top is touched lightly with fingertips, about 40 minutes. Let cake cool completely in pan on a rack. Invert onto a plate and remove parchment paper (if baking cake in advance, leave parchment paper on until ready to assemble).

RICOTTA FILLING

1½ pounds whole milk ricotta cheese, well drained in strainer

1 cup confectioners' sugar, sifted after measuring

1 Tablespoon pure vanilla extract

½ cup finely chopped Glazed Orange Peel (page 275)

¼ cup tiny semisweet chocolate chips or 2 ounces semisweet chocolate, coarsely grated

2 Tablespoons Grand Marnier

1. Beat ricotta until smooth. Add confectioners' sugar in three batches, beating well after each addition; continue beating until satiny. Add vanilla and mix well. With a rubber spatula, fold in orange peel and chocolate.
2. Using a serrated knife, cut spongecake horizontally into 3 even layers. Brush surface of each layer with 1 Tablespoon liqueur.
3. Place one layer on a 12-inch flat plate. Spread with half of ricotta filling. Top with second layer and press down gently. Repeat with remaining ricotta mixture and top with third layer; press down again. Smooth filling around sides with metal spatula (don't worry if cake feels a little wobbly; chilling firms it). Refrigerate until firm, about 3 hours.

FROSTING

4 ounces unsweetened chocolate

¼ cup unsalted butter

2⅔ cups confectioners' sugar, sifted after measuring

¼ teaspoon salt

7 Tablespoons heavy cream

2 teaspoons pure vanilla extract

12 thin strips Glazed Orange Peel (garnish)

6 candied cherries, halved (garnish)

1. In a small saucepan, melt chocolate and butter together over very low heat.
2. With a wire whisk or electric beater, beat confectioners' sugar and salt into chocolate mixture. Slowly add cream and beat until smooth and glossy. Add vanilla and mix well.
3. Cover top and sides of cassata with frosting. After cake is frosted, fill a tall glass with warm water. Dip a long metal spatula or knife into water, tap off excess and smooth out top and sides of cake, dipping spatula or knife into warm water several times.
4. Garnish top of cake with orange peel and candied cherries. Cover with cake cover and refrigerate overnight. Let stand at room temperature for about 30 minutes before serving.

SPECKLED CHOCOLATE SPONGE CAKE

Very light in flavor and texture. The cake should be made one day before filling. When thoroughly cooled, cover with plastic wrap and store in cool place. Cake can be made up to 2 weeks in advance, covered with a double layer of plastic wrap and frozen until needed. Allow at least 4 hours to defrost before filling

SERVES 10 TO 12

6 large eggs, separated
1 cup sugar
¾ cup cake flour or all purpose flour (not unbleached)
1 teaspoon baking powder

1¼ teaspoons salt
½ teaspoon cream of tartar
3 ounces unsweetened chocolate, finely grated
1½ teaspoons pure vanilla extract

1. Adjust oven rack ⅓ up from bottom of oven and preheat to 350°F.
2. Using the bottom of a 9-inch springform pan as a pattern, cut a piece of parchment paper the same size. Grease paper with vegetable shortening and fit into bottom of pan greased side up. Cut a strip of parchment 31 × 4 inches. Put a few small dots of vegetable shortening halfway up sides of pan so strip will hold in place. Grease strip and line sides of pan, greased side showing.
3. With electric mixer, beat egg yolks at medium speed, gradually adding ½ cup sugar. Beat until thick and lemon-colored.
4. Sift flour, baking powder and 1 teaspoon salt together. Add to egg yolk mixture in two batches, scraping inside of bowl with a rubber spatula after each addition (mixture should be very thick). Transfer to another bowl.
5. Wash and thoroughly dry beaters and bowl. Beat egg whites at medium-high speed until foamy. Add remaining ¼ teaspoon salt and cream of tartar; beat until soft peaks form. Gradually add remaining ½ cup sugar and continue beating until stiff and glossy. With a rubber spatula, gently fold grated chocolate and vanilla into beaten egg whites. Very carefully fold in yolk mixture. Pour into prepared pan. Tap gently on work surface to release any air bubbles.
6. Bake in preheated oven until no imprint remains when cake is touched lightly with fingertips, about 50 minutes. Cool in pan on rack for 15 minutes. Turn cake out of pan onto rack and remove paper.

FILLING AND TOPPING

2 cups heavy cream
⅓ cup sifted confectioners'
sugar
1 Tablespoon pure vanilla
extract

1 ounce unsweetened
chocolate, coarsely grated
(garnish)

1. Whip cream with confectioners' sugar until stiff. Fold in vanilla.
2. With a serrated knife, slice cake in half horizontally; spread bottom layer evenly with ⅓ of the whipped cream. Replace top layer. Coat entire cake with remaining whipped cream. Sprinkle top and sides with grated chocolate.

Note: Cake can be filled and frosted with whipped cream up to 6 hours before serving. Refrigerate until ready to serve.

ECLAIRS

For me, there is nothing quite as exquisite after a delicious dinner or luncheon as a platter of small eclairs. The unfilled shells may be frozen in a single layer on a baking sheet and covered with plastic wrap. When frozen, transfer to plastic bags and secure with twist ties; shells can be kept frozen up to 3 months. To restore crispness, place frozen shells in preheated 375°F oven for about 5 minutes.

YIELDS 24 SMALL

1 cup water
½ cup (1 stick) unsalted
butter, cut into 8 pieces
¼ teaspoon salt
1 cup unbleached flour

4 large eggs (not extra large
or jumbo)
1 Tablespoon milk
1 large egg

1. Adjust oven rack to center of oven and preheat to 400°F. Grease and flour a large jelly roll pan or two small cookie sheets (see note).
2. In a heavy 2-quart saucepan, combine water, butter and salt. Bring to a rolling boil. Remove from heat and add flour all at once, stirring vigorously with a wooden spoon. Return pan to low heat and cook, stirring con-

stantly, until a thin crust starts to form on bottom of pan, about 3 minutes; the dough should be soft and should not stick to your fingers when pinched. Transfer mixture to a deep bowl and let cool for at least 10 minutes; the mixture can be stirred with a wooden spoon to hasten cooling.

3. Add 4 eggs one at a time, beating vigorously after each addition so that the mixture is smooth before the next egg is added. Beat until the dough is shiny and smooth.

4. Fit a 14-inch pastry bag with a #9 round tip and fill bag with dough. Squeeze out dough in 2½-inch long strips, spacing at least 2 inches apart on baking sheet so that they will not touch as they expand.

5. Beat milk and remaining egg together with a fork. Using a small, flat pastry brush or goose feather, brush top of each strip with egg mixture and gently push down any peaks that may have formed. Let the shells dry at least 10 minutes before placing in oven. (The eclairs will have a shiny glaze, provided they are allowed to dry a little before baking.)

6. Bake shells for 10 minutes. Reduce oven temperature to 350°F and bake for another 10 minutes, or until puffed and lightly golden. Turn off oven and partially open oven door. Leave shells in oven to dry for 15 minutes, then remove.

Note: If using smaller cookie sheets, you will have to bake eclairs in two separate batches. Cover remaining dough with plastic wrap and leave at room temperature while baking first batch.

PASTRY CREAM

½ cup sugar
3½ Tablespoons cornstarch
6 large egg yolks, lightly
beaten

2 cups milk
1 Tablespoon pure vanilla
extract

1. In the top of a double boiler, mix sugar, cornstarch and lightly beaten egg yolks.

2. In a small saucepan, bring milk to a boil. Pour scalded milk a little at a time into egg yolk mixture, stirring briskly with a wire whisk after each addition. Cook pastry cream over simmering water, whisking constantly, until mixture is thick and smooth, about 10 minutes. Transfer to a bowl and let cool slightly; stir in vanilla. Cover with plastic wrap and refrigerate until well chilled, at least 2 hours. (Pastry cream can be made up to 2 days before filling eclairs.)

3. Up to 3 hours before serving, line up eclairs on work surface and cut in half horizontally. Fill with pastry cream and then make chocolate frosting.

CHOCOLATE FROSTING

1 ounce unsweetened
   chocolate
1 Tablespoon unsalted butter
1 cup confectioners' sugar

⅛ teaspoon salt
3 Tablespoons hot strong
   coffee

1. In a small saucepan, melt chocolate with butter over very low heat. Remove from heat and let cool slightly.
2. Sift confectioners' sugar and salt together into a small bowl. Add cooled chocolate mixture and blend well. Add hot coffee a little at a time and beat with a wire whisk just until frosting has a nice spreading consistency.
3. With a demitasse spoon, drizzle frosting over eclairs.
4. Arrange eclairs in a single layer on a platter and refrigerate until ready to serve.

ST. JOSEPH'S RICOTTA PUFFS
Sfinge di San Giuseppe

St. Joseph, whose feast day is on March 19th, is the Sicilian patron saint of home and family. Papa Casale always made these traditional pastries to celebrate this special holiday. A word of warning: a thermometer must be used to insure a frying temperature of 350°F. If the temperature is higher, a crust will form too quickly and the sfinge *will not expand properly.*

YIELDS 16

1 cup water
½ cup vegetable shortening,
   preferably Crisco
½ teaspoon salt
1 cup unbleached flour
4 large eggs (not extra large
   or jumbo)

½ teaspoon baking powder
1 Tablespoon sugar
1 Tablespoon grated lemon
   rind
1 can (3 pounds), less ½ cup,
   vegetable shortening (for
   frying)

1. In a heavy 2-quart saucepan, combine water, ½ cup shortening and salt; bring to a rolling boil. Remove from heat and add flour all at once, stirring vigorously with a wooden spoon. Return pan to low heat and cook, stirring constantly, until mixture starts to stick slightly to bottom of pan, about 3

to 5 minutes. Remove from heat and transfer dough to a deep bowl; let cool for at least 5 minutes. The dough can be stirred with a wooden spoon to hasten the cooling.

2. Add eggs one at a time, beating vigorously after each addition so that the mixture is smooth before the next egg is added. Beat until the dough is shiny and smooth. Beat in baking powder, sugar and grated lemon rind.

3. In a deep 5½-quart pot, heat vegetable shortening over medium-high heat until it reaches 350°F.

4. Using a large mixing spoon, remove approximately 2 Tablespoons of dough at a time. With a rubber spatula, scrape dough into hot shortening; do not fry more than 4 *sfinge* at a time. As they begin to form a thin crust, tap gently with the handle of a wooden spoon to break the crust and allow them to expand. Continue frying until *sfinge* are deep golden brown and have a firm crust, about 10 minutes. Remove with a skimmer and place on paper towel to drain. Repeat with remaining dough. Cool *sfinge* thoroughly before filling.

RICOTTA FILLING

2 pounds whole milk ricotta cheese, well drained in a strainer
1 cup sugar
1 Tablespoon pure vanilla extract
½ teaspoon freshly ground cinnamon (see note)

2 Tablespoons finely chopped Glazed Orange Peel (page 275)
¼ cup (approximately) confectioners' sugar

1. With electric mixer or wire whisk, beat ricotta cheese until smooth. Add sugar and continue beating until consistency is very satiny. Add vanilla, cinnamon and orange peel; mix well. Cover with plastic wrap and refrigerate until firm, about 3 hours or overnight.

2. Line *sfinge* on work surface. Cut a slit through the center top of each and fill with ricotta mixture. Arrange on a platter and sift confectioners' sugar over. Garnish each puff with 2 crisscrossed slices of glazed orange peel. (*Sfinge* can be filled, decorated and refrigerated up to 3 hours before serving.)

Note: To insure a pure white filling, use freshly ground cinnamon; the powdered variety will change the color of the filling. Cut a 1-inch piece of cinnamon stick, grind with a mortar and pestle and measure out ½ teaspoon. The cinnamon should be coarsely ground.

MENUS

I remember watching and helping my mother prepare the feasts that welcomed visitors to our home. No holiday was necessary to give mealtime a festive air; each and every meal planned for company was an occasion for having no fewer than five courses.

A meal was never served without an abundant antipasto. I can still see the trays of vegetables—fresh, marinated, roasted and pickled—with prosciutto and salami. Then there was the soup course, the pasta course, and the entree, with at least three vegetables. This was followed by fresh fruits, cheeses and nuts, and of course dessert—never just one, but always an assortment.

As I cleared the table laden with dishes, my eyes captured images that are now indelible in my mind: Aunt Lucy playing the piano with gusto, Uncle Henry unhitching his belt and adjusting the buckle a notch or two. My grandfather, Nonno Chico, sitting in the overstuffed chair, his auburn hair encircled by rings of smoke from his pungent cigar, a look of utter contentment on his face. I can see them all: Nonna Louisa, my grandmother; Aunt Katherine, Uncle Julius, Aunt Anna, Uncle Dan, Aunt Dolly, Uncle Ulysses, Aunt Tess, Uncle Bill, Aunt Angie, Uncle Tony, Aunt Evelyn, Uncle Frank, Aunt Bunny, Uncle Louis, Aunt Emma, Uncle Pete, Aunt Gloria, Uncle John, Aunt Jean, Uncle Carmine. All smiling, warmly reflecting on the meal we had just experienced and the hours we had spent together at my parents' table. And I remember Mamma's smile as they lifted their glasses to salute her efforts—a smile she returned with reddening cheeks and her own raised glass, and a nod showing she lovingly accepted their praise.

Many years have passed and the scene has changed to my kitchen: the dining-room table being cleared by my daughters, Joanne and Amy; my sister Louisa at the piano sharing her latest composition; my son-in-law Chris, offering an encouraging nod of ap-

proval each time our eyes meet; my husband John serving
cordials. The guests are sitting or standing, talking, laughing or
quietly reflecting, but everyone is smiling; nothing more need be
said. I feel the same pride, the same success Mamma did as she
accepted the chorused Salute.

I experience the same joy Mamma did in entertaining. I savor
the warmth and love generated from gathering family, and special
friends we consider family, around our table. The only thing that
has changed is today's simpler menus. The lighter pasta dishes,
the more whimsical sauces which are so quick to prepare—the
meals, in fact, that were served to me every day as a child—are
now offered and requested by the most sophisticated palates.

In any case, the menus planned in my kitchen, as in my mother's, are characterized by elegant presentation and attention to
contrasts of taste, texture, color and form. It was with these prin-
ciples in mind that the following menus were created. A number
are amazingly quick to put together; refer to them for the solutions
to your dining dilemmas.

Various wines are suggested for these menus. If any is unavailable to you, ask your wine dealer for a similar variety.

Many of my students use my suggested menus as springboards
for several meals: the pasta course may be served with just a salad
one night, and the entree and vegetables reserved for another meal.
As you read through the recipes, try creating your own menu combinations.

If you are having a dinner party, try to feature dishes that can
be prepared well in advance. An elegant menu needn't mean a lot
of last-minute fussing in the kitchen. And remember that the indi-
cated servings accompanying each recipe in this book are more
than generous to allow for healthy appetites.

Always keep the whole presentation in mind. I tell my students
repeatedly that each dish must not only be delicious on its own,
but should harmonize with the rest of the meal.

Pasta Primavera
Chicken Suprêmes with Piquant Caper Sauce
Green Beans with Tomato Sauce
Wine—Soave
Frozen Mocha Surprise

Tagliarini with Basil Pesto Sauce
Roast Chicken with Dried Wild Mushrooms
Zucchini with Garlic and Tomato
Wine—Est! Est!! Est!!!
Blueberries Flambé

Baked Ziti
Roast Chicken with Rosemary
Broccoli with Olives
Wine—Frascati
Apricot Mousse

Fried Mozzarella
Braised Chicken with Tomato and Olives
Green Bean and New Potato Salad
Wine—Verdicchio
Blueberry Cream Torte

Marinated Artichoke Hearts
Stuffed Chicken Legs
Rice with Zucchini
Cauliflower–Tomato Salad
Wine—Orvieto Abboccato
Papa's Rice Pudding

Linguine with Broccoli
Filet Mignon with Wine and Caper Sauce
Fennel and Mushrooms
Wine—Barolo
Espresso Cream Tart

Marinated Mushrooms
Beef Rolls with Tomato Sauce
Baked Rice with Ricotta
Asparagus and Carrots with Sesame Seed
Wine—Chianti Riserva
Eclairs

Conchiglie with Broccoli, Cauliflower and Anchovies
Braised Beef with Wine and Mushroom Sauce
Parsnips and Carrots
Wine—Valpolicella
Stuffed Poached Pears

Tagliatelle with Zucchini and Mushrooms
Stuffed Flank Steak
Fried Celery
Wine—Spanna
Glazed Orange Cake

Conchiglie with Tomato, Mozzarella and Fresh Herbs
Pan-Fried Lamb Chops
Beet Salad
Wine—Corvo Rosso
Stuffed Peaches

Lasagne
Stuffed Boned Leg of Lamb
Sautéed Green Beans and Cherry Tomatoes
Wine—Cabernet
Speckled Chocolate Spongecake

Belgian Endive with Prosciutto
Crusty Rack of Lamb
Potatoes with Pancetta
Sautéed Broccoli with Mushrooms
Wine—Bardolino
Linda's Grapes with Cognac

Linguine with Tomato–Garlic Sauce
Pork Chops with Vinegar
Sautéed Cucumbers
Wine—Barbera d'Asti
Strawberries all'Anna

Roasted Pepper Salad
Herbed Stuffed Pork Chops
Rice with Peas
Braised Escarole
Wine—Pinot Bianco
Pineapple–Coconut Parfaits

Linguine with Walnut Sauce
Roast Pork with Herbed Butter
Sautéed Eggplant
Wine—Frascati
Toasted Coconut Cream Tart

Sicilian Eggplant Relish
Rolled Pork Cutlets
Spinach–Ricotta Dumplings
Tomato Salad with Ricotta Salata
Wine—Soave
Biscuit Tortoni

Polenta with Fontina Cheese
Sautéed Sausage with Spinach
Wine—Barbaresco
Apple Cheese Torte

Margherita with Fried Cauliflower
Veal Scallops with Carrots and Dried Sausage
Sautéed Mushrooms
Wine—Pinot Bianco
Glazed Poached Apples with Marinated Fruit

Marinated Artichoke Hearts
Eggplant Manicotti
Veal Scallops with Mushrooms and Marsala
Asparagus Vinaigrette
Wine—Verdicchio
Caramel Custard

Green Noodles with Carrots and Mushrooms
Veal Scallops with Prosciutto and Peas
Zucchini Salad
Wine—Frascati
Seasonal Fruit and Golden Yellow Cake

Farfalle with Spinach Pesto
Veal with Tomato–Lemon Sauce
Fried Artichoke Hearts
Wine—Merlot
Ricotta Pudding

Ziti with Eggplant and Roasted Peppers
Veal Birds
Sautéed Broccoli and Mushrooms
Wine—Bardolino
Ricotta Mousse with Raspberry Sauce

Potato–Parsley Soup
Stuffed Veal Chops
Brussels Sprouts with Fennel
Wine—Corvo Bianco
Ricotta Cheesecake

Clam-Stuffed Mushrooms
Roast Veal Amadeo
Parsleyed Potatoes
Swiss Chard with Tomatoes
Wine—Amarone
Cold Mandarin Soufflé

Spaghettini with Crabmeat
Baked Halibut Steaks
Baked Zucchini
Wine—Corvo Bianco
Fresh Orange Compote

Orecchiette with Shrimp and Scallops
Fillet of Sole Florentine
Orange-Avocado Salad
Wine—Frascati
Apple–Custard Flan

Linguine with Shrimp
Poached Fish Rolls in Tomato Sauce
Green Salad with Mustard Vinaigrette
Wine—Pinot Grigio
Orange Cream

Shrimp with Caper Dressing
Swordfish with Sweet and Sour Sauce
Rice with Eggs and Cheese
Baked Celery and Mushrooms
Wine—Orvieto Secco
Grand Marnier Mousse

Fettuccine with Lobster Sauce
Baked Swordfish
Curly Endive–Spinach–Mandarin Salad
Wine–Soave
Apple Cream Whip

Index

About the Author

■ □ ■ □ ■ □ ■ □ ■

Anne Casale started teaching cooking in 1963 and has been director of her own cooking school for the past five years.

She has been a consultant for restaurants, gourmet shops and cooking schools throughout the United States, as well as a popular guest chef, lecturer, restaurant critic and food writer.

A certified member of The International Association of Cooking Schools and New York Association of Cooking Teachers, Anne makes her home with her family in New Jersey.